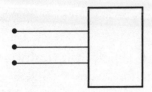

WHEN CITIZENS COMPLAIN

LAW AND POLITICAL CHANGE

Series Editors: Professor Cosmo Graham, Law School, University of Hull, and Professor Norman Lewis, Centre for Socio-Legal Studies, University of Sheffield.

Current titles:

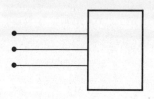

WHEN CITIZENS COMPLAIN
REFORMING JUSTICE AND ADMINISTRATION

Norman Lewis and Patrick Birkinshaw

OPEN UNIVERSITY PRESS
Buckingham • Philadelphia

Open University Press
Celtic Court
22 Ballmoor
Buckingham
MK18 1XW

and

1900 Frost Road, Suite 101
Bristol, PA 19007, USA

First Published 1993

A catalogue record of this book is available from the British Library

ISBN 0 335 15744 0 (pb)   0 335 15745 9 (hb)

Library of Congress Cataloging-in-Publication Data
Lewis, Norman, 1940–
    When citizens complain: reforming justice and administration/
Norman Lewis and Patrick Birkinshaw.
      p. cm. — (Law and political change)
    Includes bibliographical references and index.
    ISBN 0–335–15745–9 ISBN 0–335–15744–0 (pbk.)
    1. Justice, Administration of—Great Britain. 2. Law reform—Great
Britain. 3. Complaints (Administrative procedure)—Great Britain.
I. Birkinshaw, Patrick. II. Title. III. Series.
KD654.L49 1993
342.41′066—dc20
[344.10266]   92–21161
                                                                  CIP

Typeset by Colset Private Limited, Singapore
Printed in Great Britain by Biddles Ltd, Guildford and King's Lynn

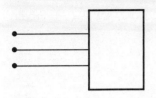

CONTENTS

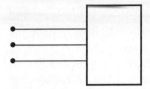

INTRODUCTION

This work arose out of a proposal which we submitted to the Economic and Social Research Council as part of their initiative on grievance redress announced in 1988. We were not, in the end, successful in gaining their support, but we decided to press ahead with our ideas anyway, albeit in a less ambitious fashion. That we were able to do so at all is due to the generosity of the Faculty of Law Research Fund at the University of Sheffield and the Law School at the University of Hull, which provided us with modest funds for travel and subsistence. We would also like to thank J.H.W. Glen and the Society of Town Clerks' Education and Research Trust.

We took the view at the time that useful though research was in relation to the actual practices of bureaucracies, what was really needed was an attempt at setting an agenda for reform across the spectrum of our public administration. Undeterred by our inability to persuade, we carried the project forward and this is the result. Inevitably we have compromised. We have attempted to set out an agenda for reform without offering a blueprint but have also attempted to describe working practices in some of our major state organs. We are conscious of many omissions: the criminal process, the police, the armed forces to mention but a few. However, we hope to have produced useful information about the processes whereby citizens can complain against their governments and their delegates. In doing so, we have not limited ourselves to the traditional ways of the law but have sought to develop a spectrum of devices whereby complaints and grievances can be pursued. We have not hesitated to criticize where we think it necessary and have thrown down a number of challenges to those who claim to have the best interests of the citizenry at heart.

As usual, our debts are numerous, but in particular we should like to thank Diane Longley for her assistance with aspects of the health service. If we have misunderstood her at any point, we apologize here in public. Other errors we leave to be detected by the reviewers.

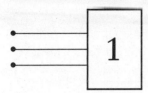

JUSTICE AGAINST THE STATE

This book seeks to examine the duties of the state to provide justice and, in particular, the optimum forms of dispute resolution. The time is clearly right for the Lord Chancellor's Department, in the current absence of a Ministry of Justice, to conduct an overview of its duties to provide effective remedies to citizens, not least in light of the general European access to justice movement. This would chime well with the Major Administration's expressed concern with equal citizenship. We hope to have presented a major contribution to policy thinking in this area, especially since we draw upon a range of both theoretical and empirical work. The large amount of empirical work that we have conducted both in Britain and abroad will be used to illustrate the types of mechanism which might be used to deal with different categories of dispute. Arguing at the outset for a coherent duty of justice provision, we go on to provide an agenda for the most suitable types of arrangement for different categories of problem: the advantages of ombudsmen over tribunals, courts over either; negotiation, mediation, or self-regulation in place of traditional methods of ordering; administrative re-examination of decisions judged against agency 'constitutions' and the like. Do central government departments require different systems from local government? Are all bodies within a particular level of government to be treated similarly? Are non-departmental public bodies (NDPBs) such that different procedures are required from those in 'direct government'? Are there problems unique to executive agencies? What safeguards are required for self-regulatory bodies? Where do the courts fit in and are the present courts the best that we can provide?

Justice is a hooray word. Everyone is in favour of it; governments take it for granted that it is endemic in our system. When egregious instances of injustice occur, then they assume that these are instances of falling from a state of grace. Yet in a peculiarly British way, we are not taken to sitting down and looking systematically at the whole of our political system. This book is a partial, but only partial, attempt to correct that state of affairs.

First, let us dwell for a moment on the concept of justice. It is, clearly, much contested, so that we need to pin down our concerns and set out the task which we have set ourselves as clearly as possible. A 'just' system would provoke a fairness agenda that would seek to ensure that adequate redress was provided for each citizen wishing to contest decisions taken by the state in their name. Now in essence this would amount to an exploration of the systems and procedures by which a just or democratic society would seek to deliver on its promises. Obviously, unless the angle of enquiry is narrowed, we would be inviting a discussion of constitutionality and its constituents, a matter which has to a large extent been covered elsewhere (see, e.g. Harden and Lewis, 1986). We therefore propose, in line with our empirical investigations, to limit our analysis to grievance or conflict redress against organs of the state. We shall be speaking therefore to what the Canadian Law Reform Commission has referred to as 'constitutionally mandated regimes'. That is to say, the classic organs of the state (though we shall have little to say about either the armed forces or the police, since they require such specialist coverage and to a considerable extent receive it) plus those which are authorized or empowered by the state. Thus we take on board NDPBs, most of the regulatory bodies, much of the self-regulatory world and, of course, local government. The logic of due process within a constitutional settlement would ordinarily implicate us in both an examination of the state's duty to provide fair redress against an abuse of power by private parties and an exploration of the criminal justice system. This would take us too far for present purposes, and in any event would be likely to cause us to lose the freshness and originality of our more limited examination. Even so, we shall have something to say both in relation to the criminal process and in relation to the issue of self-regulation and the public/private divide. The present fashion with reorganized or 'reinvented' government (see, e.g. Common *et al.*, 1992; Osborne and Gaebler, 1992) is bringing the public and the private closer together. We shall not say much about the historical and social forces which are creating this relative harmonization; that is for another book. Suffice it to say that much of the state apparatus is being marketized or privatized, which will cause us to look afresh at the problems presented for the citizen who wishes to complain. At the same time, the bringing closer of the private and public spheres reminds us of the need for the state to protect citizens against abuse by the private sphere, especially in its corporate manifestation. We shall have cause to say more about these matters from time to time and will pick them up again in Chapter 9.

THE NATURE OF JUSTICE

The absence of a written constitution is always something of an impediment to easy agreement on the nature of our polity. Even so, we can either take the view that anything that exists is 'legitimate' or has legitimacy, or we can examine our system on the basis of common understandings, spoken and unspoken promises, political rhetoric or the like. There would be little point in writing a book such as this if we took the former view and we believe that most people share common understandings about the promises which our political and legal systems hold out. Thus, as far back as the Bill of Rights of 1688, we see that 'the redresse of all grievances' is one of the prime justifications of frequent Parliaments. No one seriously believes that Parliament is today capable of redressing all grievances so that the implication is that other machinery needs to be installed to achieve that purpose. If this machinery does not redress all or most grievances, or is not capable of doing so, then we are surely entitled to a reassessment. Furthermore, the European Convention on Human Rights (ECHR) requires freedom of speech, which when unpacked is normally related to the redress of grievances. This is because if citizens wish to criticize their government, they need to be able to do so, *inter alia*, by questioning and debating with the decision maker or his representative. Interestingly, the First Amendment to the Constitution of the USA specifically links freedom of speech with the redress of grievances. All in all, then, we feel confident that the minimum content of justice is procedural fairness or, to use an American expression, 'due process'.

In Chapter 10, we briefly examine the notions of procedural justice and fairness as applied by the English courts. We shall have a number of critical observations to make at that time, but those notions pay at least some homage to the expectations of fair treatment by public bodies. It is, in our view, largely a matter for empirical observation and debate as to the proper or ideal forum for the resolution of grievances. The proper forum might be a simple re-examination of the decision by the decision-making body (albeit at a higher or different level), especially where large policy considerations are at stake. Alternatively, the full panoply of the High Court or beyond might be necessary where the matter raises important 'constitutional' issues. There is a range of permutations in between which we shall address in later chapters. The other salient device, of course, would be the inspector or ombudsman-type figure who could combine securing adequate redress with quality-control functions concerning the performance of the administrative machine.

A nicer point of contest or dispute relates to the ability of a citizen to have the decision of a public body overturned in terms of its quality. We, in Britain, have rarely come to terms with what this should mean in any systemic way. We doubt if, at the moment, there is any official or indeed scholarly consensus on the right way forward here. Our own view is that the decision must remain political, to be decided by the politicians of the day but with additional institutional assistance to help them to make rational and informed choices; choices which fit with the overall grain of the need to provide justice against the state. We make proposals later which we believe will allow politicians to make coherent decisions whenever new jurisdictions or programmes are being mooted.

Another balance to be struck in aiming for an acceptable definition of justice in this context concerns the relationship between merely procedural and 'human' rights. It has not been traditional in Britain to regard human rights as a central part of the common law, even though the European Convention on Human Rights, to which we are a signatory party, has been operational since 1953. It used to be argued that a combination of the common law, expressing the collective will of the people, and an elected Parliament, expressing the collective will of the people, would combine to guarantee effective human rights. That pretence has long been abandoned but instead Britain has claimed that it will not ratify international treaties until its own municipal law or practice is in line with its treaty obligations. It therefore seems perverse not to accept in 1990s Britain that justice against the state requires respect for human rights. We shall then assume that our concept of justice does indeed embrace such respect even though the courts have not always been eager to share that respect, as is evidenced from their failure to advance the idea, let alone protect, civil rights.

Our final point concerns the relationship, between justice and consultation with citizens over matters that are likely to affect their interests. It is significant that in this respect the *Citizens' Charter*, to which we refer at regular intervals, makes much of the need for timely consultation with interested parties. There is no doubt in our mind that the two are intimately connected and we shall periodically raise consultation issues where they seem to impinge directly on questions of citizen redress. This will be especially so where groups, not representing legal persons (i.e. those with legal personality), feel that they have been unjustly treated. It is impossible for us not to touch on these crucial issues from time to time. Even so, our focus will be unashamedly on individual citizen redress, a matter almost uncontainable in itself in one book.

A final word needs to be said at this juncture on the concept of justice. In Chapter 3, we examine the relationship between justice and the quality or efficiency of the administration. However, since social structures come into existence in order to cater for the happiness of human beings, it may be worth saying that a just society is an end in itself. Now, although justice may be a contested concept, it may well be regarded as the highest goal to be achieved. Absent just systems, who can say what people really want and expect or how it can be measured.

One further point might be added. It is that we spend very little time on 'political' forms of redress, including the handling of complaints by local councillors and Members of Parliament (MPs). This is not because they are unimportant – a matter which it would be as well for readers not to forget. Rather, it is because approaches to elected figures must be seen to be obvious to most people. In our 1987 work *Complaints Procedures in Local Government* (Lewis *et al.*, 1987), we spoke at length to such matters and found that important though local councillors were in dispute resolution, they were often regarded by members of the public as being associated with the decisions being complained against. This finding has been supported by the most recent work in the field (Hill *et al.*, 1992). MPs were therefore often approached even on local authority matters. As to MPs and their role in complaints against government departments, a recent Cabinet Efficiency Scrutiny has cast some light on previously dark corners. In the year 1990–91, nearly 250 000 letters were answered by ministers and well over 600 000 letters addressed to ministers by members of the public were answered by officials. Most of these will have been forwarded by MPs after a complaint by their constituents. MPs regard their ability to take up constituents' cases with ministers and their departments as an important part of the democratic process, reflecting the accountability of ministers to Parliament. They expect an effective response to their letters within a reasonable time. The scrutiny found that many departments have failed to meet the targets they have set themselves for prompt response to members' letters and that there was much scope for improvement in the process and handling of correspondence. Even so, the valuable role of politicians in the complaints process should not be overlooked. Having said that, our researches indicate that some MPs are infinitely more knowledgeable about the effective pressure points in Whitehall than others. For example, a simple letter to a department from an MP which does not name the executive officer or section head will often be responded to by the official who made the initial decision. Many MPs also feel that their job is done once a complaint has been forwarded, regardless of the outcome. These matters require a treatise of their own and we shall leave the matter there for the time being.

PUBLIC BODIES AND THE STATE

Having skated thinly over the concept of justice, we must now skate just as thinly over the nature of the state/public bodies. Much has been said about the 'interpretation' of the public/private divide, a matter made that much more oblique by the absence of a written constitution. In *Government by Moonlight* (Birkinshaw *et al.*, 1990), we engaged in a lengthy discussion of the nature of this dilemma and concentrated primarily on so-called 'hybrid' bodies which did not fit easily into either the public or the private domain, but which nevertheless carried out what are essentially public functions, or at least functions which would have to be carried out by the state in their absence. This area is far too complicated to be discussed at length here, but we must say a little. First, certain bodies are unequivocally public: Parliament, departments of state, local government, the army, the police, the judiciary and even NDPBs. Others are unequivocably private: Joe Citizen, Marks & Spencer, ICI, firms of solicitors and the like. In between there is a certain fuzziness and the government's own view of what constitutes a public body carries little intellectual conviction (Lewis, 1989a, p. 221ff.). We speak to the issue of Training and Enterprise Councils (TECs) later, but there are many others which cause conceptual trouble. Even the courts have been beset by this dilemma in having to decide, for example, whether the City Takeover Panel, the Advertising Standards Authority and the Greyhound Association constitute public bodies for the purposes of Order 53 of the Supreme Court (this Order describes the procedure for bringing judicial review against public bodies).

Just two further points will be made at this time; one that is merely illustrative, the other more normative. The first concerns the Office of Fair Trading (OFT), a pre-eminently public body whose name gives a flavour of its functions. One of its many roles relates to drawing up codes of practice with trade associations to protect the public interest. Many associations, such as the Association of Mail Order Publishers, the Retail Motor Industry Federation Limited, etc., do not look like public bodies at first blush. Even so, many self-regulatory bodies, as some of these are, would almost certainly be regulated by public bodies were they not to discipline their own members. In the most obvious case, that of the Securities and Investment Board, established under the Financial Services Act 1986, a conscious choice was made between the establishment of a regulatory NDPB and self-regulation by the industry. That choice is not necessarily irrevocable. Nearly all the codes of practice drawn up in consultation with the OFT allow consumers the choice of having their disputes settled by arbitration, thereby relieving them of unnecessary expense, especially since it proceeds normally by way of documentary evidence alone, which removes the need for personal attendance and can help speed up the decision and save costs. One feature of these codes is that consumers must first submit their complaint for conciliation by the relevant trade association. Incidentally, the National Consumer Council (NCC), on our assessment a public body, has suggested minimum conditions for the accountability of self-regulatory organizations. They also take the view that self-regulation should normally function in conjunction with a minimum level of legislation, even if the mandatory requirements remain vague and general (NCC, 1986). This would almost certainly cause such organizations to be classified as public bodies for the purposes of Order 53.

The apparently clear-cut distinction between a public and a private body then becomes extremely hazy upon close inspection. It may be that no easy theoretical definition of a public body can be plucked out of the air, but if our suggestion for a Standing Administrative Conference (SAC; addressed in Chapter 4) were to be adopted, then solutions would be that much closer to hand. For example, the SAC might be asked to list public bodies after a close examination and to make additions as necessary.

CONCILIATION AND ARBITRATION

Conciliation (assisting parties to a negotiated settlement by means of third-party intervention) and arbitration (binding recommendations by a third party) are not as common in public law as in private law. Also, they are not as common in the UK as they are in some other public law jurisdictions. Even so, it would be wrong to overlook such instances as do exist, an omission common in the public law literature.

Currently, the position is a little clouded, certainly as far as the public utilities are concerned. The Competition and Service (Utilities) Act 1992 provides for a Byzantine web of complaints procedures, with one possible stage being arbitration, presumably through the offices of the Chartered Institute of Arbitrators. These include billing disputes for British Telecom, gas supply, electricity, water and sewage.

Traditionally, British Rail accepts arbitration in rare cases involving breaches of their passage of carriage conditions, but there are so many exemptions to liability here as to render the numbers of cases insubstantial; they range from a high point of six cases in 1986 to a low of two in 1990. The Post Office is involved in arbitration in substantially more cases, but even so only averaging some 40 cases over a five-year period. These cases invariably involve allegations of loss of post and there is a difference in the schemes available for inland and overseas mail. British Telecom is involved in far more arbitrations than other 'public' sector bodies, so for example between 1987 and 1990 the numbers ranged between 261 and 418. The disputes will invariably be billing disputes. The arbitrator normally adjudicates on the basis of documentation alone, but there are occasions when he wishes to question the parties to a dispute. There is considerable difficulty in identifying distinctly 'public' bodies, but the Association of British Travel Agents (ABTA), for example, makes extensive use of arbitration, whereas the Law Society and many City institutions make very limited use of arbitration.

It is in the area of the utilities that the most interesting developments are likely to occur and we shall have to wait and see whether other public bodies decide to follow suit, not least in the light of the Lord Chancellor's determination to hold down the legal aid budget. The *Citizens' Charter*, too, speaks of lay 'adjudicators', but thus far the government has shed little light on its broad intentions in this area.

In conclusion, we should add just a little about so-called National Health Service (NHS) 'contracts' between service providers and service purchasers. These are not subject to the ordinary law of contract except when dealing with private providers of services. The National Health Service and Community Care Act 1990 makes this clear. But in the case of a dispute either party may refer it to the Secretary of State who may decide it him or herself or refer it to another person. Where an adjudicator is appointed, the National Health Service Contracts (Dispute Resolution) Regulations 1991 apply (see Harden, 1992, pp. 47–8).

THE PLAN

Chapter 2 begins with the nature of grievance redress and the constitutional mandate for the justification of grievance redress. We explain what we mean by 'grievance' or 'complaint' and the requirement for a system to provide adequate adjudication. The relatively recent concentration by governments on consumer or customer care within government as well as in the traditional private consumer market has begun to spill over into a concern for citizen voice within government at the level both of consultation and, more specifically for our purposes, grievance redress. The *Citizens' Charter* is perhaps the clearest current manifestation. This is an implicit recognition that justice against the state is a systemic requirement and not one restricted to the right to a very expensive day in court. The logic of this position is that the courts are merely the apex of the justice system and should not be seen as the normal forum for grievance redress. We shall argue that if this view is adopted, then we might reconsider the optimum role for the courts, which would set them apart from the rest of the justice system in terms of their function. We discuss these matters in Chapters 10 and 11, but it is worth flagging some of our ideas at this stage. Only the courts can decide issues of high constitutionality or at the level of constitutional politics, so to speak. Only they have the authority, the independence and the expertise. The resolute problems of our polity must be addressed in such a forum. Moreover, if we were to reconsider our whole system of justice against the state, then the signal role which we would expect the courts to perform might provide an impetus for them to behave more systemically and constructively rather than operating in the usual British *ad hoc* fashion. The courts would, in other words, operate as the quality control mechanism of our system of justice against the state. Because we shall be viewing the courts in this light, we shall want to ensure that they are accessible. To this end, we will have some suggestions to make for a 'Public Interest Office' where the issue raised was felt to be of special public concern.

Leaving the courts aside for the time being, we may turn again to the lower levels of the system. Providing, of course, that the citizen obtains the redress which is required, then complaints or grievances are best settled at as immediate and local level as possible. This means that, just as the White Paper on the *Citizens' Charter* declares, every governmental body should possess an accessible, visible and effective complaints procedure. If that advice were heeded, then relatively few complaints would go unredressed and few complainants would remain dissatisfied. Complaints procedures may obviously take many forms according to the nature of the organization concerned and may exhibit more or less formal features at different stages of the process. We address these issues in Chapter 8. However, not every complaint or grievance (see Chapter 2 for terminology) will be solved to the satisfaction of the complainant at the domestic level. More consideration needs to be given, in our view, to sub-court solutions at the systemic level where the grievance rumbles on.

In Britain, we have experimented with numerous alternative mechanisms: administrative tribunals, appeals to ministers, ombudsmen, codes of practice, self-regulation, enquiries and the like. What we have rarely attempted (but see Franks, 1957; Justice-All Souls, 1988) is to set down criteria for optimum dispute resolution against ideal-type circumstances and cases. There has been no attempt to replicate the systematic examination of appropriate forms of dispute resolution machinery conducted in Australia under the 'New Administrative Law' reforms of the 1970s. Since that time, alternative dispute resolution has been the focus of much discussion and experiment in the USA, particularly in relation to arbitration, mediation and regulated negotiation. There is a rejuvenation of interest in the limits of the various British ombudsman systems and a quickening of interest in European ombudsman systems. Indeed, since the Maastricht Treaty in 1991, we now anticipate a European Community Ombudsman in the not-too-distant future. We believe it is important to avoid pragmatic, cumulative responses to problems as we re-examine our approach to justice against the state. There is presently no automatic right to appeal against decisions of public officials, only the *inherent* power of the courts to review the legality of those decisions. Accordingly, appeal rights are scattered and inconsistent; they are patchwork rather than systematic.

In Chapter 3 we canvass the relationship between justice or accountability and the efficient operation of government policy. In general, along with numerous other commentators, we take the view that the two concepts are not inimical but rather two sides of the same coin. We take the opportunity to examine the contribution of justice systems to corporate planning, the attainment of performance indicators and objectives. We also attempt to assess the value of different types of procedures for quality control within the administration. One of the themes which flow through this book is the need for coherence, the need for an overview, to supervise and to keep our system of justice in a constant state of repair. We believe new bodies need to be given these tasks in order to keep the needs of the administrator/ executive and those of the citizen in an acceptable state of balance.

This leads us naturally to a consideration of the ongoing need for mechanisms to achieve this end. The lack of a Ministry of Justice has been lamented by many commentators over the years and this point of view has gained many adherents in recent times. The reasons for this will not be spelled out here, but what we will say is that some body responsive to overall justice needs with the authority to give a lead in reaffirming a commitment to institutional justice would greatly enhance the likelihood of a coherent and systematic approach to grievance redress. In Chapter 4, we examine these arguments more closely and the relationship which a Ministry of Justice might have with another body charged with the oversight of our general administrative and indeed constitutional affairs. We look at the existence of such bodies in the common law world, for example, and explain how we believe that such a development would enhance the values which we espouse throughout the book.

In Chapter 5, we attempt a conceptual analysis of the strengths and weaknesses of different types of grievance redress mechanisms with a view to producing an analysis of ideal-types of dispute resolution machinery for disputes against the state. We do this in circumstances where the institutional suggestions ought to pull in the direction of improved service standards to the public. There are many reasons for this, which we shall not examine at this point. However, to take a simple illustration, we envisage a reformed ombudsman system, particularly at the level of the Parliamentary Commissioner for Administration (PCA), who would operate in a way more in keeping with overseas models. This could be expected to produce principles of good administration against which the ombudsman could judge the performance of public bodies, thereby raising standards in the public services. The potential of the *Citizens' Charter* could move us in a similar direction.

The argument in Chapter 5 has to be assessed in the light of the other suggestions we make; for example, those in Chapter 4, concerning permanent bodies with a brief to examine the whole of the governmental machine against a constellation of notions and expectations. In other words, the recommendations made at different stages in our argument should prove mutually reinforcing, so that one way or another the culture of administrative justice would be substantially improved.

A good part of Chapter 5 will concern itself with the relative merits of ombudsmen and court-type systems. We regard this as central to any serious reconsideration of our system of justice against the state. Even so, we also begin to draw out the relationships between courts and tribunals from the point of view of their general conceptual capacities. We have already made it clear that we believe that the courts should be reserved for issues of general importance; to that we would add that we would expect them to operate as appeal courts on points of law from the lower levels of the system. Even so, for justice to have meaning in a modern administrative state, there must be ample opportunity for a reconsideration of decisions made by officials *on their merits*. It is in this area in particular that there is a lack of pattern or coherence and again we attempt to lay down criteria and institutions for reconsideration on the merits of a decision, not least where administrative discretion exists. An appeal against such decisions could take several forms: internal to the body concerned; external, say, to the minister or to an independent tribunal. We make no apologies for saying at this early stage that in principle we favour an extension of appeals to independent tribunals, though where important issues of policy exist we understand the need for exceptions. Even so, there are areas where the minister or other authority's decision ought to be final in the sense of not giving rise to a further appeal on merits. However, there ought to be far fewer of these than is currently the case.

We also develop the idea of the citizen's legitimate expectations as a consumer of public services; most notably, though not entirely, as a result of the *Citizens' Charter*. Although these developments are in their infancy, there is no doubt that a quasi-contractual set of promises – breach of which gives rise to automatic compensation – can be a very valuable device for advancing justice against the state. The great advantage, for all the shortcomings which we will speak to later, is that a measure of compensation may be made automatically available without recourse to the courts or, indeed, any less formal adjudicative machinery. Furthermore, by documenting and highlighting standards and performance measurement criteria, government can go beyond the general constitutional requirements of the courts. At the time of writing, the White Paper on the *Citizens' Charter* has been supplemented by a whole raft of individual charters from a range of governmental bodies. It may be worth saying at this stage that a range of monitoring procedures is being foreshadowed. We clearly welcome this, since establishing standards without a monitoring process would be highly unsatisfactory. And just as by improving procedures ombudsmen can render even-handed justice more likely, so can quality-control monitoring of standards.

There is also a belief in the air that competition, even in the public services, is the best guarantee of quality service. However, it is a truism to say that even in the private sector competition is rarely perfect, which is why we have an Office of Fair Trading, a Monopolies and Mergers Commission (MMC) and EC competition law. We shall therefore have a little to say on the accessibility of these bodies and devices as they affect the justice enterprise. We will also need to address the implications of encouraging competition in the form of contracting out public services. This is, of course, because the citizen will have no direct contract with the provider of the service and will usually have to rely on the governmental authority to vindicate their claims.

In Chapter 6, we move to a discussion of the world of tribunals. We discuss some of the more successful ones and indicate areas where we believe there are some serious gaps in the justice system, since we reiterate that no clear and coherent pattern can be discerned for the existence or non-existence of tribunals. They are, we believe, the great success story of British administrative law and, when working effectively, can provide an excellent, inexpensive and accessible way of redressing grievances. We canvass the idea of a general administrative tribunal for hearing complaints against government at large and also argue the need for a systematic defence of any new administrative jurisdiction not being subject to an external appeal. We also say a little about public inquiries and examinations.

This leads us in Chapter 7 to a reconsideration of the role of British ombudsmen. However, we shall say little concerning the world of private sector ombudsmen, even though the public and private realms are becoming increasingly intertwined. We do not have space available to treat this increasingly important body of law. Having explored the inherent qualities of ombudsman systems, we turn to an examination of the operation of British ombudsmen in the light of the activities of ombudsmen elsewhere. We explore the tension between what might be seen to be the competing roles of ombudsmen in redressing grievances as opposed to improving administrative processes. We take the view that much more emphasis on the latter is required than generally appears to be the case in Britain. We also suggest reforms which we believe fit in with the whole justice culture as we envisage it.

In Chapter 8 we turn to 'internal' systems of grievance redress; that is, to systems which are internal to the body being complained against. We will have made clear by this stage that more effort on such procedures is called for than is presently the case. Our work on local government complaints procedures some five years ago indicated that a great deal was still to be done to improve channels of complaints for constituents. Although some improvements may have been affected since then, it is clear that many authorities still fall far short of acceptable standards. We might add, however, that the local ombudsman plays a valuable role in this area, advising as it does on model complaints procedures for those local authorities which seek its advice. The local ombudsman has a fairly standard letter of advice, which it makes available on these occasions, addressing the following matters: accessibility, confidentiality, speed and simplicity. They also address the issues of authority-wide procedures, the desirability of appointing a complaints officer, training, monitoring and quality control. It may be useful at this point to look at the results of a small survey which we conducted in 1991 in relation to NDPBs.

We approached seventeen of the NDPBs listed in Schedule 1 of the Parliamentary and Health Service Commissioners Act 1987 with a view to examining their practices and experiences in handling complaints. We selected across a range of very different types of activities performed. We used both postal and interview techniques and received responses from fifteen of the seventeen NDPBs. By way of caution, we ought to say that eight of the bodies concerned were subject to statutory procedures for the hearing of limited classes of complaint, though none of them had an across-the-board obligation imposed. In the event, only one of the fifteen appeared to have a written complaints procedure, though many of them possessed 'defensive' internal procedures for handling ombudsman enquiries, a matter which we have found elsewhere in the public sector. Nevertheless, some encouraging developments were observed. One example is the Housing Corporation, which contains a performance review division which is Financial Management Initiative-linked (for FMI, see later chapters) with quality assurance and targets and turn-round times attached. Such items are just the sort of levers which the ombudsman should be capable of pulling and just the sort of thing into which open channels of accountability could feed.

Eight of the NDPBs had, at that time, no experience of an ombudsman enquiry. Now granted that some NDPBs are substantially regulatory in character and are less likely to attract complaints from members of the public than others, there is nothing so unique about any of them which causes us to believe that published complaints procedures are irrelevant. We take the view that the official justice system would have far less to do if proper concern was taken to hear and receive complaints from the general public. To draw a parallel, it is rare for someone to want to take Marks & Spencer to court. Be that as it may, we assess the utility of different types of complaint processes, the use of codes of practice, publicity for procedures, *de novo* review by senior officers, the experience of social security adjudication officers, case conferences, the relationship between

employment grievance procedures and 'consumer' complaints, and conclude with a summary of best practices and caveats. We draw particular
attention in Chapter 5 to the use of consumer advocates within the administration, a development of some standing in the USA.

Chapter 9 focuses on the regulation of utilities with an element of strong
public concern. Self-regulation is also addressed at this point, as is the role
of the OFT and its relations with other regulatory regimes.

In Chapter 10, we deal with the formal justice system in the shape of the
courts. We examine their traditional role in curbing administrative excess,
and we address their strengths and weaknesses. We do not restrict ourselves
to the British courts, given the growing importance of both the ECHR and
the European Court of Justice (ECJ). Even so, we examine an alternative
role for the courts in the light of the extended regimen of coherent
administrative justice which we advocate. We reiterate that the courts'
primary function should be that of constitutional quality control. We
examine the case for regional courts and propose the office of 'public interest
defender'.

The final chapter contains our conclusions and is effectively an agenda for
reform.

CONCLUDING REMARKS

What we attempt here is two-fold. First, we examine present arrangements
in the field of justice against the state across the spectrum. Naturally in a
work of this size, we cannot offer comprehensive coverage, but we hope to
draw a fairly accurate map of the processes currently in operation. In doing
so, we identify both structural weaknesses and best practices. This enables
us to undertake the second task, the one we feel to be most important. That
is to set out an agenda for a complete and comprehensive system of justice
against the state. It is unashamedly an agenda for reform. Not everyone will
agree with every part of it, but we hope that we can partake in the broader
debate. We have no doubt that our present system, for all its many strengths,
is too *ad hoc*, too piecemeal and too unpatterned to be entirely satisfactory.

We advocate not just an examination of our system of public law justice
as a whole in seeking coherence and overall fairness, but an examination of
the institutions, which should ensure that the system stays in constant repair,
moves with the times and exposes fewer and fewer gaps. We hope our
readers will regard this as a worthwhile exercise.

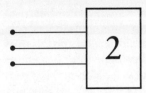

THE REDRESS OF GRIEVANCES

You must never complain; some of them did complain and they were killed by
the Destroyer

(After I Corinthians X, 6)

We take it as elementary that redress of grievance is a basic social necessity.
There has not been a group, tribe or society among which grievances have
not arisen and which did not require resolution; the more effective and
speedy the resolution, the better for the overall peace. We do not deny that
unresolved grievances or conflict have their constructive role to play in social
development; nor do we deny that methods adopted to resolve grievances
may only deal with the symptoms and not the disease. Grievances may
remain subliminal, or suppressed, or those who feel them may be reluctant
to raise them for a complex web of reasons. The group in question may
encourage the raising of some kinds of grievance, or grievances on some subjects but not on others. One tier of government may encourage the raising
of grievances about another tier of government, but not about its own
activities. Or the way a group is structured simply prevents certain kinds of
grievance being raised to the level of consciousness, or prevents situations
being perceived as ones over which a grievance may be expressed. So much
is elementary.

By concentrating upon grievances, we do not wish to convey the impression that the redress of grievances takes pride of place in a pecking order
of social tasks, that it assumes automatic priority over other important
functions, such as effective regulation of behaviour to minimize anti-group
or disruptive tendencies or to counter abuses of a dominant position,
economic or otherwise. Nor do we wish to argue that the resolution of

grievances is the most important task in what Karl Llewellyn (1940) termed the 'Law Jobs', i.e. those tasks which are necessary as minimum components of co-existence in any group. These jobs he described as disposition of trouble cases: the grievance remedial task; channelling of people's behaviour to avoid or minimize conflict; establishing a group's decision-making processes to provide authoritative answers to problems or disputes; establishing a policy-making framework to provide direction and incentive for the group; and lastly developing the human skills to achieve the smooth and fair operation of the previous tasks (Llewellyn, 1940). We would be the first to accept that all these tasks are of equal importance to that of grievance redress and, in our own work in different ways, we have directed our attention to the relationship between law and policy-making for instance. However, grievance redress has a particular pull on our attention, both because of our legal backgrounds and because of its pivotal role in the performance of the other law jobs (Birkinshaw, 1985a). Furthermore, we have both noticed in a wide variety of contexts that an absence of effective grievance procedures is commonplace among our public institutions, hybrid institutions and privatized utilities. We are clearly of the view that a failure to provide effective redress is not only indicative of a failure of legitimate democratic expectations, but that it is also symptomatic of other shortcomings, of various levels of seriousness, in the provision of services; accountability for the exercise of power; efficiency and effectiveness in administration; a lack of public procedures to develop policy and to overview its implementation and to carry out an open performance review.

WHAT CONSTITUTES A GRIEVANCE?

The term 'grievance' has been used to cover anything from what is in effect a request for information to a sense of unremedied wrong which might have the capability to topple a government. The term 'complaint' is also used frequently as an analogue of grievance: are the two the same? Our basic approach is to treat them as interchangeable terms and to give a broad interpretation as to what constitutes a complaint or grievance, otherwise we will be befogged by jurisdictional casuistry. However, distinctions have been drawn between the two terms and it may be beneficial to outline the differences in approach (Rawlings, 1986a).

A grievance to some connotes a sense of wrong or injury to one's interests, dignity or rights, either felt personally or on behalf of another and which sense of injury has not been rectified or assuaged through any process or procedure. It clearly does not include a simple request for information, though obviously where a request is refused, that may well become a grievance. If a grievance is distinguishable from a complaint – and to repeat that in this work we do not make the distinction – the difference probably lies in the fact that a complaint is more closely associated with the raising of an objection before there has been any attempt to resolve the matter. Where resolution is attempted and fails – even if it constitutes a simple request to review a decision informally – then it becomes a grievance. Here we are concerned with both complaints procedures and grievance procedures. Throughout the book, we shall treat the terms 'complaints' and 'grievances' interchangeably. We repeat that we do not wish to introduce excessive legalism and a broad approach will be adopted. The Commission for Local Administration (1978) referred to the expression 'complaint' covering not only a grievance but also a 'query'. We would expect the query to embody an expression of dissatisfaction.

We must also point out the obvious fact at this stage that a complaint or a grievance, where it remains unresolved, may not only assume varying degrees of severity, from the trivial to the government toppling, but the subject matter may be infinitely variable. It may also be obvious, but when complaining against a bureaucracy, one tends to notice that complaints or grievances fall into categories – delay, treatment by an official, failure to exercise discretion in one's favour, serious abuse by an official – which may well constitute a disciplinary offence, misapprehension of facts by an official or misinterpretation of rules being common categories but not the exclusive ones.

GRIEVANCE REDRESS AS A STATE RESPONSIBILITY

Is grievance redress a state responsibility? Historically, the Crown in England, as did executive powers elsewhere, claimed a prerogative to dispense and administer justice, a prerogative claimed at various times as against other systems of justice dispensation, e.g. that of the Church. Most famously, the Crown claimed in the person of James I a right to dispense justice personally by sitting as a justice in his own courts. This claim was rejected, surprisingly successfully, by the Chief Justice in a famous landmark decision of the early seventeenth century, a decision which emphasized the 'methodological autonomy' of legal reasoning and the highly refined, artificial and acquired skills which its practice demanded (*Prohibitions del Roy*, 1607). What has been accepted since then is that the courts of law are the final arbiters of legality, the supreme interpretators and expounders of the law, and courts, while professing independence, are state bodies. Furthermore, we should not overlook the fact that the prerogative was claimed jealously not only to maintain control of dispute resolution at the higher levels but also to help achieve a common outlook in values and to maintain the King's peace. A vital aspect in grievance remedying is that it provides valuable information to the authorities on what is going on and what is going wrong.

The provision of constitutionally mandated regimes for dispute resolution was achieved by the common law, and the King's courts, taking over responsibility for dispute resolution from other systems of justice. Of course, the common law system did not simply replace other systems of law; it merely absorbed them, as in the case of canon law and equity (the latter being a form of personal justice of the monarch dispensed by the Lord Chancellor historically), systems of local law – a specific example concerned local forestry and customary laws in the eighteenth century (Hay *et al.*, 1975; Thompson, 1975) – and to a significant extent the Law Merchant. This latter was a special body of commercial law administered through its own courts. When exigencies of state affairs or those brought about by pressure of work necessitated it, special tribunals could be established to expedite the disposition of trouble cases. Existing judges would preside over these tribunals; in a way, the Star Chamber was such a body, but less well known was the resort to special tribunals to deal with disputes in the rebuilding of London after the Great Fire of 1666. They were presided over by King's justices. In other words, special or local systems of justice would be brought within the province of the common law, the common law of the state, while at the same time the state's judges would be commissioned to administer justice through more localized or informal fora than a court of law.

Today, where an activity or service or area of administration are provided by the state or public sector, a common pattern has been to establish tribunals or ombudsmen under a statute to deal with disputes. In Chapter 5, we examine the strengths and weaknesses of these two devices relative to one another. In some cases, statutory ombudsmen, which includes those set up pursuant to statute as well as those specifically established within a statute, have been created for 'private' areas of activity, e.g. for building societies, the legal profession and financial services. In other areas, an ombudsman or some other grievance remedial device such as the Press Complaints Commission has been established on a 'voluntary' basis as a necessary component of self-regulation with state approval; if they were not accepted by the interest group, there was the threat of statutory schemes imposed upon them by the government. The spectre of Parliament taking an active and permanent interest in the affairs of a professional body is usually sufficient to prompt the body into some form of visible and credible self-regulation.

Historically, then, the state (and on our discussion of the concept, see Birkinshaw *et al.*, 1990) has had a central role in grievance redress, whether through the provision of courts or other procedures. If not directly involved in providing, it will often be involved in pressurizing for the creation of appropriate mechanisms and overseeing them. An interesting example of this occurred in the case of the UK's first privately run prison on Humberside. It is a showpiece for privatization in a subject area commonly perceived as one which, like defence and security, is the preserve of the state. In the prison, a Controller appointed by the Home Secretary is responsible for disciplinary offences and the prison has its own Board of Visitors, although there is close supervision by the Home Office. The regime is very similar to that which exists in state prisons (see Chapter 8). Quite clearly, one of the most significant trends of the 1980s was the realization of administrative overload and the consequent hiving-off or privatization of state responsibilities and activities. If one were to take the arguments of free marketeers to their conclusion, then all those activities currently performed by the state should be hived-off to private bodies. As we have remarked in detail elsewhere, this is not in reality the removal of the state, rather its reformulation (Birkinshaw *et al.*, 1990). Nor can the state simply off-load and ignore, the consequences; an effective *system* of redress and justice is a state responsibility and an irreducible state responsibility. Governors may not accept that claim as a moral necessity; but they would have to confront it as a matter of political reality in the face of system breakdown, disruptive conduct or growing public discontent. Let governors ignore justice and any, or all, of these will follow. Among free marketeers, it may be fashionable to decry the state, but rarely the nation. Provision of justice systems is a subject which ultimately the nation must address if the provision is to be coherent and cohesive. This does not mean that the nation or state, for we do not discern the distinction, has to take direct responsibility for their provision in every detail or to provide every procedure. This point should be seen in the context of two observations.

First, other dispute resolution mechanisms apart from the courts will frequently be invoked, a point alluded to above, because an expanded state provides more opportunities for injustice against citizens; and in discussion of an expanded state, let us discuss the essence and not the rhetoric. Indeed, not only judicial bodies but also political bodies will be unable to cope and provide relief in the vast majority of cases. Even if the state does not provide other procedures, it cannot safely ignore the supervision of those generated by social or economic intercourse in the 'private sector'. Supervision is a necessary minimum component to ensure independence and efficiency. Secondly, ADR schemes will flourish – ADR being Alternative Dispute Resolution mechanisms.

Both of these developments are responses to administrative overload in the provision of justice. We will examine ADR in a moment, noting that its origins lie in the wish of lawyers to bypass congested court dockets or to fashion more appropriate procedures for particular disputes. In a British context, the two have combined together to produce a variety of grievance remedial devices outside the usual processes of judicial and political decision making. So we see the resort to tribunals, public inquiries, ombudsmen, administrative mechanisms such as the Broadcasting Complaints Commission, regulatory agencies and consumer councils or forms of self-regulation. The *Citizens' Charter* continues this tradition. On the public side, what this amounts to is very often a knee-jerk reaction by the state to provide a safety valve to redress grievances. All too frequently, there is as little systematization about the appointment of such bodies as there is in the allocation of decision-making functions more generally in the British polity. We would add that there has been more reshaping of the public sector in the last decade than at any time since the latter half of the nineteenth century. For a variety of reasons, the state has to provide fairness systems across the broad spectrum of its activities and those the superintendence of which it cannot avoid. To the courts falls the responsibility of being the checker or that of overall quality-control maintenance. The ADR movement really develops from a concern among practitioners and legal academics about the provision of effective mechanisms outside the courts to provide a service to their clients to settle their disputes, clients who are caught in the clutches of a seriously overworked legal system. ADR is concerned with a failure by the official legal system to cater for the multiplicity of disputes modern society generates; the resort by the state to devices outside the legal and political processes reflects the official acknowledgement that its procedures cannot cope. What we have to consider in this book is the extent to which official thought has been given to creating the optimum form of procedure for different kinds of disputes and what needs to be done to establish what the optimum procedures are.

Excluding for the time being reports into specific areas of activity such as prisons, there have been four major reports into administrative justice in Britain; the last reported in two stages. The first two were government reports. The first, the Donoughmore Report (1932), was essentially preoccupied by the extent of the delegation of legislative and adjudicatory powers to Ministers and tribunals in the post-1918 British state. It was really concerned with the supremacy of regular law, meaning the courts, and the supremacy of Parliament. Its contribution to the debate on justice in the administrative state was strictly limited. The Franks Report of 1957 was established to inquire into statutory tribunals and inquiries; by the designation 'statutory', it was to address the more visible dispute resolution mechanisms created by the state. The Whyatt Report of 1961 was instrumental in bringing to life the ombudsman in this country. The last was the Justice-All Souls Committee report on *Administrative Justice* in 1988.

We examine these reports in later chapters but we should note that the 1988 report continued the tradition set by Donoughmore and Franks (and at least they were government-appointed) of working within a given framework and not raising fundamental questions about the nature of administrative justice in the contemporary state. The report raises issues that should have been raised and properly addressed in the 1960s. The fact that they were not raised at that time was not the fault of the authors of the 1988 report; they did, however, adopt a very safe posture from which to approach their review, no doubt in their desire to be taken seriously by the governors and officials whose tendency to status quo, or opposition to radicalism which they have not sired, would be reassured by the unquestioning approach of the committee's authors. This is not to say that the report did not contain critical material or helpful suggestions. It simply avoided fundamental questions which must be addressed in a rapidly changing state structure.

The questions which we would place at the top of the agenda are the following. First, in order to assess the nature and efficacy of administrative justice in the contemporary state, we have to have some idea of what the structure of the modern state looks like. As well as plotting the visible mechanisms along with the informal processes, we must identify the devices employed by the state to perform or facilitate its administration including its resort to private bodies or interest groups: the public places and the private places. We have catalogued these developments elsewhere (Birkinshaw *et al.*, 1990). Obviously, we move along a spectrum from government bodies properly so called, to public corporations and then into the world of non-departmental bodies or quangos. In looking at many government agencies, we must be alive to the fact that bodies sounding functionally similar (e.g. an agency or commission) may in fact be carrying out very different functions with obvious implications for grievance handling. For instance, an agency may be a regulatory agency or it may be a service provider as in the case of the Benefits Agency, or it may be both. We have to take the elementary point that a procedure suiting one functional type of institution may not suit another. This point has been made in relation to the traditional departments of state (Birkinshaw, 1985b).

Secondly, what are different procedures good at doing, or, to put the matter another way, when should particular kinds of disputes be referred to specific kinds of procedures? These questions have been asked before, of course, but usually within the confined ambit of discussion whereby it is agreed that a complicated point of law is more appropriately dealt with by the courts. A dispute over fact or merits for an individual entitlement or amount which does not justify court intervention, or which requires specialist treatment which courts are not equipped to provide should go to tribunals. Where no trappings of independent adjudication are required or where claims on a finite, cash-limited fund are involved, and not an infinite source of revenue, it may well be acceptable, reserving for the time being any discussion upon the content of 'acceptable', to keep the matter within a department, or more obviously under departmental control, rather than hand it to a tribunal. Where the problem at hand concerns the application of policy to an area or region, the initial impact does not affect so much the individual and so is not susceptible to a series of justiciable disputes; its impact is at the group level and a public inquiry or a public meeting may well be more appropriate. Where policy needs to be developed in a sensitive area or the law applied in a specialist and sensitive manner, it may be more appropriate for a minister to hand the subject to an independent agency which may also be given the role of dealing with complaints. What has not been addressed at the official level is how this discussion applies to developments that are characteristic of post-1970s change in Britain, although there are studies relating to the use of tribunals in different roles as well as specialist agencies engaging in regulatory activities (Baldwin and McCrudden, 1987). This development includes the proliferation of ombudsmen, the resort to self-regulation under governmental or statutory codes of guidance, the widespread privatization and regulation of utilities and the expansive use of private sector bodies to achieve public purposes.

The third question concerns the content of the state's obligation to provide for redress of grievance. We have already expressed our views that as well as bearing responsibility for those services or areas of administration which the state delivers, a responsibility which includes effective and responsive grievance procedures, the state cannot simply delegate responsibility to a private undertaker and withdraw. There will be questions about the nature of delegation and ministerial responsibility over the extent and mode of delegation, the residuary responsibility of the state, questions of licensing, competition, quality maintenance, supervision and the assuaging of public discontent. We have long argued that there is rarely a clear-cut division in any event between the public and private; there are rather varying levels of compenetration and dependency between the state and significant economic and commercial and professional organized interests (Birkinshaw *et al.*, 1990). As we find elsewhere, the state may privatize but it cannot turn its back. This book seeks to eke out the contours of the contemporary state and to establish the duty upon the state to provide fairness regimes and quality control throughout its activities.

Other countries have recent experience of an overhaul in their system of administrative justice. As we write, we are of the view that an overhaul of the kind that was undertaken in Australia in the broad realm of administrative justice would be a valuable starting point in any discussion of administrative justice. Such a discussion is all the more timely, given the impetus of the *Citizens' Charter* and fundamental reforms in our public institutions. What does the Australian experience – known in fact as the New Administrative Law – have to offer?

The 'New Administrative Law' (NAL) dates in fact from 1976. The reform comprised an Administrative Appeal Tribunal (AAT or GAT), through which an increasing number of administrative decisions has been subject

to *de novo* review, i.e. review on the merits of a case and not simply on
the legality of a decision. The latter basis of review is the usual extent of
judicial review in the UK, certainly in England. In the UK, tribunals
may review the merits of a decision, but rarely at the level of a ministerial
discretion as is the case in Australia. Further additions were a Commonwealth ombudsman system, a dramatically reformed system of judicial
review and, last but not least, freedom of information (FOI) laws which
have crucially influenced other aspects of NAL. On this latter phenomenon,
two Australian commentators have delivered the following judgment:

> The most significant change has been the increase in the availability of
> information about what the government and officials do. These changes
> . . . have a number of effects. First, people have access to information
> on the structure of departments and agencies, and on the procedures,
> guidelines and policies according to which administrative decisions are
> made. Secondly, they may apply as of right for access to information
> about individual decisions or classes of decision, and thereby discover
> whether particular decisions have or have not been made affecting them.
> If they discover that a decision has been made which affects them, they
> can request a statement of the reasons for that decision. Finally, there
> is additional machinery by which the decision itself can be reviewed.
>
> While the existence of review machinery is important, the fact that
> the public have rights of access to information about administrative
> procedures and an entitlement to reasons for particular decisions
> affecting them will, in many cases, obviate the need for the use of the
> review machinery. The majority of conscientious officials makes every
> effort to act in accordance with both the law and policy guidelines.
> (Thynne and Goldring, 1987, p. 240)

Evidence from Australia shows that FOI increases efficiency in so far
as adverse decisions against departments forces officials to exercise great
care to maintain better records and that what is written will be clearly and
unambiguously understood several years later. Furthermore, FOI has led to
improved filing and the need to develop filing registers. Based upon our own
researches in the USA and Australia, there appears little truth in the belief,
promoted in May 1992 by the Prime Minister as a reason for rejecting FOI
in the UK, that FOI results in increased reliance upon oral communications
and a reluctance to commit discourse to permanent record. Such a reliance
would in any event increase the likelihood of legal or ombudsman intervention by way of attacks on the exercise of discretion, fair procedure or maladministration, respectively.

Under the NAL, the Commonwealth ombudsman can receive complaints
directly and can commence investigations on his or her own initiative. The
ombudsman theme we pick up on in a later chapter. Likewise, we address

the detailed operations of the AAT and its power to review a decision, even of a minister, on the merits and the activities of the Administrative Review Council (ARC) at a later and more appropriate stage. The Administrative Decisions Judicial Review Act 1977 requires that reasons for decisions be provided on request – this in fact is a practice followed by a number of departments and agencies which provide a statement of relevant facts and findings without any formal request when informing a person of a decision adversely affecting them. The person affected is then in a far better position to decide whether or not to seek internal or external review than is a person who remains ignorant of the grounds on which an official has acted.

Thynne and Goldring (1987) claim that the NAL has produced a change in the climate and culture of complaining. The reforms have not only increased the number of mechanisms available for reviewing administrative action, they have also helped to reduce psychological and cultural barriers against complaining by 'victims of the system'.

We should note in passing at this point (see Chapters 4, 5 and 6) that although the NAL says little about the shaping of policy-making procedures and administrative justice, the ARC along with the Attorney-General's Department and Senate Standing Committees comment upon the desirability of appeal mechanisms from administrative decisions created by new legislation and whether appeal should be made to the AAT. Draft legislation, both primary and secondary, is passed to the ARC by the Attorney-General's Department for the ARC's advice on whether administrative decisions should be subject to appeal on the merits. Senate committees also examine draft legislation, including delegated legislation, to ensure that there is no over-reliance by the executive on expansive discretion affecting an individual's rights or interests without safeguards by way of appeal to independent bodies. It needs only to be said at this early stage that the ARC has conducted an investigation into the distinctions between the AAT and the Commonwealth ombudsman and their procedural *modi operandi*. We address their study, which is a very useful addition to the topic of appropriate fora for challenging administrative decision making in Chapter 5.

What we see in the Australian example is a much more thorough examination of administrative justice than anything we have witnessed in a British context. We also have the benefit of over a decade of practical experience of the NAL. We would not press the case for the introduction of the Australian reforms without more in this country. However, we would put forward the Australian experience against those who would argue that a fundamental re-examination of administrative justice in the contemporary state is not possible or fruitless and that wholescale change is neither possible nor desirable. We will let the reader decide where he or she stands on these matters. We should also note that in Canada there has been widespread reform in administrative agencies and means of redress provision under the influence of constitutional reform via a Bill of Rights, anti-discrimination legislation, FOI legislation, privacy protection legislation and human rights legislation. These developments have taken place at a time when the Canadian Law Commission has taken a leading role in researching into and recommending reforms in administrative law, and research papers have included studies into the Australian AAT and *Towards a Modern Federal Administrative Law* (1987). This latter dwells, *inter alia*, on the fate of administrative justice given the decline in ministerial responsibility as a ruling practice of government and the emergence of independent and semi-independent agencies of government.

Both the Canadian and the Australian developments have been heavily influenced by the US model and by the work of the Administrative Conference of the United States (ACUS), which is constantly making recommendations and giving advice on administrative justice in the federal system of government and administration. We examine the work of ACUS in Chapter 4.

ALTERNATIVE DISPUTE RESOLUTION

We referred above to the Alternative Dispute Resolution (ADR) movement. ADR has been concerned more about easing the congestion caused by over-full court dockets and the delay and expense associated with litigation than with the state as a justice provider. As the Dispute Resolution First Aid Kit for Attorneys makes clear, its major target is really lawyers seeking more effective means to facilitate resolution of their clients' problems:

> ADR has quietly slipped into the mainstream of legal practice. For some, the mention of ADR signals debate over whether some means for dealing with conflict is faster or better than litigation, while for others, ADR represents a reminder of traditional notions of legal negotiation and settlement. Both views miss the point. Over the past two decades ADR has become a cornucopia of processes, procedures and resources for responding to disputes, all of which supplement rather than supplant traditional approaches to conflict. Contrary to its label, ADR is not an alternative or substitute at all; it adds useful tools to an attorney's existing professional tool box.
>
> (Mackie, 1991, p. 1)

Other ADR advocates, on the other hand, as well as emphasizing relief of court congestion and reduction in expense and delay, suggest wider considerations in ADR. For example:

- to enhance community involvement in the dispute resolution process
- to facilitate access to justice
- to provide more 'effective' dispute resolution.

> (Goldberg, cited in Mackie, 1991, p. 3)

Although much of the ADR movement has been commercial and family law dominated – particularly in relation to arbitration, conciliation and negotiation – we share the aspirations of the above list and welcome them on to our own agenda. We believe passionately that an economically influenced sceptism about any model other than a market model of justice ought not to be allowed to drive out the noble tradition which sees justice as a community-based aspiration, not as an economist's plaything.

ADR has taken on board the ombudsman system, particularly as its utility is developed in the field of consumer redress. This has been accompanied by a rejuvenation of interest in the limits of the various British ombudsmen and a quickening of interest in the European ombudsman, particularly post-Maastricht. However, it is important that pragmatic, cumulative responses – especially if invoked without any thought to overall design – are avoided in our systems of public law and in the devices which may help to achieve greater justice in the modern state, be those devices ombudsmen or procedures or processes whose duty is the resolution of grievances.

CONCLUSION

We have endeavoured in this chapter to address a variety of preliminary but important points. First, we have given a wide interpretation to grievance and complaint and note that we intend to use the terms interchangeably. It covers all forms of raising objection, disputing a matter or even expressing dissatisfaction by way of making a query. Frequently, the point where information is requested will be the point where a complaint may be made or where information about a complaints procedure may be supplied. Secondly, we argue that the provision of justice systems to deal with grievances and their oversight, even in the age of ADR, is a state responsibility. This is clearly the case where the activities of the state or its surrogates impinge on its citizens. It is also equally true where powerful economic actors in monopoly or privileged or simply influential positions have the power to affect individuals' lives. Thirdly, official and for want of a better expression semi-official thought has not adequately addressed the problem of identifying the optimum provision of justice systems and the optimum form that procedures should take in a changing state structure. The raw equipment may be there partially if not in its entirety; is it being put to best use? Finally, other countries have undertaken major reforms from which we might learn.

Governors have regarded efficiency as the ultimate pursuit of government in the 1980s and 1990s. Are efficiency and justice compatible?

3

ACCESS TO JUSTICE AND THE QUALITY OF ADMINISTRATION

What is the connection between 'access to justice' and the quality of administration? What contribution, if any, does access to justice make to the enhancing of accountability and the promotion of efficiency? Accessible and effective grievance remedial devices are a necessary component of accountability; the errors of decision makers can be corrected, oversights highlighted, abuses rectified, shortcomings avoided. But does access to justice promote efficiency? Government has become more receptive to the 'learning process' involved in grievance resolution; vital information can be gathered from complaints and grievances which can be used as an aid to future administration and provision of services. Mistakes, or the possibility of mistakes, may thereby be reduced. In May 1992, the Chief Secretary to the Treasury emphasized that service delivery was expected to be enhanced in the public sector without additional real resources. The *Citizens' Charter* would bring about increased efficiency in part, we would add, assisted by effective grievance procedures. The charter would play a vital role in the Public Expenditure Survey and allocation of public expenditure.

But the doing of justice may promote inefficiency. That will be the case where a concentration upon an individual's rights disrupts a major programme involving considerable human resources and expenditure, e.g. procedural irregularity in public hearings before approving a motorway scheme, demolishing a development after an unlawful compulsory purchase order, or the presence of a serious vitiating fault in a process of consultation which resulted in amended regulations or laws that have been acted upon by thousands of individuals, incurring massive public expenditure.

In all these cases, an insistence upon 'justice' in a complainant's favour would lead to varying degrees of administrative catastrophe. Public law mitigates such dilemmas by making the award of relief – where a case is established for relief – discretionary. An individual's entitlement has to be weighed against public welfare. In other cases, the disruptive outcome is avoided by the judiciary exacting less onerous duties of fair procedure so that no 'unfair process' has been pursued, or by limiting the range of those who can argue their case in court. In private law, particularly in the area of negligence, an individual right stands to be vindicated; the element of judicial discretion, where a right exists, is far less prominent. To avoid what may appear as catastrophic consequences for a single act of negligence, for example, the courts may limit the range and extent of a duty of care owed by, say, the police to citizens where the former have failed to arrest a dangerous criminal, or they may place the test of culpable behaviour at a high threshold. Or a duty may be curtailed by physical proximity, as in the case of escaping prisoners, so that only those in the vicinity of the prison may sue for negligent supervision. Further, courts may decide there is no duty to prevent particular forms of injury, such as 'pure economic loss' as opposed to physical damage or for nervous injury or shock to distant relatives and friends of those injured by a defendant's negligence.

What this amounts to is that in public law and in private law, judicial limits will be set to what justice demands. These limits may be more discretionary and utilitarian in the case of public law than in private law, though even in the latter the law works on certain calculations of public benefit tempering individual entitlement. It may well be that we should have an expanded public law of delict or tortious liability; but for this we would have to look to the statute book and not judicial decision.

What we must address is not the pursuit of a grievance to a conclusion which brings justice at the possible cost of administrative catastrophe, but rather how valuable lessons or 'learning experience' may be derived from effective grievance procedures, and how such procedures and other techniques contribute to an overall increase in efficiency. The emphasis is upon the reduction of grievance by the setting of appropriate standards of performance in which the public may participate, by systems of audit and monitoring (i.e. the monitoring of grievances for quality control) and by the provision of complaints procedures which provide knowledge about performance shortfall and overall improvement as well as resolve individual grievances. We believe that justice and efficiency are not mutually exclusive; rather, they are mutually supportive where appropriate procedures are set in place to address a wider range of duties than simply remedying a complaint. Given our interests, the latter task is not one we would belittle. What we have to do is put complaining in a wider context. In short, can justice and efficiency serve each other and be mutually supportive? Or is the widespread provision of justice mechanisms destructive of efficiency? By its own actions, the government would not see this antipathy, as witness the reforms in the privatized utilities which have provided for the setting and meeting of appropriate standards of service and the mandatory creation within industries of grievance procedures (see Chapter 9). Another dramatic example comes from British Rail, where the Central Transport Consultative Committee reported in August 1992 that complaints had risen by 66 per cent since the introduction of the *Citizens' Charter* (*The Times*, 5 August 1992). These figures suggest the need for more effective complaints procedures than currently exist; after such consciousness-raising, their absence would be seen as an act of inefficiency in itself.

JUSTICE, EFFICIENCY AND GRIEVANCE REDRESS

Making mistakes that upset individuals or groups can be costly. Failing to rectify those mistakes, or providing the opportunity for them to be rectified, can be disastrous, both in terms of maintaining legitimacy and in terms of efficient delivery of services and programmes. A central preoccupation of the government since 1980 has been the promotion of efficiency in the delivery of governmental programmes. Efficiency is taken as achieving the same result at lower cost or lesser use of resources or achieving better results at similar costs. This objective has placed emphasis upon managerial performance; to instil an ethos of sound sensible management and cost-cutting from successful private enterprise to the public sector. As well as achieving efficient administration, it is concerned with trimming the public sector where possible or reshaping the public sector for more effective delivery of service and customer care (Common *et al.*, 1992).

We have long argued that effectiveness precedes efficiency; efficiency implies performance and performance implies objectives, or more accurately, the meeting of objectives. The meeting of objectives involves an assessment of effectiveness. Efficiency must be seen in terms of its contribution to effectiveness in meeting stated objectives (Birkinshaw *et al.*, 1990). Furthermore, the terms 'input', 'output' and 'outcome' suffuse the contemporary assessment of governmental programmes in the conduct of accountability analyses. Input refers to the amount of resources invested in a programme; output refers to the immediate result of that investment (e.g. the speed with which applications are dealt with); outcome, on the other hand, addresses the overall impact and success of a policy behind a programme – reducing unemployment or crime rates.

That said, our focus in this chapter is an investigation into the contribution that grievance procedures and other justice forms make to enhancing efficiency and improving service delivery. As such, grievance procedures

are a part of a much bigger package, the features of which have been prominent in all spectra of political thinking. The range of debate covers the Prime
Minister's *Citizens' Charter*, Opposition publications, the published views
of 'think tanks' of both the left and the right and the contributions of
consumer bodies. The spirit was probably best captured by the Prime
Minister's words in the charter, although support for the sentiment has been
articulated in other political groups:

> The White Paper sets out the mechanics for improving choice, quality,
> value and accountability. Not all apply to every service. But all have a
> common objective: to raise the standard of public services, up to and
> beyond the best at present available.
>
> (Cabinet Office, 1991, p. 2)

In the very next paragraph, the Prime Minister states that he wishes to
build upon the 'well-spring of talent, energy, care and commitment in our
public services' so that these qualities may be released to ensure that citizens
can have services in which they have 'confidence, and all public servants can
have pride'. We shall do no more than point out at this stage that the charter
says little about service provision in the private sector, apart from beefing up
the powers of utility regulators and competitive tendering, although the
Director-General of Fair Trading has made some important observations in
his report for 1990:

> My Office is neither a price commission, nor some sort of super
> consumer advice centre able to sort out individual problems. Our efforts
> are largely concerned with *preventing* problems and *improving* the
> trading environment.
>
> (OFT, 1990, p. 18; and see Chapter 9)

Looking through the exhortatory language, the charter sees public
services being improved by the setting of standards in all areas of service –
'Explicit standards, published and prominently displayed at the point of
delivery'. Standards will be progressively improved as services become more
efficient. Increased efficiency will be characterized by greater openness in
the running of services – though there is no mention of a freedom of information statute and subsequent statements have rejected such laws for central
government. It will be increased by the supply of full and accurate information about the provision of services, ensuring choice in service, non-
discrimination, accessibility and suitable explanations and procedures for
redress when things go wrong. This sounds acceptable and it would be
churlish to cavil at it. Passing over the question of adequate resources to
achieve these desiderata for the time being (although the charter informs us
that public spending amounts to £5000 on each adult per annum), the
charter draws upon the experience of a variety of agencies and practices

which have set the mould for governmental practice and service well into the twenty-first century. These reforms, for reforms they are, have projected into the centre of public performance the realization of greater competition and efficiency in public performance, i.e. borrowing what are seen as fundamentals of the marketplace and transposing them into the public sector, and the setting of performance standards that will act as targets so that progress may be checked, usually by way of independent and external audit, in the meeting of performance standards, privatization, buying 'public services' from private contractors and a clear commitment to improve value for money. The charter adumbrates consumer-conscious provisions such as 'Evidence that the views of those who use the service have been taken into account in setting standards' and 'Well sign-posted avenues for complaint if the customer is not satisfied, with some means of independent review wherever possible.'

In this, the charter is consumer-conscious in a way that previous central government managerial initiatives were not. At the least, the situation should be avoided where a procedure existed in the DHSS to deal with maladministration; for fourteen years nobody was informed about it! (Select Committee on the Parliamentary Commissioner For Administration, HC 158, 1991–92, Qus. 4 & 5; *Guardian*, 2 August 1991). We look at the consumer dimension more closely in Chapter 5.

IMPROVING EFFICIENCY IN ADMINISTRATIVE PERFORMANCE

It is necessary to say a little about the Next Steps agencies and the Financial Management Initiative (FMI) introduced in the early 1980s in central government and then spreading throughout government agencies and the public sector. The FMI contains some very important practices, viz. the setting of objectives of departmental administration, the establishment of performance indicators and the installation of monitoring and scrutiny programmes to gauge the meeting of objectives and performance. This involved the Efficiency Unit, which works alongside the Treasury and Office of the Minister of the Civil Service and its successor, working closely with ministers to develop the latter's departmental strategies for better management and the use of efficiency scrutinies and targets to ensure improved delivery of specific results and services, *not least services to the public*.

FMI took on board the scrutiny studies, introduced by Sir Derek Rayner, which looked at the running costs of programmes to ensure that they are within their budget and which assessed the delivery of policy objectives. 'In doing this they raise questions about the clarity of the objectives set and the effectiveness of the arrangements designed to deliver them.' They are also centrally concerned with accountability. The studies are designed to set out ways of achieving better value for money by improving the quality of service and use of resources, or by making savings without loss of essential output. A scrutiny is typically a ninety-day review. Three months after the review report – which is a detailed fact-finding exercise establishing what happened as opposed to what was supposed to happen – the department produces an action plan setting out how the scrutiny recommendations will be implemented, by when and by whom. A report from the department follows two years later specifying what has been achieved. Recent scrutinies with direct public impact include the community programme and community benefit; legal aid; health care (NI); improving the standard of service to the public in social security regional organization; and ministerial correspondence on, *inter alia*, complaints which we address in detail elsewhere in Chapter 8.

THE NEXT STEPS INITIATIVE

Next Steps is concerned with the development of executive agencies to deliver services to the public and which are outside the traditional Whitehall departmental structure. It seeks to separate the functions of policy development and service delivery. It follows the ideas contained in the Fulton Report of 1968, but 'the commitment to its implementation is new' (Davies and Willman, 1991, p. 1). Its origins were anti-public sector: a means of cutting back the public sector and facilitating privatization.

The central belief was that policy formulation (and responsibility for that) and effective management of service delivery were incompatible within a traditional department. This was because the restrictions on ministerial responsibility were 'incompatible with commercial competitiveness' (ibid., p. 3). Further, the efficient delivery of public services could not be obtained from within a traditional department, the structures and ethos of which inhibited good management.

Accompanying the Next Steps Initiative (NSI) was a Cabinet Office publication *Service to the Public* (1988). This acted as the benchmark for consumer-oriented management techniques in the public service. What was required was 'a rigorous examination of whether provision matches need and a strong determination to demonstrate what has or has not been achieved' (para. 5.1). Aims and objectives were to be set out and information collected on the extent to which those aims were being met. Methods of evaluation would be clearly defined. Publicized complaints procedures would act as aids to evaluation – 'for most departments the most commonly quoted indicator of performance is the number of complaints they receive' (para. 5.5). Consumer groups could be used to channel complaints and to convert them into constructive criticism. It presaged many of the developments in the *Citizens' Charter* and suggested the use of client surveys, a point developed by the National Audit Office, staff training and fuller explanations to the public.

There is evidence to show that central government is reacting to the growing interest in the effectiveness of services 'as measured by customer satisfaction to be found in the private sector and in public utilities at the local level' (Davies and Willman, 1991, p. 44). Davies and Willman cite the example of the framework document – the foundation document – of the Inland Revenue as an example of a framework document which has a customer awareness, albeit that many taxpayers may cavil at their designation 'customer'. The Contributions Agency has held consultation exercises with its consumer or client groups. This is all welcome, but a far more concerted effort must be made to allow the consumer voice to contribute effectively to the setting of performance indicators and to the monitoring of performance. We develop these points in Chapter 8.

While in some agencies – and also it should be added in some local authorities – it is possible to witness 'regular and careful listening to the customer' (Peters and Waterman, 1982), what is lacking is a legal duty to take seriously what they say in setting performance indicators and in monitoring performance. Nor do we believe that plans announced in relation to the *Citizens' Charter* which will involve the appointment of private consultants who will investigate to ensure that the provisions of the charter are being satisfied by agencies and bodies covered by the charter make good this democratic deficit.

The momentum for change facilitated by the introduction of agencies has tremendous potential for enhancing public service if the characteristics which distinguish the public from the private are recognized rather than minimized (Davies and Willman, 1991). Chief among these is the concept of citizenship and the right to equality and fairness, to accountability and responsiveness and humane treatment.

For the most part, we applaud the publication of corporate plans, the annual reports and framework documents themselves – though we note that the publication of these and so much more would be a legal requirement in the USA, Australia and Canada. Although the government has promised to be more open, it has avoided placing central government under FOI legal duties. This must lead to consideration of whether the new found consumerism in governmental strategy might be found wanting if subjected to FOI scrutiny. Indeed, it is interesting to observe that the discussions leading to the implementation of the *Citizens' Charter* are not to be opened up to public observation.

Redress of grievance, so much a part of government thinking, is an essential component in achieving accountability for service and performance. But there must be full and effective accountability for policy formulation; at present, this aspect is deficient. It will be all too easy, where many complaints are made, to sack or remove the manager, when the real problem is with departmental or governmental policies involving underinvestment.

We repeat that along with more focused lines of demarcation within government, clearer and more concentrated thought on fair and open grievance procedures will assist managerial responsibilities.

THE *CITIZENS' CHARTER*

Described as 'the most comprehensive programme ever to raise quality, increase choice, secure better value, and extend accountability', the government believed the *Citizens' Charter* would set standards for other countries as well as Britain. It would redefine the contract between the citizen and the state. The charter covers central government, local government, health care and utilities. The four main themes in the charter are to be achieved by market-led policies, which include more privatization, wider competition, further contracting out and more performance-related pay. It then outlines mechanisms which are of greater relevance to our present concern. These are: comprehensive publication of information on standards achieved, more effective complaints procedures, tougher and more independent inspectorates, and better redress for the citizen when things go badly wrong. Approaches would be tailored to specific services and local areas and detailed charters would be published for some individual services. In health care, for instance, there is particular reference to choice of general practitioner (GP) and being able to change GP easily, respect for privacy, dignity, cultural and religious beliefs and access to personal information about them. In health in particular, it would, the charter states, not be sensible to set centrally national standards which every health authority would be compelled to adopt. To which one might add that the more general local standards are, the more useless they will be in improving performance.

All public services will have to ask themselves what they are doing. They will have to publish their commitments to standards of service which will be independently monitored. Where there is a failure to reach the published standards, the newly empowered citizen can seek alternative services or compensation having ventilated any grievance through an appropriate procedure. Complaints can be used to gauge performance and to assist monitoring. The number of complaints about a school or unemptied dustbins or badly maintained roads will indicate that standards, if set at an appropriate level, are not being met, or if they are being met they require resetting. If, we would add, standards cannot be met within existing resources, then that may well indicate an insufficient budget and insufficient resources. This may well reflect a serious miscalculation with the policies of a department, the Treasury or the government.

The ministerial and administrative arrangements concerning the *Citizens'*
Charter we leave until Chapter 5. An advisory panel will provide generally
applicable guidance on the way in which standards should be specified.
These will seek to ensure quality control and quality assurance in the provision of services by relevant bodies. Increasing use is being made of standards
set by the British Standards Institute in setting such standards as BS 5750
(Barron and Scott, 1992). For exemplary service providers, an official seal
of approval known as the Charter Standard and Charter Mark may be
awarded.

The competitive marketplace suffuses the charter; the fear of competition engenders more constructive responses to complaints than authority,
it is believed (Pirie, 1991). So that to take a couple of examples, contract
compliance and penalty clauses will apply to services as diverse as hospital
treatment undertaken by contract with health authorities and local authority
housing repair contracts with sub-contractors or Direct Service Organizations (DSOs). A scheme such as this is operated in Liverpool by a housing
association dealing with people in acute need. Repairs are carried out by a
contractor on an approved list of contractors who is contacted by a tenant
and the bill is sent to the association. For some services, rail and London
Underground for instance, specific service targets can be set under existing
statutory provisions. Privatization – which has taken place in forty-six
industries since 1979, accounting for 'about two-thirds of the former
state sector of industry' – will continue. In education, schools and local
education authorities (LEAs) will come under a variety of duties to publish
information. These were published as the *Parents' Charter* in 1991 and are
now contained in the Education (Schools) Act 1992, s. 16.

Proposals concerning the purchase by public authorities of services to the
public from private contractors similarly empower the citizen to measure
performance against published performance indicators for standards of
service. In fact, some local authorities are requiring accreditation with
standards set by the British Standards Institute as a contract condition.
Failure to meet the standard will entail extra cost for the public and private
provider. Once again, greater efficiency will be enhanced by discovering
what grievances exist about services so that weaknesses may be remedied
before catastrophe ensues. Indeed, in the case of local authorities and other
agencies that are compelled to contract out, it will be in their obvious self-
interest to have worthwhile procedures to alert them to a defaulting or
inefficient contractor in order for the authority to take the necessary action.
However, in many cases, for example, government department/agency
relationships, health authority and service provider relationships, although
the relationship is described in contractual terms, it is not one that is legally
enforceable.

There is no doubt that the *Citizens' Charter* suggests ideas which are rich in potential to improve service and it makes suggestions for customer consultation and grievance redress which appear to go substantially beyond tokenism. But caution should be counselled; in drafting the *Parents' Charter*, the National Federation of Parents and Teachers Associations was not consulted. Appropriate procedures must be developed through which consumer values and choices may be identified so that they may then be incorporated into performance targets. A customer service manager in local social security offices has been a fairly long-standing practice, but issuing staff with name badges where they have contact with the public, although a simple sounding idea, does in fact cut against the traditional ethos of civil service anonymity and reminds us of a point we made above in relation to Next Steps: that the culture of the civil service is changing with the development of more and more agencies specializing in service delivery.

Complaints will be handled under a code of guidance which will contain a tight target for resolving complaints and 'clear information on further procedures if the customer is not satisfied with the response' (p. 42). Codes sound nice, but they may not be very effective. A code of guidance for complaints was drafted by the Commission for Local Administration and research conducted in the 1980s revealed that the code was effectively ignored in a large number of authorities (Lewis *et al.*, 1987). We need reassurance that the procedures will be implemented effectively and taken seriously by service providers to be both effective from the point of view of those who complain and to provide reliable data to assess the performance and shortcomings in delivery of service by the providers of services, those whose task it is to monitor performance and those whose duty it is to set targets. In passing, it is interesting to observe that in drawing upon existing complaints mechanisms, the charter claims that the procedure for prisoners maintains prisoner confidentiality, an assertion expressly refuted by the Woolf Report into prison riots in 1990–91 (Woolf, 1991, para. 14, 330 *et seq.*).

We certainly agree that complaints procedures need to be close to the ground and that the first point of contact must be accessible and clearly identified rather than removed and centrally located. However, we have often voiced our belief that, in local authorities, there should exist above a service complaints procedure an authority-wide procedure, possibly in the chief executive's office and containing members of the opposition as well as the leading party and independent outsiders. Its role would be not only to deal with the more difficult grievances, but also to take more strategic action for a particular service and services generally, based in part on the lessons to be learned from individual incidents. It is a clear example of the close proximity between grievance redress, the doing of justice, strategic planning and increased efficiency. We make detailed comments upon the suggestion for a Lay Adjudicator scheme in Chapter 8.

The charter declares its intention to augment the powers of audit, a subject we deal with below, although it concentrates upon local government and the health service – authorities will have to publish their responses to auditors' reports. There are no positive proposals for central government which include the executive agencies, although they are caught by the developments which we described and which led to the charter. Nor is there any reason to believe that the charter's thinking will pass them by.

The charter may well be a formidable expression of a particular philosophy, but we feel that it has set the framework for the future develop-ment of public service, just as the Next Steps has defined the future role of the public sector and central government. Whichever political party is at the helm of government, the general ethos has been established. Along with Next Steps, the *Citizens' Charter*, strange as it seems, may be used to advance very different political ideologies: from a market-dominated narrow consumerist vision as at present to a model which is rich in the ideals of participatory democracy. Although the charter sees the citizen primarily as an economic actor seeking to maximize choice and, one may add, in a manner which may be destructive of the uniformity of provision of public services, nevertheless the opportunities to embrace the richer vision and to develop service standards 'which appropriately reflect the attributes and qualities which' citizens value (NCC, 1991, p. 7) are there. We have not seen a government before making such declarations of intent to listen to the citizen and to base standards of service on their feedback and complaints and making such a public commitment to their promise. Much will be revealed in the unpackaging. But there is every reason to hope, for instance, that sustained analysis of service will not only produce better value for money, efficiency and effectiveness, but that expenditure on service will be matched more keenly to the perceived value and importance of the output. This could allow for a direct public impact upon the value and desirability of preferred governmental outcomes, i.e. an influence upon policies. 'Parts of the public sector which have been allocating huge resources to things of little benefit may well begin to husband those resources more assiduously' (Pirie, 1991, p. 24). To which we would add that they may be allocated more democratically if grievance procedures bring home the deficiency lying in inadequate investment rather than in poor delivery – a point made by the Central Transport Consultative Committee when commenting upon the large increase in complaints against British Rail following the introduction of the charter. This begs the question of effective user participation in the planning (dare one use that term?) of service provision. We would add that the market-dominated and individualistic philosophy which informs the charter is clearly not of a participatory democratic nature. Its model of just desert lies in contract, not need. 'Needs' are viewed as either subjective wants to which there is a contractual entitlement, or paternalistic bureaucratic judgements about others' 'well-being' (Barron and Scott, 1992).

Indeed, in the first annual report of the charter in November 1992, the Minister responsible for the report described it as a shift towards management by contract and by explicit objectives (Waldegrave, 1992), with the primary focus shifting to the contracting out of civil service functions. Here too, there will be an increasing distinction between the purchase and provision of services as applies in the NHS.

In passing, and we pick up on this theme in Chapter 11, the justice system itself (i.e. the administration of the courts) comes out particularly badly if the criteria of the charter are applied to it. The National Consumer Council conducted consumer research which identified a series of desirable reforms in court administration which basically follow the thrust of the charter, although they in fact predate it (NCC, 1991d, annex 3). The Lord Chancellor's Department does have performance indicators for the court processes, or aspects of it, but as of 1991 these were not publicized:

> The case against wider disclosure is that the system is still in the course of development, makes fairly crude assumptions and is not yet an adequate guide to performance. On the other hand, targets which are known to lawyers and judges as well as court staff are more likely to be met and if they are met can be registered.
>
> (NCC, 1991d, annex 3)

And, if registered, we believe, they can be refined and improved. Ignorance means that the public, those for whom justice exists, do not know whether internal performance indicators are being met. Their complaint, therefore, appears unspecific and unquantifiable.

AUDIT

The *Citizens' Charter* emphasizes the importance of efficient independent audit to expose weaknesses and to confirm good internal systems. Auditors do not usually enforce standards, but in the case of local government the auditor can go to court to obtain judicial orders and declarations. Departments and agencies of central government are audited by the Comptroller and Auditor-General (CAG), who heads the National Audit Office (NAO) and who reports to the Public Accounts Committee (PAC) of the Commons. As well as conducting value for money (VFM)/efficiency audits, the CAG's remit has broadened to include effectiveness audits, i.e. assessing how successfully programmes have been meeting the policy objectives of government. In the case of departments and agencies, such a role will be important for assessing the 'quasi-contractual' relationship between the two bodies (Davies and

Willman, 1991). Furthermore, the CAG will examine performance indicators drawn up by the Treasury and departments to establish whether targets are reasonable. The charter has far more to say about local government auditing than that of central government. This is ironic given that some of the most trenchant criticism, of both the CAG and the Audit Commission for local government, concerns central government. In the former case, it was pointed out that the Social Fund spends a third of its resources on its administration! The latter criticism related to the fact that the 'poll tax' cost almost three times as much as the old rates system to collect.

In the case of the CAG, highly critical reports on the reduction of housing benefit (13 June 1989) and the failure by officials to gauge the impact that the reduction would have on recipients, the Social Fund, homelessness and standards of service in local social security offices (and see HC 207 1989/90 for the PAC), have highlighted serious shortcomings in service delivery and government policy, shortcomings which if avoided would have minimized much hardship and unnecessary suffering to individuals. These seem to us to be a case of justice denied.

A glaring example of the use of CAG reports to itemize systemic failures leading to shoddy service occurred with the use of the investigation into DSS benefit offices by the PAC. The report named the worst fourteen offices in Britain to highlight delay, poor service, incorrect payments and a two-day wait for destitute claimants before they were dealt with (twenty-sixth report of the PAC, 3 July 1991). The lessons to be learned from these reports are of enormous importance and in the case of the NAO they are presented to the PAC of the House of Commons and can be the subject of investigation and report by that body.

The CAG has acknowledged that pursuit of customer service may conflict with value for money considerations – cuts may lead to removal of service or affect frequency and quality. Public perceptions and priorities may well change. Hard choices have to be made, the CAG has said, in what is not a 'market' situation in any real sense. The task facing the NAO is to inject a great deal more customer care and customer consultation into providing customer services of all kinds. Of the five concepts in the charter, viz. quality, choice and competition, standards, value for money and accountability, it is the latter where the CAG sees its major role in serving Parliament and the public and providing independent assurances and reports.

Accountability is at the heart of the contract with the customer. 'It is one of the areas where present arrangements are not good enough and where improvements will be needed' (Dewar, 1991). Indeed, CAG reports have increasingly emphasized the customer service aspects of value-for-money reports on, for example, the National Insurance Fund and huge over-and-under payments (NAO, 4 June 1992), and on the failures of the Resettlement Agency to meet its financial targets in running residential centres for the homeless – with the result that money was returned to the Treasury rather than being spent effectively on a very vulnerable group. In these reports, residents' views were surveyed by Mori for the CAG (NAO, 21 May 1992).

Furthermore, the NAO has criticized the use of league tables of performance as simplistic unless they are heavily qualified. The NAO has emphasized that not only 'front-line' staff but 'back-up' staff must be customer-oriented. Here we feel that complaints procedures would be particularly important in exposing not only rudeness, delay and cancellation, etc., but also faults of a systemic nature – the practices of solicitors in legal aid provision for instance as well as court services.

> VFM examinations in these areas are not theoretical exercises based on some ideal and unrealistic expectations. They are directed essentially at what can be done within available resources and do not question agreed policy objectives . . . They require direct access to all relevant internal information and analysis.
>
> (Dewar, 1991, para. 15)

A key element involves asking the customer directly. This is not done as often by departments as it should be on the basis that it will raise expectations unrealistically. Furthermore, independence may be desirable in consultation processes such as Crime Prevention Through Partnership between the police and local citizens. Where the NAO conducts customer surveys, they are made available to departments and agencies and are planned with them. They form plans for action and NAO supports their findings by seeing what steps departments have taken to compare their work with best outside practice, including private sector practice. The NAO emphasizes that improved customer service takes time, effort and commitment.

The *Citizens' Charter* announced that local authorities must publish their responses to auditors' reports and that the Audit Commission (AC) is to publish new 'league tables of local authority performance with similar tables for health services', the latter of which have come within the Audit Commission's purview. A local council will have to set out what action it proposes to take after a full and public council debate. Information will have to be produced in a way that will make it easier to compare different authorities' performances (see Local Government Act 1992, s. 1) – it should be noted that this idea was unsuccessfully attempted in the Local Government Planning and Land Act 1980. The Local Government Act 1992 will allow the Audit Commission to identify individual authorities to highlight, presumably, good and bad practices. It already publishes such information in general, anonymous terms for authorities' guidance. This is known as the Quality Exchange and includes the processes for assessing customer satisfaction and the results of such exercises (see Audit Commission, 1992).

In passing it should be noted that the local auditor has far greater contact with the public, who are able to make complaint to the auditor directly about a matter of audit, than does the CAG (see Chapter 8).

The Audit Commission, which employs 1000 staff, is under a duty to promote studies to encourage economy, efficiency and effectiveness in local government and health authorities. The commission has published a management paper *Managing Services Effectively – Performance Review* (1989a). In its recommendations on key indicators, targets and monitoring it predated the *Citizens' Charter* by two years. It also published an 'Implementation Guide' to give practical advice and which identified 'Quality Indicators' for most local authority services.

The commission's reports are models in establishing best practice in service delivery, thereby assisting in the setting of realistic targets and checks, and in helping to assuage enormous discontent in a way that grievance procedures by themselves could never hope to do. In its report on *Managing the Crisis in Council Housing* (1986a), it set out the benefits of following its recommendations:

> . . . perhaps £80–100 million could be saved in excessive management costs; the number of empty council properties could be reduced by 20,000–25,000; cost of bed and breakfast accommodation could be more than 25 pc lower; rent arrears might be reduced by £100 million, or even more; the funds available for maintenance could be increased by as much as £1 billion.

The report also spells out the difficulties caused by inadequate procedures to respond to applicants, which has important implications for complaints procedures:

> . . . tenants do not know who to contact directly, so they resort to putting complaints in writing and phoning the office; messages are lost and a correspondence backlog builds up; staff are less responsive to immediate problems; and naturally tend to respond to pressure from the more assertive tenants and members of the authority on the 'oil the squeaky wheel' principle. This simply leads to a worsening of the situation, distortion of priorities and extra costs, as voids and the resulting vandalism increase.
>
> (ibid.)

The commission's report on *Housing the Homeless* (1989b) advises that there should be adequate systems to monitor and forecast demand. Too frequently inadequate resources are devoted to housing advice services which can be a cost-effective way of reducing homelessness. To avoid disputes, standard formats for interviewing and guidance notes for interviewing officers should be produced; otherwise, it is difficult to see how an authority can apply policies consistently. In the vast majority of authorities visited, interviewing officers had excessive case loads adversely affecting the efficiency and efficacy of their work. This often meant that there was no preventative/advisory work and frequent closure of the office only allowed contact by telephone 'with the result that those entitled to assistance were turned away and those not entitled were given assistance' (ibid., p. 26). It is interesting to see echoes of this criticism in research conducted into the review and appeal procedures operating within social security administration, specifically on the high workload of adjudication officers and improper consideration of claimants' cases (Wikeley and Young, 1992).

To take one further example in *Healthy Housing: The Role of Environmental Health Services* (Audit Commission, 1991a), local authorities are advised on the effective use of their finance. This is partly a question of setting priorities and adopting a proactive strategy defining those strategies. These should be based on information – much of it from complaints – on the nature and scale of problems in an area and on those individual properties which require action. 'They should be backed by a work programme which defines clear objectives, sets targets at all levels of the service and provides for performance monitoring against targets.' Targets should cover response times and have efficient inspection procedures. Tenants should be provided with information on the authorities' actions and with advice and help to avoid loss of their homes. Specific times should be set to respond to complaints, which are the major cause of inspections.

Here as in many other reports, if the local service is hindered by central government policies, the Audit Commission is not reluctant to allocate the criticism where it belongs. In fact, the commission is more critical of government policy than the CAG, who is prohibited from questioning the merits of government policy by his governing statute. The commission's report on *Making a Reality of Community Care* (1986) is really very damning in criticism of the bifurcation of government policies towards community care: on the one hand, more responsibility was devolved to authorities, on the other, social security policies were undermining that very initiative by subsidizing private residential homes. Implementation of a policy was split between unco-ordinated agencies and authorities and the end result, for which the government bore responsibility, was 'disarray and inefficient use of resources'. The victims will be some of 'the most disadvantaged members of society' (ibid., p. 5). This is not only a denial of justice but also seriously inefficient.

Criticism of central government policies is present in a series of papers published in 1990 on the police. *Footing the Bill* (Audit Commission, 1990a) was critical of the way central government financed provincial police forces: 'they make planning difficult, reduce local accountability and work against VFM'. In *Calling All Forces* (1990b), the commission noted that few forces had specified the targets of service they expect. Most officers did not know how long it took operators to answer calls from the public or the delay before officers arrived at an incident – about 40 million calls for help are made a year including twelve million 999 calls. Generally, there was 'remarkably little analysis and monitoring of the outputs of policing'. The commission was in no doubt that the police forces could do more to take the public into its confidence and to provide a more informed basis for public debate.

Further papers recommended reorganizing police forces to provide territorial subunits which would be fully accountable for the quality of day-to-day policing in local areas, thereby removing 'overlong lines of command'. The objectives of the papers are to achieve appropriate levels of delegation to assist in establishing responsibility and accountability on officers. The police have been the subject of many complaints concerning their actions and the utility of the system for dealing with complaints against the police – including the Police Complaints Authority, which acts as a supervisory authority to police investigations rather than as an ombudsman – has been severely criticized (see Goldsmith, 1991). The commission's papers seek to address the shortcomings in efficiency, the lack of specified objectives and targets, monitoring of performance and the organizational weaknesses which must be successfully tackled and upon which effective complaints procedures and accountability devices may be built. Numerous reports, and indeed the Home Secretary's statement in May 1992 on a review by a Royal Commission of the police, is indicative of increasing unease about police efficiency. The point must be highlighted that this unease has a direct relationship to the absence of suitable accountability mechanisms, sufficiently effective grievance procedures and appropriate opportunities to remedy injustice against the police outside the courts. There should be suitable procedures to deal with these concerns long before the courts are invoked.

In its annual report for 1991, the commission stated that it was directing auditors to spend more time assessing the extent to which authorities had adopted stated objectives and performance indicators and how effectively they were being monitored. The commission follows up for six years the results of its project investigations. It would be wrong to assume that this was 'knocking' local government. Indeed, the commission has been quick to emphasize the crucial role of local authorities in areas of critical importance, such as in *Urban Regeneration and Economic Development* (1990c). Local authorities must act in consort with central government and the private sector. Local authorities should carry out:

> . . . a clear sighted assessment of the needs of each deprived urban area: a *local regeneration audit* (LRA), developed in conjunction with the private sector and the local offices of central government

departments . . . Local authorities themselves can play an important leading and coordinating role.

(ibid., p. 2)

The local regeneration unit (LRA) will be monitored to see what changes in targets and objectives need to be made and will involve a formal review process. It will be published, although the report says nothing about local involvement except through the local authority. The report is critical of central government efforts to bring about urban regeneration in the past, especially in the experience of some urban development corporations which effectively excluded local authorities, e.g. the London Dockland's Development Corporation (LDDC), which is in fact facing a vast class action by local residents for environmental damage and pollution. The report praises the virtues of partnership, but we would endorse the thrust of earlier work which indicated the importance and the benefits of allowing local participation in decision making affecting local areas. The 'feedback' in reviewing the LRA must contain a community element and there must be safeguards to ensure that decision makers take a 'hard look' at contributions from local communities (Lewis, 1992; Harden and Lewis, 1982).

In 1991, the commission published *How Effective is the Audit Commission?* (1991b). Since its inception in 1983, £662 million had been saved by authorities as a result of authorities acting on auditors' advice (p. 17). Interestingly, the commission's effectiveness was assessed as part of the five yearly review of non-departmental bodies. The results of this review 'are not in the public domain', although it appeared that the government was satisfied with the commission's work (p. 20).

FAIR PROCEDURES AND EFFICIENCY

The Audit Commission is concerned with improving systems to achieve greater value for money and efficiency, improvements which lend consequential assistance to the promotion of fairer and more accessible complaints procedures. Perhaps we can make a few points at this stage about procedures which seek to give a fair hearing to a grievance – though not necessarily vindicating that grievance – and which also fit into an arrangement whereby information about the specific grievance, and more generally about performance shortcomings, or indeed about problems concerning the objectives of the institution, may be obtained. The information gathered from such complaints and their resolution should provide valuable instruction and data for the setting of objectives, performance reviews and performance indicators. We have found this to be the case in numerous bureaucratic environments. We wish to save until Chapter 6 our discussion of tribunals and more recent replacements, i.e. the Social Fund Commissioner, who act as court substitutes, the latter of which has a very instructive programme of safeguards to make procedures as fair and as efficient as possible.

In this context, however, it is worth making special reference to the Woolf Report on prison riots (Woolf, 1991), which stated that in a prison community, and we would add that his observation has a much wider relevance, 'Proper structures are necessary to achieve justice.' These should be straightforward, expeditious, effective and independent. The report's section on complaint redress and discipline is in the direction of the role of justice and access to it and the contribution these make to perceptions of fair treatment, efficient administration and a secure environment, albeit in the closed society of prison. The report is also of value as a study on the different procedural routes to the attainment of those ends. We regret, however, that there was no recommendation for a prisoners' ombudsman. As an institution, ombudsmen are capable of far more than remedying grievances, because their investigatory powers allow them potentially to uncover systemic failings which other procedures do not.

If, however, there is one important lesson to be gained from the ombudsman experience in the UK, it is that we have not provided the means to give maximum impact to, and to make optimum use of, the ombudsman as a device for improving administration and administrative decision making. We have not given the necessary emphasis to the role of the ombudsman as a 'seeker out of systemic causes of injustice in a way that courts and tribunals are ill equipped to do' (Graham, 1991). We develop this point in Chapter 7.

By way of emphasizing a number of points we have been making, it is interesting to observe, for instance, that in a recent work on regulatory law in the USA, the author advocated an office in the White House or Congress to co-ordinate regulatory activity and to devise overall strategies of regulation and to advise against undesirable ones. Central importance was placed on the ombudsman feeding the benefit of that office's experience of grievance redress into this co-ordinating and planning programme. Access to justice was seen as being directly related to an overall strategy of performance enhancement and successful policy formulation (Sunstein, 1990). This, it should be noted, was advocated for a federal system where there is no ombudsman for national (or federal) government as there is in the UK. The use of an ombudsman overseas in this capacity, however, has been noted and the efforts of such ombudsmen widely lauded in the field of policy and strategy formulation. Even in a British context, use of an ombudsman-like figure for wider strategic purposes is not unknown. The Broadcasting Standards Council (BSC) is under a duty to monitor programmes to make general reports on standards *and* the BSC also has power to initiate its own complaints against programmes. This latter power is ostentatiously missing from other ombudsman schemes in the UK.

With these reservations in mind, it is interesting to note some instructive examples from complaints procedures available under the Financial Services Act (FSA) 1986. In the case of the Securities and Futures Association, for instance, the Complaints Commissioner deals with complaints that are not resolved by the SFA's Complaints Bureau and oversees the general working of the system of complaint handling. He or she is empowered to make recommendations regarding the future handling of complaints and to make random checks to see how the bureau is processing its workload. As Graham says, the commissioner is a very good example of a quality-control device which is similar to the Legal Services Ombudsman. Indeed, with the ombudsman-like procedures under the FSA, complaint handling is seen as an 'integral part of the regulatory structure' for financial services: 'all members of SROs [self-regulatory organizations] and the SIB are required to have complaints procedures and to ensure that their officers and employees are aware of them' (Graham, 1991).

The Investment Management Regulatory Organization's complaints procedure goes further, requiring members to submit a quarterly summary of complaints – those that remain unresolved three months after receipt, as well as those that are resolved. Where it cannot be resolved by the member, the customer must be notified that he or she can take the complaint to the relevant SRO (IMRO) or the independent adjudicator.

> SIB has highlighted the importance of complaints procedures for providing information to the regulators. According to the SIB's annual report for 1989–90, the complaints procedures for SIB, SROs and RPBs have been carefully reviewed and a number of improvements made . . . It shows how complaint handling can be built into a regulatory programme.
>
> (ibid., p. 44)

Numerous statutory and non-statutory devices exist for the resolution of grievances. Some are almost ombudsmen; others are purely informal *ad hoc* arrangements (see Chapters 7 and 8). One of the clearest examples illustrating the lack of appreciation of the value of grievance resolution as an aid to enhancing efficiency is contained in the privatization legislation.

Privatization of monopolies, or near monopolies, has brought with the new regulatory regimes which superintend the industries a variety of grievance remedial devices. The concentration initially upon the remedying of grievances as a discrete activity to the virtual exclusion of the learning potential and lessons for future improvement in overall service provision in the industries can be observed from the fact that, apart from telecommunications, the regulatory and remedial functions are split between two bodies.

A further dimension is the responsibility of the Office of Fair Trading to deal with complaints from industrial users. Experience of grievance redress is spread over a range of bodies, and there are the usual array of advisory bodies for particular constituencies, i.e. small businesses, the disabled, etc. in telecommunications. Achieving efficiency and the analogue of competitive practice is the responsibility of the regulatory authorities.

The regimes for gas, electricity and water are still feeling their way, but we believe that not all has been done to maximize opportunities to provide for effective redress of grievances and to ensure that the information acquired in grievance redress is used as effectively as possible to assist in performance review and policy development. We shall examine the Competition and Service (Utilities) Act 1992 in Chapter 9, where we note that we remain to be convinced that the procedures that do exist in the privatized sector have been thought through sufficiently, or are as effective as they ought to be *qua* redress of grievance itself. The regulatory regimes do in fact reveal a great deal that is of interest in the interrelationship between efficiency and justice and we reserve until Chapter 9 a detailed discussion of those regimes.

That information from grievances needs to be fed into the policy-making process is, we believe, elementary; in its own way the public inquiry into land use and major development attempts something along these lines. A more significant vehicle, perhaps, for public involvement before decision asking and before grievances arise, takes place in the setting of water quality objectives under the Water Act 1989. Public involvement will help legitimize decision making. But we also believe that a body should be charged with correlating the information and maximizing the utility to be gained from lessons provided by efficiency audits, value-for-money audits, and effective redress of grievance – in short, to protect the 'justice' side of efficiency.

CONCLUSION

In this chapter, we have focused our attention on the relationship between justice and efficiency. We have argued that a commitment to a just system does not impede efficiency any more than it might impede enhanced quality of public performance. If we are alive to the fact that justice is not simply a matter for the courts – it concerns the righting of wrong, unjustified, ill-informed, ill-considered or unconsidered decisions – then we must give thought to the best kind of procedure operating at the optimal level within the organization providing a service.

Too frequent an intervention from the courts, or reversals by tribunals or adverse recommendations from ombudsmen, will make the system seize up and produce inefficiency. It will not be able to get its basic job done. Procedures operating within departments, agencies, authorities or whatever, are not primarily concerned with the reversal of decisions; more often they have as their essential duty explanation or modification, reversal being a relatively drastic option, but there none the less. If effective procedures are not present, greater problems will follow, leading possibly to system breakdown. If they are present, they will, if used properly, have an invaluable role to play in both rectifying wrongs/mistakes before they are incapable of resolution by the service provider and in providing information to managers. For those grievances that cannot be assuaged internally, then procedures operating at a higher level and exogenously should not only give an authoritative determination. Part of their role should be to feed back advice into the service area on its system delivery. In this task, courts are on the periphery and not, as presently structured, ideally suited.

Monitoring, evaluation and value for money are all (legal) vehicles too often overlooked in our changing bureaucratic world. All of them have their part to play in achieving justice; they are part of a spectrum to which we have spoken at regular intervals.

4

THE SUPERVISION OF JUSTICE

One of our main themes has been the need for coherent and systematic address being paid to our system of justice against the state. Our present arrangements are patchwork quilt and pragmatic. The only 'new' body established in recent years to oversee even part of our justice arrangements is the Council on Tribunals, following the recommendations of the Franks Committee (1957). The Lord Chancellor's Department, for reasons which we shall outline shortly, has never enjoyed the status or culture to oversee our whole system of justice against the state.

What we advocate, in line with our expressed sentiments, is a range of bodies charged with keeping access to justice in repair. Although we argue for a Ministry of Justice at the apex of the system, we think it right that there should be a number of intermediary bodies each charged with responsibility for crucial parts of the system. We take this line for a number of reasons. There has to be formal and final responsibility for pulling together the several strands of justice. That must be a political body in the form of a minister who would have to be a cabinet minister in order to make clear that justice is at the heart of our system. Even so, that portfolio would make considerable demands on the office holder, who could not expect to be *au fait* with either the specialist knowledge or the passions of those committed to other parts of the system. In addition, it seems important to us that specific agencies should be charged with the advocacy of justice and its constant improvement. No single ministry could be expected to perform in that way, even allowing for the inevitable division of labour in the great offices of state. We turn to the nature and functions of those bodies shortly.

Even as recently as 1975, the late Professor Harry Street was lamenting that 'nothing has been done to improve the quality of the administrative process at its earliest stage' (Street, 1975, p. 102). For the administrative process read the lowest level of justice. Since that time, a number of things have changed at the level of local government. New tribunals have been established (e.g. the Valuation and Community Charge Tribunals), new appeals to ministers, new responsibilities on reporting and monitoring and even a freedom of information law. Furthermore, the local government ombudsmen have effected a number of improvements, some of them in the light of the report presented on complaints procedures in local government in 1986 (Lewis *et al.*, 1987). Little has been done in relation to non-departmental public bodies (NDPBs) save for the fact that a number are now subject to the jurisdiction of the Parliamentary Commissioner for Administration (PCA). In central government, the picture has been relatively bleak until the last few years. The Next Steps agencies have changed the picture somewhat (Efficiency Unit, 1988). We refer to these developments in Chapter 5.

However, for present purposes, what needs to be noted is the relatively greater amount of information made available to the public about the working of this very substantial area of central government. Not only are the agencies' 'framework documents' or 'mini-constitutions' public property, but so in many instances are business plans. In particular, targets and performance indicators are laid down for the delivery of public services. This is a considerable advance on previous practice even if it falls short of a Freedom of Information Act. Even so, at the time of writing, there is much to be done in the field of adequate grievance procedures, quite apart from the failures in the field of consultation and 'rule-making'. Again we have a patchwork quilt with some agencies performing considerably better than others. Since they were established, the *Citizens' Charter* has been born and all government bodies, including the agencies, are intended to comply with its ruling sentiments. These sentiments include grievance procedures and improved consultation as part of the generic concern with customer care. We now have a cabinet minister responsible for these matters and we must wait to see how much change will occur. What appears to be the primary weakness at the moment is that any developments will be the result of informal pressure, both peer group and otherwise. Legislation is very much the last resort, certainly as far as central government is concerned, though parliament has recently passed the Competition and Service (Utilities) Act 1992, the Education (Schools) Act 1992 and the Local Government Act 1992. A similar reluctance to legislate to increase accountability within central government occurred in relation to the Next Steps agencies, where a silent revolution in central government was undertaken without legislation. Such legislation as there has been since has been scant (we refer further to Next Steps later in the book, and see Chapter 3).

Again, Harry Street is worth quoting:

> I insist that the law can play an important part. It must ensure that there is a fair inquiry: the citizen must be given a reasoned decision and a full finding of facts must be published. Compliance with these legal requirements greatly reduces the risk of arbitrary or erroneous decisions. The civil servant's knowledge that part of his handiwork is subject to scrutiny by High Court judges will make him take more care over the quality of his decision.
>
> (Street, 1975, pp. 102–103)

Street is here talking primarily about public inquiries, but it is clear that his argument extended across the spectrum of decisions in the public arena. Sadly, the law too rarely plays a part. If it had, then we could have expected at the very least a general statutory requirement for public bodies to produce visible complaints procedures, albeit that they would need to be tailored to the circumstances of individual administrative cultures (see IPPR, 1991). Indeed, this is exactly what our empirical work has indicated in those circumstances where clear complaints procedures have been adopted. In other words, different agencies have different structures and different organizational patterns which resist uniform grievance procedures. Any general legislative obligation to produce grievance procedures would need to bear that in mind. Even so, some common features are identifiable, e.g. clarity, publicity, ease of access, internal review by an official not associated with the original decision, etc. Although to some extent there have been welcome improvements since Professor Street was writing, there are still too many decisions taken by public servants without the possibility of a hearing of any kind. We suggest a number of responses to this situation, one of them being the desirability of a Commons committee charged with examining each new discretionary jurisdiction. We note in Chapter 5 that such an arrangement already works well in Australia. Along with the other suggestions for institutional reform that we make, such a committee should prove invaluable. As we argue, that committee should be charged with asking why an appeal should not lie to the General Administrative Appeals Tribunal (AAT), which we discuss in Chapter 6, failing which some other appeal mechanism. We make it clear that such decisions must be political at the end of the day, but having a body to examine discretionary activity in the round should ensure more consistency and certainly more debate.

Although Professor Street rejected the panacea of an AAT, he was disturbed that ministers have internal and unpublished arrangements for settling problems which are largely concealed from citizens:

If a dissatisfied claimant is persistent enough he will have his appeal from the decision heard by a superior in the civil servant hierarchy according to a system clearly laid down within the department. On the other hand the poor uninformed citizen will be told nothing of this opportunity for review of the decision against him arrived at by a civil servant of fairly low grade, and therefore will not have his case reconsidered.

(Street, 1975, p. 109)

Although being unsympathetic to an AAT, Professor Street does advocate more of a system than presently exists, even if he accepts that some review/appeal could properly remain within the administrative regimen from time to time. By insisting that those decisions which remain with ministers should entail the disclosure of findings of fact and the giving of reasons, he was hopeful that the courts would be able to question mistakes of law much more frequently.

THE COUNCIL ON TRIBUNALS

At this point, we should say a word or two about the Council on Tribunals. The council was set up by the Tribunals and Inquiries Act 1958 following the report of the Franks Committee (1957). It now operates under an Act of 1992 and an accompanying statutory instrument. Its functions are threefold; to keep under review the constitution and working of the tribunals specified in Schedule 1 of the parent Act and, from time to time, to report on their constitution and working; to consider and report on matters referred to it (by the Lord Chancellor or Secretary of State) with respect to tribunals whether or not specified in the Schedule; to consider and report on these matters with respect to administrative procedures which involve or may involve the holding of a statutory inquiry. For present purposes, we shall largely ignore the third provision.

Traditionally, the Council on Tribunals has been thought by those of a radical disposition to be somewhat on the tame side, but in recent years it has struggled valiantly to provide an oversight role over administrative justice as well as to extend their terms of reference more than their political masters would allow. Perhaps a flavour of its work and influence, taken from its Annual Report of 1990–91 should be recorded. During that year, the council made critical observations on the arrangements for hearing immigration appeals and recommended changes to the law consonant with a concern for human rights. It published a report on *Model Rules of Procedure for Tribunals* to guide departments and tribunals so that they might adopt or select from the menu. Although the Council appears never to have taken a position on the adoption of an AAT, it has recently reiterated its opposition to an unnecessary proliferation of tribunals. It has stressed this particularly strongly in the field of social security where the Social Security Appeals Tribunals are well-established and extremely experienced. Incidentally, social security is instructive in illuminating the possible range of procedures – internal and external – which can be usefully adopted for the ventilation of grievances (see, e.g. Wikeley and Young, 1992). The council was also extremely active in canvassing a general right of appeal to Child Support Appeal Tribunals established under the Child Support Act 1991. The appeals regimen established under this Act is instructive and attracts our general support. It is therefore worth dwelling on. Without wishing to delve into substantive detail, there is provision for someone dissatisfied with a decision taken by the Child Support Agency to appeal to the Secretary of State for a review of the decision. This review is conducted by a child support officer of the agency who took no part in the original decision. From his or her decision, there is a general right of appeal to the tribunal and thence to the Child Support Commissioner (a lawyer of standing) on a point of law. Without prejudice to our position on a GAT, this type of arrangement appears to satisfy all the canons of satisfactory administrative justice. It seems likely that the role of the council was influential in the arrangements adopted.

What is perhaps significant is the general stance of the Council on Tribunals as a result of the deliberations which led up to the arrangements. They expressed clear preference for the expansion of existing tribunals whenever possible, rather than creating new ones. This could be done by adding new panels of members with any necessary additional training. Secondly, although appreciating that a system of internal administrative review might improve standards of administration, such a review should never be regarded as restricting the right of appeal to an independent tribunal. They announced that they would be 'vigilant in monitoring any future proposals with this in mind'. In this vein, they were also critical of the lack of an independent appeals body for homelessness complaints. They were influential in amending the Code of Practice issued under the Housing Act 1985, which recommends an appeal panel at member level with a chairperson who is independent of the decision process and with access to legal advice. This did not meet all their concerns. Similarly, they appeared to side themselves with those who favour an independent appeals system (preferably the Social Security Appeal Tribunals (SSATs)) for housing benefit reviews.

There is little doubt that the Council on Tribunals has developed greater visibility in recent years and is doing enormous amounts of good work. In particular, its strong emphasis on new rights of appeal are to be applauded, even if these emphases seem occasionally somewhat circumscribed. It appears from its reports that it is concentrating on official intervention which affects people's 'rights, particularly those affecting livelihood and status' (Council on Tribunals, 1991a, 3.27). We were informed that the council does not comb through all legislation with the mission to ensure that all new jurisdictions are appealable to a tribunal unless a sound argument to the contrary can be mustered. As we shall see shortly, this is the position adopted in Australia and one which we would endorse. None the less, the council is inching in that direction. For instance, it has recently asked for changes in its governing statute. In particular, it would like to see statutory recognition of its function of advising on legislation proposing new adjudicative procedures including tribunals. This is presently being resisted by the government. We return to certain aspects of the council's work in Chapter 6.

Unfortunately, government has too often failed to give the council the kind of support it needs as witness the special report which it produced in 1980 (Council on Tribunals, 1980b). This report contained a number of recommendations which the council at that time wished to see implemented in order to strengthen its role. The boldest of these was its ability 'to act as advisory body over the whole area of administrative adjudication'. It saw the need for an independent body to offer advice to government on what kinds of disputes are appropriate and inappropriate for adjudication by tribunals. It saw itself as that body. However, with its traditional staffing establishment and budget, it saw itself contrained to day-to-day issues, being unable to undertake work broader in scope. Other recommendations included the statutory duty to be consulted on primary legislation. In fact, following this report, the Lord Chancellor did issue a Code for Consultation to other government departments and it is currently in the process of being updated. Furthermore, the special report urged that in the case of both primary and secondary legislation, there should be a statutory duty for the minister to make public the observations expressed by the council. This would be after the fashion of the Social Security Advisory Committee established by the Social Security Act 1980. In fact, the report said that sometimes the minister informed Parliament that the council had been consulted, thereby giving the impression that it was in agreement with him, even when that was not the case.

Without wishing to cast aspersions on the secretariat of the council, we do not regard it as satisfactory that it is staffed exclusively by civil servants on secondment, primarily from the Lord Chancellor's Department. Our discussions indicate that having the council itself as a buffer between the secretariat and the government makes its independence more likely. Even so, there is, in our view, no substitute for a formally independent secretariat committed to the pursuit of justice for its own sake and which does not have an interest in civil service careers.

Allied to this concern is the fact that the Council on Tribunals does not have a research budget or a research department. We are conscious of the scholarly and painstaking work conducted by the secretariat which, in the last year for which we have figures, produced 112 papers of substance for consideration by the council as well as being in constant correspondence and contact with government departments and other bodies advising on a wide range of policy matters. It has had the benefit of an academic research co-ordinator for a short period and the secretariat is now taking up responsibility for research co-ordination. That is to say that it is primarily concerned with encouraging external research and disseminating information on research being conducted. While applauding this development, we feel it is no substitute for 'proactive research' of the kind frequently conducted both by the Australian Administrative Review Council (ARC) and the Administrative Conference of the United States (ACUS). It is to these bodies that we now wish to turn. However, before we do, we ought to say that the council in its 1980 special report recommended that they be given a full-time research officer and a research budget. They had been impressed, they say, by their visits to both ACUS and the ARC. Ironically, perhaps, they remarked after their visits that the Council on Tribunals has 'had considerable influence on constitutional developments in related fields in other countries'!

THE AUSTRALIAN ADMINISTRATIVE REVIEW COUNCIL

The ARC was established in 1975 as an independent advisory body having general oversight of the current system of administrative review. It is intended to monitor and promote the rational and effective operation and development of administrative review. One of its major responsibilities is to provide advice to the government which will ensure that the present system develops on a principled rather than an *ad hoc* basis (Justice-All Souls, 1988; Lewis, 1989b).

The ARC is charged with considering and making recommendations to the Attorney-General on a wide range of issues relating to administrative review, including the jurisdiction of the various agencies reviewing Commonwealth administrative action, such as the Commonwealth ombudsman, the Administrative Appeals Tribunal (the GAT or AAT) and the courts. It is also concerned with the rationalization and consolidation of existing review tribunals as well as primary decision-making procedures to ensure that discretion is exercised justly and equitably. The ARC has, for some time, attracted attention in the public law world for the boldness of its approach and in recent times its accumulated experience has allowed it the confidence to take on particularly fraught issues. For example, quite apart from its most recent recommendations on the role of the ombudsman, to which we return, it has also provided advice on decision-making procedures for the allocation of finite resources, always a very delicate matter (ARC, 1991b).

Importantly, the ARC is empowered to determine its work programme and is not restricted to carrying out references made to it by government. Compare the Law Commission in Britain which has been restrained from conducting wide-ranging examinations of administrative law. Other significant points to note are that the ARC is served by a secretariat which includes four full-time research staff including a director of research. Its membership has always been very high-powered and its influence depends greatly upon that strength and the quality of its work which has consistently been of the highest standard.

No description of the ARC would be adequate, however, without mention of the other scrutiny bodies which round off the administrative review process within the Commonwealth jurisdiction. In this respect, the relationship between the ARC, the Attorney-General's Department and the Senate Standing Committees is crucial. Between them, these bodies comment upon the desirability of appeal mechanisms from administrative decisions created by new legislation. In other words, new legislation, both primary and secondary, is looked at to see if there are any good reasons for not giving the GAT *de novo* appeal rights; that is to say, whether the issue should be heard afresh by the appellate body. We will see in Chapter 6 that most discretionary administrative decisions can be appealed to the GAT.

The examination of classes of administrative decisions in order to ascertain whether they should be subject to appeal on the merits is specifically included in the ARC's Charter. The ARC performs this function in relation to existing legislation where, in accordance with consultative arrangements between the ARC and the Attorney-General's Department, the Attorney-General refers the proposed legislation to the ARC for advice. The Attorney-General has the standing function of considering whether the GAT should be vested with jurisdiction to review decisions made in the exercise of proposals for legislation. The terms of reference of the Senate Standing Committee on Regulations and Ordinances include the scrutiny of delegated legislation to ensure that it does not unduly make the rights and liberties of citizens dependent upon administrative decisions which are not subject to review on the merits by a judicial or other tribunal. Similarly, the terms of reference of the Senate Standing Committee for the Scrutiny of Bills requires much the same for primary legislation.

Justice-All Souls has recently supported the idea of a British-style ARC, a matter first seriously mooted by Sir Douglas Wass (1984) in his (1983) Reith Lectures, though Professor Street had earlier rejected calls for a British *Conseil d'État*. Lord Scarman (1974) had hinted at a body roughly constituted like the ARC and indeed even the Council on Tribunals itself had pointed in that direction:

> Whatever balance is eventually achieved between the sovereignty of Parliament and the courts as the guardians of the liberty of the subject, there would appear to be a significant role for an effective independent, statutory advisory body in the field of administrative adjudication, with both detailed knowledge and more general insight linked in a systematic manner.
>
> (Council on Tribunals, 1980a, p. 22)

As we shall see, however, it saw itself as that body. Lord Justice Woolf (1992) has recently expressed similar sentiments.

Justice-All Souls 1988, then, recommended that there should be an independent body, whether statutory or established as a Royal Commission, separate from the executive functions of government, charged with the duty of reviewing all aspects of administrative law and the process of administrative decision making throughout the UK. This body would comment and recommend but would not itself have executive powers. Justice-All Souls was concerned that such a new body would acquire status and dignity at an early stage and would not be as poorly treated as the Council on Tribunals. They appeared to think that the PCA had fared better and concluded that this was partly explained by his links with Parliament. As we explain in Chapter 7, we think that the PCA may in fact have been hindered by being seen as an appendage to Parliament rather than as a citizen's defender. Be that as it may, we agree that an annual report to Parliament would be desirable were such a body to be established.

We repeat what we have said elsewhere, that such a body would be less influential outside the general framework of the 'New Administrative Law' in Australia; that is to say, reform of the court structure and judicial review, an expanded ombudsman system and other recommendations which we shall make from time to time. In other words, the reforms need to be interlocking so that the whole system of justice against the state is examined in the round.

One further point is worth making, albeit that it is a very significant point. It is that, certainly until recently, the ARC has barely impinged upon the main problem of constitutional politics, viz. the policy process, though in May 1992 the ARC tabled its rule-making report in Parliament. This recommended extending the 1970 reforms into the area of decisions of a legislative character. Central to the recommendations is the requirement for mandatory consultation with the community prior to the making of important rules (see ARC, 1992).

We have largely restricted ourselves here to the adjudicative process, the main focus of the book. Even so, we have made it clear that there is no easy cut-off point between adjudicative and policy items. Although the defence of a revised public law system to address policy debates would require a separate book (though see Harden and Lewis, 1986), we cannot rationally argue the case for a body such as the ARC without recommending that it is given jurisdiction for matters of justice beyond the merely adjudicative. It is not clear what the stand of Justice-All Souls was on these matters, but we believe it fair to say that the policy process did not figure prominently in their otherwise very valuable report. To take on board these broader issues, we need to examine the experience of another model.

THE ADMINISTRATIVE CONFERENCE OF THE UNITED STATES

ACUS was established by public law in 1964 as a permanent, independent federal agency to study the efficiency and fairness of the administrative process in the federal government and to recommend improvements to the President, Congress, etc. ACUS has also from time to time been given special tasks by the Congress.

> . . . the Administrative Conference of the United States may:
> (1) study the efficiency, adequacy and fairness of the administrative procedure used by administrative agencies in carrying out administrative programs, and make recommendations . . . as it considers appropriate;
> (2) arrange for interchange among administrative agencies of information potentially useful in improving administrative procedure; and
> (3) collect such information and statistics from administrative agencies and publish such reports as it considers useful for evaluating and improving administrative procedure.
>
> (US Code, Title V, s. 574)

ACUS has a council which oversees its work and is headed by a chairman appointed by the President for a five-year period. The council oversees the work of ACUS, setting the agenda for plenary conference sessions, which are, in the American fashion, open to the public. Such a session takes place at least annually and here the members debate and vote upon proposed recommendations. These will have been developed by committees composed of members of ACUS, with the help of outside consultants. After a committee proposes a recommendation, the council must approve it for full ACUS decision. Once ACUS makes a formal recommendation, it is published in the Federal Register and Code of Federal Recommendations.

A number of very important developments have occurred as a result of the activities of ACUS and it has been particularly active in the past ten years. Quite recently, ACUS has been examining the potential uses for alternative means of dispute resolution (ADR) in a number of different areas. Such examination has involved the use of 'mini-trials', mediation, dispute review boards, case management and arbitration as informal voluntary alternatives to formal hearings before the federal agencies. There is a flavour here once again of the *Citizens' Charter*, albeit that the British version seems at the moment at least a little less rigorous. However, more to the point, we are bound to feel that an independent body is less likely to cut corners than is a government pledging to reform its ingrained habits.

Furthermore, it would be a mistake to imagine that ACUS was limited only to dispute settlement. It has been active for much of its life in the 'rule-making' process, whereby the federal agencies engage in policy making (see, e.g. ACUS, 1991). Indeed, ADR becomes 'Reg-neg' (i.e. regulatory negotiation) in this context, where new-style American corporatism has made an unexpected appearance. Reg-neg involves bringing together representatives of potentially affected interests to cooperate in trying to draft a proposed 'rule' (the British equivalent might be delegated legislation, circulars or mere administrative rule/guidance). The agency would normally expect to publish as a proposed rule any agreement arising from the negotiations. The nearest equivalent in Britain is perhaps the examination in public under the Town and Country Planning Amendment Act 1972 in relation to structure plans. Even then, the differences are considerable.

It is hardly surprising that ARC is active in examining procedural aspects of the policy-making process given the history of US administrative law and in particular its unique contribution to world administrative jurisprudence through the rule-making process. In this respect, it has, until now, ranged wider than the Australian ARC and gets closer, in our view, to what is required in a British setting.

A BRITISH STANDING CONFERENCE

Britain is beginning to look isolated in not having a system of considered oversight of its administrative processes. The Council on Tribunals has come a long way in recent years, but much remains to be done and we agree with Justice-All Souls (and implicitly with the Council on Tribunals itself) that the council would find it difficult to change its ways without a root and branch overhaul. As it is, it does much very good work in the field of tribunals and enquiries and could work collaboratively alongside a new body such as ACUS or ARC. What we have in the past recommended is a Standing Administrative Conference (SAC; Lewis, 1989b), but the terminology is unimportant. It is clearly irrational to wait for a system crisis to occur and then respond to it with whatever panic the moment produces. It is difficult to mount an argument against setting up some kind of conference or council which has as its central remit the task of looking at the effectiveness of our system of administrative law and practice. Whether we are interested in value for money or accountability or both, we ought clearly to be engaged in systems for corporate planning and performance review.

Another point worth stressing is that all the ancient arguments about democracy and the rule of law presuppose some notion of due process. A modern state with a modern bureaucracy and a healthy concern with constant reappraisals of public policy needs, we believe, a system of due process writ large. This should be a central concern of the SAC. Indeed, if we make a cultural claim to due process, then a development such as is foreshadowed here ought in no way to be seen as a threat to Westminster styles of government. Whatever scepticism others might have about the new constitutionalism, a SAC ought to be seen not only as an element of pluralism reawakening expectations of healthy debate and rigorous analysis, but as an information aid to Parliament itself.

In a work of this sort, it would be indulgent to go further into the policy process and the potential contribution of the SAC to a broader dialogue, especially as we have covered much of the ground elsewhere. However, one issue does spring to mind with which such a body could assist. This concerns the shifting boundaries between the public and the private sectors, most of all in the last dozen or so years when privatization and contracting out have occurred on a large scale. The government's own thinking on the matter is controversial to say the least (H.M. Treasury, 1991). However, we have recently seen a proliferation of partnership agreements between government and the private and voluntary sector in the execution of economic and social policy (Birkinshaw *et al.*, 1990). Self-regulation has also seen something of a resurgence recently and may indeed be genuinely desirable, but it poses important questions about the nature and extent of the public, the constitutional, sphere. Not only must these issues pose questions about the adequacy of parliamentary procedures for accounting, value for money and the like, but they also invite questions about the desirability of opening up government advisory committees as well. This is a hugely complex area which will never be given a decent airing in the absence of a body such as the SAC with a strong research capacity, public backing and a distinguished membership. Some of the difficulties thrown up by these recent developments will become more apparent in Chapter 9 concerning the regulation of utilities, etc., and Chapter 10 where the courts are struggling with the difficulties of whether to classify certain hybrid bodies as sufficiently public to allow Order 53 Rules of the Supreme Court to be invoked.

Perhaps it is worth concluding this section by another reference to the recent work of the Australian ARC. At the time of writing, the ARC had just concluded its *Multicultural Australia Project* (1992). This has been directed to examining whether the ethnic communities experience difficulty in accessing the administrative justice system. We need not go deeply into the report save for mention of the role of the Commonwealth ombudsman, whose general jurisdiction and practice we describe in Chapter 7. The recommendations concerning the ombudsman have, incidentally, largely been repeated before the Senate Standing Committee on Finance and Public Administration (Ombudsman Inquiry). These recommendations are particularly important for us in this section, since they envisage him supporting the general oversight role of the ARC, something presently alien to UK ombudsman systems. These recommendations include the following:

1 That he publicize the fact that his office is available as a central reference point for those who are dissatisfied with a government decision, but who do not know what remedies are available.
2 That he adopt a leading role in the dissemination of information about administrative review, particularly the basic message that one can complain or appeal.
3 That he give increased attention to the investigation of systemic problems.
4 That he receive additional resources to enable these recommendations to be implemented.

We find this particularly helpful, since it not only highlights the utility of such supervisory bodies as the ARC/SAC but recognizes the role of other institutional partners in ensuring that constant attention is paid to the whole of the state justice system. The lesson is not lost on us, nor we trust on our readers.

JUSTICE AND HUMAN RIGHTS

As we have already seen, the UK's current attitude towards human rights is somewhat ambivalent. We believe the time is overdue to reaffirm our commitment at the level of domestic law. Like others, we support the inclusion (and indeed the extension) of the European Convention on Human Rights into our legal system. For present purposes, we shall regard this as uncontroversial. What we need to say a little about here, however, concerns the supervision of the human rights exercise. In its *Constitution of the United Kingdom*, the Institute for Public Policy Research (1991) recommended the establishment of a Human Rights Commission. The tasks envisaged for the commission included the initiation of legal proceedings against those who contravened the Constitution's Bill of Rights; to advise Parliament and ministers whether current policies, practices or proposals offended against human rights; to investigate practices and procedures which may be incompatible with the Bill of Rights; to initiate proceedings even where there has been no individual complaint and to produce codes of practice to assist those who are bound to uphold the Bill of Rights. In making these proposals, the IPPR drew on the legislative experience of a number of Commonwealth countries.

We are entirely sympathetic to the sentiments underlying these proposals. Our only concern relates to the proliferation of bodies with responsibility to oversee the justice system. For our part, we are inclined to the view that most of the functions envisaged for such a commission could be performed by the Standing Advisory Committee, particularly if it were to establish a discrete section with human rights responsibilities. The exception would relate to the initiation of proceedings, but since we recommend the establishment of a Public Interest Office (PIO; see Chapter 11), which would have the power to take up a case to the courts or a GAT where the public interest was at stake, this should not present a problem. The human rights side of the public interest would naturally be included in the PIO's remit. The PIO would be part of the Ministry of Justice, to which we now turn.

A MINISTRY OF JUSTICE

As long ago as the Haldane Committee (1918), there were criticisms of the division of responsibilities between the Home Office and the Lord Chancellor's Department in relation to the justice system. There has also been concern expressed at the failure to appoint a cabinet minister specifically to promote justice as an ideal. Given our concerns, it is scarcely surprising that we should side with the reformers. Let us begin with the Haldane Committee in the knowledge that many of the criticisms there expressed have gained force and momentum since that time: 'There is no functionary at present who can properly be called a Minister responsible for the subject of Justice' (Haldane, 1918, p. 63). Although Haldane envisaged retaining the office of Lord Chancellor (partly owing to its ancient dignity), which we think makes little sense, he was clear that a strong case had been made for the appointment of a Minister of Justice. He stressed the difficulty of getting the attention of government to legal reform. Since that time, the Law Commission has been appointed but, for all its virtues, it is largely constrained to examine 'black-letter' or technical law and rarely raises its eyes unto the hills. Given what we have already said, the Law Commission is an inappropriate body to conduct such a task.

Interestingly, Haldane was struck by the 'total inadequacy' of the organization which controls the general administration of the very large staffs, together with their voluminous business, and who are required to give effect to the decrees of the Courts of Justice throughout the country. We say interestingly because the *Citizens' Charter* has much to say about improvement in court lists and indeed the general processes of the court system. At the time of writing, the Lord Chancellor's Department (LCD) is being upbraided by the responsible minister for its tardiness in producing a charter for the LCD.

Having spent considerable time outlining the vast array of the Lord Chancellor's responsibilities, some of them political, some judicial and many administrative, Haldane concluded that present arrangements were less than satisfactory. There was little chance that he could pay personal attention to most of the matters under his general remit.

As we have indicated, there are numerous conclusions which Haldane drew with which we would not wish to be associated, but the thrust of the criticisms was clearly correct:

> The Minister of Justice would probably sit in the House of Commons, and he ought to be accessible to those who have suggestions to make. Besides his administration of the staffs of the various courts in England, his Department should contain experts charged with the duty of watching over the necessities of Law reform, and of studying the development of the subject at home and abroad.
>
> (Haldane, 1918, p. 74)

Justice-All Souls (1988) did not come out in favour of a Ministry of Justice, seeming to believe that it would somehow interfere with or be in opposition to a body such as the SAC. We think that to be quite mistaken, since the SAC would have a friend at court, so to speak, if such a ministry was given the unequivocal task, *inter alia*, of promoting law reform and pursuing a more perfected system of justice. For its part, such a ministry would have the best possible advice on which to base its programme, at least in the field of public or constitutional law.

More recently, the IPPR (1991) came out strongly in favour of a Ministry of Justice. Their proposal was to replace the office of Lord Chancellor with the office of Minister of Justice, 'a more overtly political Minister who has no judicial function and will not have to be a qualified lawyer'. Such a minister would have responsibility for courts and legal services with the Director of Public Prosecutions serving under him. The Attorney-General, on the other hand, would continue to be appointed by the Prime Minister and would continue to be the principal legal adviser to the government. He would also continue to have responsibility with respect to the conduct of litigation to which the government is a party. They saw the new ministry as taking over the legal functions now carried out by the Lord Chancellor's Department and the Home Office. They adopted the view that the Home Office's present responsibility for criminal law and procedure, and for the enforcement by statutory bodies of aspects of the civil law protecting individual rights such as the race discrimination legislation, sit uneasily with its control functions such as the police, prisons and the immigration services. Likewise, they believed, the Lord Chancellor's direct responsibility for the appointment of the judiciary and his position as a Law Lord, sit uneasily with his political role as a member of the government:

> This fragmented, and in some instances inappropriate distribution of functions should be brought to an end with the creation of a single strong Ministry responsible for all of the 'Justice' functions, separate from any responsibility for law enforcement.
>
> (IPPR, 1991)

Although we are here only concerned with the public law aspects of a Ministry of Justice, we are entirely in accord with these sentiments. We need perhaps simply add that we think that the historic traditions of the Lord Chancellor mean that he is far too close to the professions, and in particular the Bar, to undertake the kind of proactive reforming role that we deem necessary to provide a coherent system of the supervision of justice against the state.

CONCLUSION

The purpose of this chapter has been to indicate the type of machinery which we believe is necessary if a coherent and systematic public justice system is to emerge and be maintained. Progress is already being made. Much more needs to be done and the totality needs to be kept in constant repair if we are to be true to our cultural ideals. Let us conclude with a quotation:

> But what is government itself, but the greatest of all reflections on human nature? If men were angels no government would be necessary. In framing a government which is to be administered by men over men, the great difficulty lies in this; you must first enable the government to control the governed; and in the next place oblige it to control itself. *A dependence on the people is, no doubt, the primary control on the government: but experience has taught mankind the necessity of auxiliary precautions.*
>
> (ACUS, 1985, p. v)

We believe that something like the machinery which we advocate would represent vital auxiliary precautions.

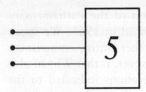

5

OPTIMUM FORMS OF DISPUTE RESOLUTION

Once the pledge has been made by the state to produce justice for all citizens, then it becomes necessary to give consideration to the most appropriate form and forum for different kinds of complaint and grievance. No serious attempt has been made in the UK to examine this issue. The 1950s and 1960s saw some important developments in this area but nothing rigorously systematic occurred. After the furore over Crichel Down in 1954, the Franks Committee was appointed in the following year to consider and make recommendations on the constitution and working of tribunals other than the ordinary courts of law and the working of such administrative procedures as include the holding of an inquiry or hearing by or on behalf of a minister, *and in particular the procedure for compulsory purchase of land*. The upshot was the Tribunals and Inquiries Act 1958 (now 1992) which is, without doubt, a major landmark in administrative justice. However, it, following Franks, was limited to areas where recourse to a tribunal or public inquiry was already available. Within that framework it sought to improve the quality of justice through openness, fairness and impartiality. It left the remainder of the administrative justice system largely unremarked and made no attempt at structuring ideas on optimum forms of dispute resolution. It did not attempt to identify conditions which made administrative tribunals desirable in any given situation.

The next major development of any significance was the celebrated Whyatt Report in 1961. This report was influential in helping to bring about the first classical British ombudsman in the form of the Parliamentary Commissioner for Administration (PCA), established in 1967. We speak about the strengths and weaknesses of this and other British ombudsman systems in Chapter 7. What is often forgotten, however, is that Whyatt also recommended that, unless strong policy considerations indicated to the contrary, an appeal to an independent tribunal from discretionary decisions should be available as of right. To this end, Whyatt favoured the establishment of a general administrative appeal tribunal of the sort eventually adopted in Australia in the 1970s as we noted in Chapter 2. This recommendation has, however, lain dormant in the UK, as has a full-scale review of administrative justice as recommended by the English and Scottish Law Commissions in 1969. An ersatz review was undertaken by the Justice-All Souls Committee which, after many years of rather slow and punctuated deliberation, reported in 1988 (Justice-All Souls 1988) (see Chapter 2).

The Justice-All Souls Report contained many important recommendations, albeit that none were particularly original. For present purposes, its major flaw – that of ignoring the policy-making process almost in its entirety – is unimportant. However, it remains unsatisfactory in several respects. Not only is the treatment of ombudsmen somewhat conservative and unimaginative, but no satisfactory treatment is given to the ignored second thigh of the Whyatt Committee, viz. the automatic right of appeal from a discretionary decision. Even more significantly, no attempt was made to identify the strengths and weaknesses of different forms of administrative justice – tribunals versus inquiries versus ombudsmen. It is not a conceptually informed document; rather, it is one which looks at present arrangements and suggests 'necessary reforms'. The task, then, still remains to attempt an analysis of ideal types of dispute resolution machinery for complaints against the state.

The present position is lucidly summarized by Professor Bradley (1985, p. 702):

> There are three main ways in which disputes arising out of state services and controls may be settled: (a) by conferring new jurisdiction on one or other of the ordinary courts; (b) by creating *ad hoc* machinery in the form of special tribunals; (c) by empowering the appropriate minister to make the decisions. In the latter case, Parliament may be content with the normal process of departmental decision or may require the minister to observe a special procedure, for example, to hold a public inquiry, before the decision is made.

It has been remarked upon time out of mind that the reasons for adopting one of these three rather than the others is haphazard and largely unsystematic (see, e.g. Birkinshaw, 1985a). Certain prejudices may be seen to be at work in a number of respects; for example, the minister wishing to be shielded from interference by outside bodies as a general principle. However, there is little rhyme or reason in the existence of any particular set of tribunals for securing justice against the state. Some of the more vital areas for citizens, such as social security, have traditionally and understandably been subject to formal appeal systems. The systems have rarely satisfied the classical criteria of openness, fairness and impartiality, and have recently been under sustained attack in the UK. However, most impartial observers would demand an independent assessment of entitlement in an area so crucial to the quality of people's lives. Elsewhere, there are no independent tribunals where we might expect them, while they appear in areas where no obvious criterion of special merit can be easily observed. Independent tribunals may spring up as a result of special pleading, a late committee amendment in the House, as a *quid pro quo* for some concession required by government and so on. This is clearly unsatisfactory, lacking in principle and lacking in justice.

THE SEARCH FOR JUST SOLUTIONS

We have made the point from time to time and will make it more forcefully later that the court system should be the quality-control mechanism of our public life. The courts are expensive, to a considerable extent arcane, and absolutely essential to holding a constitution together; to holding the nation to its larger promises. They should be invoked only when serious issues are at stake. That primarily means where some dispute over citizen rights is at issue, where natural justice is under threat or where some serious challenge to the legitimacy of state action is mounted. Due process within the administrative/state machine should normally be sought elsewhere. To a considerable extent, that should be within the processes of public administration itself, though those processes need to be buttressed by auxiliary mechanisms in the form of ombudsmen, tribunals, enquiries and the like.

The first, and obvious, point to make is that any grievance against a public body ought to be remedied by that body itself without further prompting. It seems to us remarkable that no single statutory duty currently exists on public authorities to produce and publicize a grievance procedure whereby members of the public have a clear picture of the shape of an organization and who professes to be responsible for decision taking. The location of a higher level of appeal and the processes for raising or expressing a grievance ought clearly to be a statutory responsibility of all public bodies. Freedom of information would clearly help in this respect, since those jurisdictions which have adopted such a degree of openness require that the organizational framework be clearly identified. This involves identifying clear lines of responsibility for decisions taken and to be taken. At the moment, in central government terms at least, the *Civil Service Yearbook* is the nearest we get to this state of affairs and, valuable though it undoubtedly is, it is hardly compendious and hardly readily available to the public at large.

We have no doubt that a formal duty to publish a complaints or grievance procedure should be established. Within that general duty, it would be for the organization concerned to determine the precise nature of the procedures thought suitable. We give extensive treatment to these issues in Chapter 8. However, in the interests of presenting a complete picture of a just administration as we envisage it, one or two other points should be touched upon here. The first is that we ally ourselves completely with those who argue that a free and open society should defend its decisions rationally. In other words, reasons for decisions should almost always be forthcoming for decisions taken in the public sphere. There are any number of models available which the UK might wish to copy in order to enhance fairness, and we believe efficient administration, in government. We have decided to suggest the adoption of the Australian example, not least since the Commonwealth of Australia operates a Westminster model of government.

The introduction in the Commonwealth administrative law package of the 1970s of a statutory obligation imposed on decision makers to give reasons for their decisions upon request has properly been regarded as one of the most significant reforms contained in the package. In a memorandum produced by the Administrative Review Council (ARC) in 1978 to explain the statement of reasons requirement, the ARC said that the requirement was intended to overcome the real grievance persons experience when they are not told why something affecting them has been done and to enable persons affected to see what was taken into account and whether an error was made so that they may determine whether or not to challenge the decision. A series of judicial decisions has explained the value of the requirement as being two-fold. First, to stimulate the decision maker to consider carefully the lawfulness and correctness of the decision to be made in the circumstances and thereby improving the quality of decision making. Secondly, to ensure that decision making rests on a rational foundation by stimulating the decision maker to identify and formulate the reasons which motivate the decision. The improvement in decision-making standards has been attested to by senior administrators (ARC, 1991a). What is equally clear is that furnishing reasons for decisions may also help to prevent unnecessary appeals or complaints in connection with the making of decisions.

Under the 1977 Act, a person aggrieved by a decision to which the Act applies has a right to receive a statement of reasons for the decision. Subject to a few exceptions, any decision of an administrative character made under an enactment meets the description of a decision to which the Act applies. A person aggrieved includes a person whose interests are adversely affected by the decision. This standing test is to be given a liberal construction [*Australian Conservation Foundation v Minister for Resources* (1990) 19 ALD 70]. The statement to which a person seeking reasons is entitled is a statement in writing setting out the findings on material questions of fact, referring to the evidence or other material on which those findings were based and giving the reasons for the decision. The duty is enforceable via judicial review. This may be thought to be unnecessarily cumbersome and suggestions have been made to simplify the enforcement machinery. Be that as it may, a provision similar in nature to that of the 1977 Act ought to be adopted in the UK. During the period within which the Act has been in force, the number of requests for statements of reasons first built up to a peak of more than 2000 in the mid-1980s, but then gradually fell away. This is thought to provide significant evidence that the duty to furnish reasons on request has had the desired effect of improving the standards of decision making.

Internal grievance handling, then, openly operated, should remove the overwhelming body of sources of complaint. Two more matters might be mentioned to complete the picture, which are more extensively treated elsewhere. The first is that the administrative regimen of public bodies would be operating in a context where a reformed ombudsman system should be in place. Principles of good administration would presumably be required of public bodies in such an event, so even greater pressure would be brought to improve the standards delivered to the public. We speak to the issue of internal monitoring of grievances by public bodies in Chapter 8, but it is worth anticipating the argument by saying that monitoring of complaints by public bodies ought to produce a degree of quality control which should do nothing to impair the quality of administrative justice. Although the present position in Britain is unsatisfactory, the *Citizens' Charter* initiative may possibly herald the beginnings of some improvement. At the time of writing, the government is considering the appointment of independent consultants to ensure that no slippage occurs in terms of charter promises. That is to say, they are conscious that pretty promises might be made by public agencies without ensuring that those promises are honoured at the daily level. The task of the consultant monitors would be to make both random and systematic checks to ensure compliance.

The second point to make is that if our proposals for a Standing Administrative Conference (SAC) were adopted, then it would be surprising if such a body did not concern itself from time to time with the procedures adopted by government for handling complaints by the public. One way and another, then, the culture of administrative justice would have been substantially improved. To that extent, external appeal might be less important, at least at the quantitative level, than might otherwise be expected. However, before we turn to the issue of external constraints, another form of redress mechanism needs to be canvassed.

In recent years, the British courts have been developing a doctrine called 'legitimate expectations', an issue which we develop in Chapter 10. Briefly put, where a public authority leads someone to believe that it will act in a particular way or that a particular state of affairs will continue, that someone may, in appropriate circumstances, rely upon that belief. This now appears to be in the process of moving from a judicial to an administrative doctrine. This necessitates that we say a little about the Next Steps Executive Agencies (Efficiency Unit, 1988) introduced earlier in Chapter 3.

Next Steps is concerned with the establishment of agencies to deliver services to the public and thereby separate out policy making in Whitehall from service delivery through the agencies. The expressed intent is to improve the quality and efficiency of services; something that the traditional civil service has been thought not to do particularly well. The general thrust of Next Steps is that agencies should be discrete organizations with a defined task or tasks. They are headed by a chief executive and the framework document should constitute their constitutions. This sets out the relationship between them and their sponsoring departments and contains their aims, objectives, and performance indicators. The relationship between the agencies, their departments and the Treasury is complicated and still unfolding. However, monitoring of their performance is fairly rigorous. Even so, there is no clear evidence as yet that the monitoring is directed to ensuring more than close control on public expenditure. Many of the agencies still have no quality performance indicators as opposed to quantitative ones. We spoke of this issue in Chapter 3 in comparing inputs, outputs and outcomes. That said, there is enormous *potential* for monitoring with a view to examining the delivery of services from the point of view of the customer/consumer. Some of the agencies have established steering groups or advisory boards with an external membership. They are, however, mainly the technical agencies such as Companies House and the Vehicle Inspectorate, where the external frame of reference will be commerce or business interests. The wider consumer as citizen does not as yet figure in these developments. This is not to say that customer preferences are not sought and we return to this issue shortly.

The present government stresses closeness to the 'customer' as a primary consideration in the delivery of services. There remains the concern, however, that the commercial customer is given priority over the customer as citizen. Certainly, there has been little in the way of public debate either over the constitution of the framework documents themselves or over the performance indicators. Which indicators are chosen is clearly of vital importance, but too little in the way of political debate accompanies their establishment. A test of the *Citizens' Charter* will be how much this state of affairs changes. The same may be said of the issue of quality control, i.e. how much information from complaints and grievances will be fed into the working practices of the agencies so that weakness in service delivery may be identified and addressed. It is worth mentioning in passing that the Parliamentary Commissioner for Administration (the PCA or ombudsman) will have jurisdiction in relation to most of the activities of the agencies. Indeed, in so far as their targets and indicators are publicized, he might well enjoy greater influence than he did before the agencies were established. In other words, the concept of 'maladministration' may be widened to embrace the disclosed targets and indicators (see Select Committee on PCA, 1991–92).

In many instances, a combination of the framework documents and performance indicators will effectively promise particular levels of performance, upon which of course many customers or consumers will feel entitled to rely. Leaving aside the issue of whether at some stage in the near future the courts will develop the doctrine of legitimate expectations into this area, we may well anticipate that the administration itself will be prepared to enter into so-called 'contracts' with citizens, breach of which might produce their own remedies. At the time of writing, the government has produced its first thoughts on a *Citizens' Charter*. The general thrust of this idea is that performance promises will be made by the public sector, breach of which will allow for compensation to be provided to an injured party on a scale laid down by government itself. There is undoubtedly mileage in such ideas, which we believe ought to be widely encouraged. We discuss these initiatives further later in the chapter.

INDEPENDENT TRIBUNALS

We have already touched upon the question as to whether, in principle, all discretionary decisions in the public sector should be subject to independent appeal. We have seen that this has found favour in several quarters while failing to win general acceptance in the UK up until now.

At the risk of oversimplification, we can say that the traditional rules governing review of administrative action produce the situation where the courts are in effect concerned with the procedures adopted for taking decisions and with interpreting points of law, while the merits of the decision are left to be determined elsewhere. In British terms, this means either that there will be a specific *ad hoc* tribunal for rehearing argument on the merits or they will be left to be determined, in one way or another, according to administrative or executive discretion. We will have more to say about tribunals and their desirability in Chapter 6.

Given that unbridled discretion can lead to arbitrary decision making, we can now take it as read that checks and balances ought to be put in place to ensure that administrative decision making is as fair and rational as possible. We make it clear that, to this end, a whole raft of devices needs to be considered and we try to make our position clear on where each of these devices fits into our overall scheme of things. However, one point in particular needs to be developed at this point. It concerns the relative strengths and weaknesses of ombudsman systems as opposed to appeal on the merits. There is no point in pretending that there will not be overlap. There often will be, and we wish to argue that this is no bad thing in itself. Given, too, that ombudsman systems tend to have more than one object and that one of them is attending to allegations of injustice suffered by individuals at the hands of government, this should cause no surprise. However, we ought at least to have a set of general principles in mind as to which machinery can best perform which function in the overall scheme of things.

THE RELATIONSHIP BETWEEN OMBUDSMEN AND APPEALS ON THE MERITS TO TRIBUNALS

Much of what follows is again unashamedly based on Australian Commonwealth experience. In particular, we have borrowed heavily from the ARC's Report to the Attorney-General in 1985 (ARC, 1985). For present purposes, we shall assume that administrative tribunals in the UK can be grouped together and treated like the Australian General Administrative Appeals Tribunal in terms of relationships with the ombudsman system.

The primary function of ombudsman systems is to investigate independently complaints from individuals relating to defective administration by departments and authorities. Their role is to make recommendations in order to improve administrative processes and to provide justice for aggrieved individuals. The ombudsman operates in a relatively informal and confidential manner, and in a private setting. In contrast, tribunals adjudicate, to a considerable measure in an adversarial fashion, on the merits of a specific decision made by an administrator. As a review body external to the administration, a tribunal's role is to provide justice to aggrieved individuals and guidance for primary decision makers by making determinations as to what is the correct or preferable decision in a particular case. The tribunal, although far less formal than a court, nevertheless sits in an open and judicial fashion, with the applicant entitled to a hearing and to have access to the materials upon which the tribunal will base its decision.

In Australia, the broad investigative charter of the ombudsman was explicitly distinguished from AAT-type review in the Explanatory Memorandum to the Ombudsman Bill 1976:

Thus the function of the Ombudsman is quite different to that of an appeal tribunal . . . these bodies are empowered to hear appeals from decisions and where they think fit, to overrule these decisions and substitute their own. They are limited to considering decisions, and are not ordinarily concerned with other administrative functions. They are, moreover, confined to specified classes of matters, whereas the Ombudsman has power to investigate the whole field of administrative activity of government.

In fact, the straightforward distinction between reviewing on the merits and finding defective administration is not as simple as it seems. This is a point which was also picked up by the Justice-All Souls Report which referred to 'the substantial degree of overlap which exists between the two systems' (Justice-All Souls, 1988, para. 5.27). They refer to those instances where the ombudsmen have produced remedies quite similar to those of the courts. For instance, in addition to the many small cases where benefits are paid belatedly or unreasonable tax demands are abated, there are also certain cases in which the ombudsmen's intervention leads to the payment of substantial sums of money. Justice-All Souls was speaking primarily of the demarcation between the ombudsmen and the courts, but the same, and perhaps larger point, applies to the tribunal system. They seemed to accept that the individual had and should continue, in many cases, to have a choice as to the preferred avenue of redress. The Commission for Local Administration, in its evidence to the committee, argued that the individual should continue to have freedom of choice as between the ombudsman and trial-type forms of redress. They had found, in their experience, that no problems had been created in practice.

The committee, in underwriting the *status quo* without analysing its potential in any detail, expressed the view that the ombudsman in many situations is a more effective way of securing redress against the administration than recourse to the courts (tribunals). They are clearly right, but as the ARC persuasively argued in its report, the relative strengths of the several institutions need to be assessed to ensure that the most effective system of administrative justice is produced. With the assistance of the ARC's *22nd Report*, this is what we would now like to attempt. This is an ideal-typical model and we are assuming that an ombudsman system is operating at its optimum potential rather than reflecting what is currently done in the name of present UK ombudsmen. To that extent, we are assuming that most of the reforms of the ombudsman system which we associate ourselves with in Chapter 7 are in place.

In setting up ombudsman systems, most governments have worked on the rough and ready distinction of courts and/or tribunals dealing with law and in the latter case 'merits', while ombudsmen merely investigate failures of administration without reference to the merits of the decision. Even if an ombudsman would personally have come to a different conclusion from, say, a tribunal on the merits of the decision he or she would not be entitled to interfere in the absence of a failure of administration; what, to some extent in the UK, we refer to as 'maladministration'. As the Australian ARC pointed out, however, it is doubtful whether this distinction is a valid one, even though the functions of the two sets of institutions are largely different 'in terms of their nature, functions, scope, procedures and remedies' (ARC, 1985, para. 10). If we take a basket of ombudsman jurisdictions around the world, what we find is that there are some jurisdictional powers which an ombudsman possesses and which most 'judicial' systems do not, while there are some areas of very clear overlap.

In the former category, we find jurisdiction afforded where, even though a decision was taken in accordance with a rule of law or a statutory provision, the outcome was unjust, oppressive or unreasonable. 'Reasonableness' in this context means considerably more than it means for UK courts when exercising their ordinary judicial review functions. We elaborate on this in Chapter 10. Many ombudsman systems also afford jurisdiction to find fault or error where a decision, albeit in accordance with normal administrative practice, is simply thought to be 'wrong'. On the other hand, most ombudsmen may find a failure of administration where a decision appears to be contrary to law, improperly discriminatory, was taken for an improper or irrelevant purpose and the like. These are areas where the courts or tribunals exercise traditional jurisdiction. The distinction between the two sets of institutions, *in terms of grounds of review at least*, may be thought to be elusive. The end result of using either institution may be substantially similar in terms of remedy and redress *despite the different methods and procedures adopted*. Points of intersection, then, clearly exist. Even so, there are *characteristic* differences to which we should turn before we look at the acceptability of a person aggrieved choosing the appropriate jurisdictional forum.

One clear distinction emerges at the outset. Where the decision maker is left with a choice between several as opposed to merely one course of action when making a decision, the ombudsman will not find such a choice to be defective providing the correct procedure has been followed. If the ombudsman recommended the substitution of one decision with what he thought to be preferable, this would be, as Professor Richardson once remarked, 'unwarranted obtrusion into the proper exercise of administrative judgment' (Commonwealth of Australia Ombudsman, 1982, p. 39). Leaving aside the situation where courts or tribunals merely adjudicate on the law, then the judicial process as such, let us say primarily the tribunal process, is dedicated to determine for itself the correct or preferable decision based upon the facts as they appear to the tribunal itself. Another clear distinction relates to the procedures adopted by the two sets of mechanisms.

The nature of ombudsman review is investigative. Procedures are characterized by the requirement that an investigation be conducted in private and according to the discretion of the ombudsman himself. An investigation may not infrequently be conducted without the presence of any of the protagonists. Now this obviously can occur where a court or tribunal is the chosen forum, but it cannot rationally be said that this characterizes the judicial process. Again, although the ombudsman will make the result of his investigations available to the parties, they will not necessarily see the documents upon which he has acted. This is, of course, not the way a court of law proceeds, even though ombudsmen traditionally have at least the power of the courts to call for documentation, evidence, to swear oaths and so on. Again, the ombudsman normally makes enquiries of the parties concerned separately, without the others being present, also in sharp contrast to the judicial process. In fact, the ability of the ombudsman to investigate all documents which he thinks might impinge upon an alleged failure of administration contrasts sharply with the practice of tribunals and courts to restrict themselves to documents which can generally speaking be identified as relevant to the issue by the combatants. The ombudsman may himself also make preliminary enquiries and settle or abandon the issue at any time.

The other side of this coin (and we shall take the Australian AAT as our guide) is that tribunals generally only receive complaints in writing, hearings are public, the parties or their representatives are entitled to appear, to inspect documents presented in evidence, and to present their case in a semi-structured, at least ordered, fashion. Although the remedies sometimes made available by tribunals and by the ombudsmen turn out to be similar, ombudsman recommendations for the most part are not enforceable, even if in reality they are normally complied with. However, given the concern which the ombudsman has with the quality of administration, his recommendations will often be very different from those of a court or tribunal. In particular, they may recommend that a rule of law, provision of an enactment or practice upon which a decision, etc., was based be altered. In fact, then, such a recommendation might be made together with a recommendation for *ex gratia* compensation, which gives the ombudsman, on occasion, greater influence than a court or tribunal. Furthermore, the ombudsman, unlike the judicial process, can choose to monitor the behaviour of the agency or department subject to criticism and seek to publicize failure to act on the recommendation.

Here is one of the strengths of an ombudsman system. But there are weaknesses, too, which mirror the strengths of the judicial process. This is seen most clearly in relation to cases where there are strongly disputed questions of fact at issue. Despite access to documents and general impartiality, the investigative nature of the ombudsman process makes it unsuitable for exercising an adjudicative role in an adversarial context. This is particularly true where there are substantial discrepancies in the versions of the facts presented by the parties, particularly in cases alleging misleading or defective oral advice where there are no written records of an event and a lack of independent evidence. There is another associated point which is worth stressing in illuminating the essential differences between the two sets of institutions. A court or tribunal must decide on the facts in front of it, subject to some extent at least, to rules of evidence and to the forensic skills of the parties or their representatives. Although the ombudsman must also have scrupulous regard for the facts and must not presume either for or against the administration, there is in reality *a higher investigative duty* at stake. Was the administration defective? Were there better or more appropriate ways of conducting public business? This represents a considerable differentiation. Again where a complaint relates to various actions of a department or agency which form a pattern of conduct, all or some of which are not within the judicial competence, the ombudsman represents the better course for a complainant.

The Australian ARC adds four more areas where it believes the ombudsman is a preferable forum to the judicial process. Again we are in agreement with their suggestions, which are as follows:

a. where the complaint relates to action, or to a facultative, procedural, preliminary or collateral decision, of a department or authority rather than a substantive decision. e.g. the exercise of evidential powers to obtain material upon which a substantive decision may be made.
b. where a decision is of a quasi-legislative character and affects the complainant as part of a group rather than specifically as an individual [note *not* the present position in the UK].
c. where the matter relates to internal administration or the exercise of a power of delegation which does not, of itself, affect an individual's interests or
d. where a decision only takes effect for a short period of time.

(ARC, 1985, para. 57)

Most ombudsmen systems are directed either not to investigate a complaint where an alternative avenue exists or they are given a discretion in such an event. The latter is more common and, in our view, more desirable. It is not always clear from searching through ombudsman reports what guiding principles inform the decision to investigate or not in such a case. The Australian ombudsman has again provided useful criteria which we are happy to adopt. The following were described as relevant in deciding whether to investigate a complaint, notwithstanding the existence of an alternative avenue:

1 The costs involved in pursuing the alternative avenue of redress.
2 Personal factors such as age or state of health which affect a complainant's ability to demonstrate his or her entitlement to relief.
3 Whether the facts might be better established by utilizing the fact-finding procedures provided for under ombudsman legislation.
4 Whether the remedies which the alternative review mechanism is capable of providing are adequate or appropriate (Commonwealth of Australia Ombudsman, 1982, pp. 12–14). A simple illustration might be where there is a statutory restriction in the form of limited damages or compensation. The ombudsman, obviously, is not restricted in terms of the remedies which seem to be appropriate.

By way of elaboration, we would say that since the ombudsman is a cost-free mechanism from the point of view of the complainant and since the initiative to investigate lies with the office of the ombudsman, these might also prove crucial factors. The reverse side of the latter point is, of course, that the applicant in the judicial process has to show more enterprise and motivation, may incur expense and will need to gather evidence in support of the application.

In some jurisdictions, particularly where an issue important to the administration is at stake, it may be likely that even were a complainant to win a case before a tribunal, the administration might wish to challenge on appeal, thereby causing further expenditures of resources on the part of an aggrieved individual. This might be just such a case where an application to the ombudsman might represent a more attractive proposition. The administration should always be allowed to ask for a declaratory judgment in such a case if the issue was important enough to it.

It seems to be universally accepted that overlap between the two sets of institutions is inevitable, and, for the most part, acceptable. The major division of opinion relates to whether there ought to be a discretion to refuse an application as outlined here (the position in most of the English-speaking world) or whether a choice of forum should be left freely available (e.g. as in France, Finland and Sweden). The latter is probably not acceptable in the UK, though we have no doubt that aggrieved individuals ought to have a range of distinct review venues in which they can pursue administrative justice according to the particular circumstances of the case. There does need to be, it seems to us, collaboration between the ombudsmen and the judicial process to avoid unnecessary duplication. The establishment of a Ministry of Justice would be helpful in this respect.

It would be valuable, in our view, for a body such as a SAC to examine the issues addressed in this section in a national setting as being indispensable to providing a comprehensive system of administrative justice. In doing so, it might wish to lay down criteria or codes for our ombudsmen to address in deciding whether or not to exercise their discretion to proceed with an investigation despite the existence of an alternative method of review. Consideration would also need to be given to the possible mutual referral of cases as between the two sets of institutions with the consent of the applicants or individuals concerned.

A satisfactory system of administrative justice needs to begin with fair and open procedures within the administration itself and extend up to the highest courts whose (accessible) determinations will be the most authoritative on the nature of administrative and constitutional propriety. In between, there is a range of possibilities and a plurality of experiments which might be conducted. As we have already suggested, there may be areas where the minister or other authority's decision ought to be final in the sense of not giving rise to a further appeal on the merits. An example would be where issues of high policy importance were at stake. Even so, these occasions ought to be far fewer than is currently the case. Without wishing to prejudice what we have to say in Chapter 6, this means extending the tribunal system beyond its present limits to some considerable degree.

The ombudsman system, operating at its highest potential, is an indispensable element of justice in the contemporary state. It can dig where the courts and tribunals cannot trespass. It can point up systemic weaknesses and suggest improvements. Even so, it can do much to provide justice to individuals outside the juridical process. We simply need to think harder about the optimum roles for the two sets of institutions. They are both necessary and must be as accessible as we can make them.

Of the alternative justice arrangements which need to be considered, one type seems to us to be most significant and to that we now turn.

THE CITIZEN'S LEGITIMATE EXPECTATIONS AND THE STATE'S PROMISES

We have already touched upon the doctrine of legitimate expectations as a judicial construct. This is in effect a judicial attempt to examine the citizen's imminent expectations of government, at least in a limited category of circumstances. What is now beginning to develop is a broader political philosophy about the citizen's legitimate expectations about the way government should behave. This is often accompanied by the highly dubious language of 'contract', which is by no means a legal term of art, but it expresses the belief that a set of promises be made by the state apparatus concerning the quality of services delivered to the public (see Harden, 1992). Most often this takes the form of performance indicators or standards which the government department or agency is to meet. Breach of these promises/standards may result in a measure of compensation for those adversely affected. From the traditional legal system's point of view, these developments are potentially important and innovative. The significance is primarily two-fold. The first is that by documenting and highlighting standards and performance measurement criteria, government can clearly go beyond the general constitutional requirements of the courts. The courts are clearly not equipped to judge adequate standards of managerial or commercial performance. Yet by assessing what it regards as an adequate level of service, government offers citizen complainants a more or less detailed criterion for judging the failure of service delivery. Secondly, these developments offer the potential for speedy and accessible recompense outside the traditional court structure. Whatever the future of these experiments, there is no doubt in our mind that they offer the potential for important gains in terms of accessible justice against the state.

Before developing this theme, a minor detour might be of interest. Although the impetus for this new movement has undoubtedly been the government's *Citizens' Charter* (Cabinet Office, 1991), precedents already existed in the shape of compacts made between several local authorities and their service departments and the consumers of those services. The idea, then, is not entirely new; only the scope and degree of apparent commitment marks a watershed. The second point to make is that, in the hands of the Major government, these aspects of the *Citizens' Charter* go hand in hand with a commitment to further privatization of state activities and the contracting out of as many public services to the private sector as possible. We are not able to develop the importance of these commitments here, but several points are worth making before we move on. The government is convinced that competition is the best guarantee of quality service. The example of Marks & Spencer is usually at the forefront of these claims. However, it is a truism to say that competition is rarely perfect, which is why we have an Office of Fair Trading, a Monopolies and Mergers Commission and a raft of (not least EC) competition laws. We shall therefore have a little to say elsewhere on the accessibility of these pro-competition agencies and devices for the justice enterprise. We shall also want to say a little shortly on the implications of these claims for the contracting out of public services.

THE *CITIZENS' CHARTER*

The July White Paper of 1991 spoke to a range of mechanisms for improving the lot of the citizen, some of which we have touched upon. Of the others, the only one which is outside the scope of this book is performance-related pay for civil servants. What remains are: published performance targets, both local and national; comprehensive publication of information on standards achieved; more effective complaints procedures; independent inspectorates; and a somewhat amorphous category entitled 'better redress for the citizen when services go badly wrong' (Cabinet Office, 1991, p. 5).

One of the earliest ringing declarations is that there 'should be no secrecy about how public services are run, how much they cost, who is in charge' (ibid). Naturally this point of view coincides with our own, yet in a country with a strict Official Secrets Act and no Freedom of Information Act, such a proclamation is bound to ring a little hollow. Another oddity of the Charter is the statement that public servants should not be anonymous. How this squares with ministerial responsibility, the lynchpin of the constitution, is also difficult for us to understand. We must simply await events. What appears to be the case from an early examination of government intentions, however, is that local government, the remaining nationalized industries and a few other assorted bodies should be subjected to a much more customer-oriented regime than central government departments and their offshoots. If so, this is an advance but a one-foot forward advance with the other firmly rooted to the spot, protestations to the contrary notwithstanding. It must be said, however, that at the time of writing, the government has announced plans for contracting out a range of central government services and/or putting them out to competitive tendering. The impact of such developments on service to the citizen is awaited with interest.

The July 1991 charter has been followed by a series of *ad rem* charters for individual services. At the time of writing, they amount to 28. The Prime Minister has also appointed a panel of advisers on the charter initiative with a unit having been set up in the Cabinet Office to co-ordinate the programme of action arising from the White Paper. We do not have the space to address all the issues outlined even in the White Paper, but wish merely to assess the validity of the initiative at large in providing greater potential access to justice. Let us therefore outline just a few of the claims, standards and promises which are envisaged in the knowledge that there is nothing to prevent all public services setting out their own detailed standards after a thorough examination. Thus, for instance, in relation to hospitals, it is envisaged that the maximum time patients should normally have to wait will be displayed for everyone to see in hospital waiting rooms. As to British Rail, an appropriate target might be that 92 per cent of all trains should arrive within five minutes of the published time. The Passenger's Charter for British Rail also describes an *ex gratia* system of refunds and vouchers for delayed and cancelled trains. British Telecom's customers can now claim compensation if new telephone lines are not installed within two working days of the agreed date. The Council Tenant's Charter allows tenants to execute repairs where the local authority has not done so and to charge the authority for the work. Similar provisions apply to housing association tenants. And so on.

Other aspects of the charter intended to improve quality and therefore access to what is a citizen entitlement are better information, clearer standards of service expectation, points of comparison where there is no direct competition, and audit and monitoring. We shall say just a little about each of these in turn.

The setting of standards is and of itself a vehicle for providing greater information. But there are further proposals which would strengthen the amount of information available. For example, the Housing Corporation is to issue a stronger Tenants' Guarantee which will set benchmarks for assessing the quality of service in rents, allocation, maintenance and repair. Performance information will be made available to tenants, who will also be consulted regularly through satisfaction surveys. In schools, too, better information for parents will be made available to exercise their rights to freedom of choice. Valuable though these moves may prove to be, it is difficult to understand the philosophy which pulls us in this direction while still opposing a Freedom of Information Act.

As to standards, this is very much the centrepiece of the charter idea. We have already touched upon the promises to be made within the National Health Service. British Rail, too, is to provide clear standards relating to punctuality, reliability, cleaning, the answering of telephone enquiries and the like. In the Post Office, performance standards will in the future be set by the Secretary of State rather than by the Post Office itself, as formerly. Furthermore, a new independent regulator is to be introduced for the Post Office who will monitor performance against targets, and will be responsible for making an independent assessment of complaints about Post Office services. He or she is also to advise the Secretary of State on levels of redress for service failures and on the level of access charges to the postal network in cases where there is a dispute.

A whole range of monitoring procedures is promised in the charter and we would simply say that establishing standards without adequate monitoring arrangements would be highly unsatisfactory. Let us, however, merely say a word about local authorities. The government is proposing to strengthen the audit and inspection services. For instance, local authorities will be obliged to publish their response to auditors' reports and the Audit Commission will be asked to publish league tables of local authority performance.

A second Charter White Paper was promised for the autumn of 1992 (see p. 38 above).

COMPLAINTS AND REDRESS

The matter of complaints and redress is central not only to the charter's concern but of course to those of this book. It is fundamental to the

Citizens' Charter that all public services, including local authorities, should have clear and well-publicized complaints procedures. Not only should such procedures be open and accessible, but a code of practice for the handling of complaints should be produced. Within this general commitment, a range of experiments is promised. The NHS may be asked to produce an arbitration scheme for claims of medical negligence, while for the family health services, patients may choose to use lay conciliators. Prisoners, on the other hand, are to receive reasoned written replies within clear time limits, etc.

We naturally greatly welcome the government's belated conversion to complaints procedures, but we remain convinced that a general statutory duty supplemented by codes of practice is what is required. At the moment, this does not seem to be contemplated. What is of considerable potential interest, however, is the reference to independent complaints machinery where internal procedures fail. The government is to consult on the introduction of a new scheme under which local lay adjudicators would be appointed to deal with minor claims for redress which the body complained against has not settled in a speedy and satisfactory way. This proposal is extremely interesting, but it remains to be seen how far such a scheme could be introduced without the facile second-guessing of political decisions, especially in relation to the allocation of scarce resources. At the time of writing, progress on this aspect of the charter appears to be stalled. Closer examination suggests that the government does not really contemplate full-blown arbitration in such cases; rather, they see the 'adjudicators' as complainants' friends, perhaps operating more as mediators or advisers. One thing is clear, there are many instances of informal justice schemes operating around the world which the government could investigate. We shall mention just one as being illustrative of informal complaints handling.

The United States Postal Service provides an interesting example of complaints handling in the form of the 'Consumer Advocate'. Every post office makes available customer service cards or complaints cards, though complaints may also be made by telephone or letter. Customers who remain dissatisfied after regional or local reassessment may complain in writing to the Consumer Advocate who directs the Consumer Services Division. The Consumer Advocate performs the following functions:

1 Representing the individual mail user within the Postal Service.
2 Recommending policy changes to improve an individual user's mail service.
3 Maintaining liaison with consumer groups.
4 Taking expeditious action on customer enquiries and complaints.
5 Determining that the responsible officer takes corrective action.
6 Providing regular reports, based upon consumer service card data; these are used for service monitoring purposes.

We believe this is a valuable development and would be appropriate for at least some of the larger UK government agencies.

Automatic compensation and redress is, in many ways, the most intriguing new idea as far as we are concerned in offering the potential for replacing court-type forums by something much more speedy and accessible. Already council house tenants enjoy a 'right to repair', which allows them to get certain repairs costing up to £200 done where their landlord fails to do so. British Telecom's customers can now claim compensation if new telephone lines are not installed within two working days of the agreed date; there are guaranteed standards with an attendant compensation scheme in the water industry. OFGAS is introducing a new package of key standards which includes compensation for customers (and see Chapter 9). In the NHS, the charter envisages guaranteed waiting times for operations. If the original hospital cannot meet the deadline for treatment, the district health authority will seek provision elsewhere, including, if appropriate, from the private sector. As to British Rail, an expanded compensation scheme has been agreed with the government so that, for example, if trains are cancelled or unreasonably delayed, passengers may apply for a refund. Season ticket holders will receive compensation, mainly by extensions to their season tickets, for days where there is no effective service.

Some of the government's ideas are at present a little hazy and it is also clear that effective compensation, for example in relation to British Rail, would probably cost as much as remedying the defects in the service in the first place. Even so, many of the charter's ideas are fresh and stimulating. Properly developed they have the potential for an important addition to our mechanisms for achieving justice against the state.

CONTRACT AND LEGITIMATE EXPECTATIONS: A PRELIMINARY ASSESSMENT

Perhaps the first thing to remark is that the present concentration on the 'contractual' relationship between state agencies and their 'customers' is not all it appears. Contract suggests choice, freedom and rational discourse. Not only is this not normally the case in relation to the provision of state services, but doctrinally there is normally no contractual liability for failure to deliver most public services (Harden, 1992, ch. 5). This is perhaps all the more reason to provide alternative and accessible forms of redress. Some of the suggestions for redress in the form of vouchers, cheap or free travel or even compensation are imaginative and will hopefully have a valuable part to play in the years to come. So also we should give a tentative welcome to a number of the other schemes which have been outlined. For example, the proposal for independent representation for complainants in the social services, the appointment of lay members to the various inspectorates, and most interestingly of all, the lay adjudicators to arbitrate in disputes between the citizen and the state agency on a voluntary basis. All these proposals will be followed with keen interest.

A number of queries remain, however. The first is that the *Citizens' Charter* defines the public sector on page 6 of the White Paper. Leaving aside the fact that the 'rump' of government departments after the executive agencies have been hived off are not really the subject of the charter, there is no reference to non-departmental public bodies (NDPBs) let alone the various state 'hybrids' such as the Training and Enterprise Councils (TECs). This is all the more reason for establishing our SAC to monitor such issues.

An associated point perhaps is that contracts with the private sector need much closer scrutiny than they have so far received. Where does the citizen, for example, stand in relation to a complaint about services where they have been contracted out to the private sector? There is, of course, no legal relationship between a citizen and such a contractor in the absence of tortious damage caused. Is it really satisfactory that only the state organ or agency can move against the private party? It is apparently becoming standard practice when councils contract out street cleaning to have penalty clauses in the contract activated by the number of complaints received. We should like more attention to be paid to this matter.

There is a considerable body of reference to consultation with customers and consumers but as yet it appears not to enjoy any institutional expression. The Next Step agencies are a case in point: 'all agencies will regularly consult customers and clients about the services they provide' (Cabinet Office, 1991, p. 36). In fact, some agencies are very much better than others, while some (e.g. the Benefits Agency) seem to experience considerable difficulty in determining who their customers are. Again, a little more rigour might be appropriate and once again we would favour legislation which made the duty to consult obligatory. This would bring us into line with a number of other countries who have attempted to bring the rule of law up to date.

Finally, for all the advances foreshadowed by the *Citizens' Charter*, there seems still to be a scarcely veiled attack on local government. This seems to us to be retrograde, since many services are best delivered locally. For justice to be real there needs to be confidence that those who provide local services have responsibility, resources and a degree of autonomy. It will be difficult for them to provide adequate services justly delivered if they are constantly being badgered by the centre. Interestingly in the late summer of 1992, the Audit Commission reported that 95 per cent of urgent repairs were carried out by local authorities within target times – often as little as a few hours. Most tenants were also offered choices when significant work was carried out in their homes. However, only 13 per cent of district councils had tenant representation on estate management bodies.

All this being said, many of the ideas expressed in the charter are fresh and interesting. They have the potential to increase the range of devices available to citizens to secure justice against the state. Voluntary, 'contractual' compliance is the most favoured option, with a backstop arbiter independent of the courts as the ultimate compliance mechanism. It would be surprising, however, if such an arbiter were thought to be as appropriate for central government departments as for local government and the remaining nationalized industries.

THE CITIZEN AS CUSTOMER

Many of the foregoing ideas are institutional expressions of the relatively recent fashionable concern with the 'customer' of public services. Many commentators date the emergence of this movement with the publication of *In Search of Excellence: Lessons from America's Best Run Companies* (Peters and Waterman, 1982). We need to say a little more about this movement here and to illustrate it with some examples. The treatment is necessarily a little untidy but we are concerned to provide a flavour of what is possible for assisting the citizen as consumer. We would hope that a body such as the the SAC would be able to take these issues on board and make concrete recommendations for improving the quality of justice against the state.

Identifying customer needs accurately is important for our purposes, since such identification ought to lead to fewer genuine grievances. We have already seen that some consultation devices exist to serve that end but that in general they are less developed in the field of citizen welfare than where commercial services are being offered.

The quest for good customer service may be used as a surrogate for real competition, especially where public services represent a monopoly. Traditionally, of course, customer or citizen views have been sought through the political process but, for all its advantages, traditional politics is too blunt an instrument for sensitive assessments across the board. A range of consultative devices has been tried in Britain and across the world, but recently customer surveys and market research have begun to figure prominently.

Although market research in the public sector is now particularly fashionable, it is not new. For example, Tony Benn, in addressing the Conference of the Market Research Society in 1970, called for the application of market research techniques to social and welfare problems (see, e.g. Common *et al.*, 1992). This practice has now become quite widespread, not least in the field of social security and employment services. It is an undoubted good that people should be asked for their comments on both the service presented and that desired. However, surveys have a down side and should be used in conjunction with other techniques, both of law and politics.

Elected representatives may well feel undermined by surveys as cutting across their functions. In the absence of FOI, politicians and managers are also able to refuse to disclose the findings of consumer surveys, especially where the findings are unacceptable to their image about quality of service provided. Unless the questions are tightly controlled, the findings might be unpalatable to ministers on another ground; namely, that they may be used as an argument for improving services and thereby increasing public expenditure. On the other hand, if they are tightly controlled, then the general public is answering behind a gag. And, of course, unlike the political process, a questionnaire cannot be cross-examined. However, as Common *et al.* (1992, pp. 80–81) point out: '. . . user involvement in a variety of ways, from passenger surveys on buses to parent-governors of schools is now on the agenda of senior management'.

As to staff attitudes on services, the public service's response is very mixed. Recent years have not been conducive to taking note of the views of public servants, especially trade unionists. Yet front-line staff are the people closest to the customer. Companies House is something of a leader in this field. At its London office, a junior manager collects and notes the views of staff each day and services have been changed or introduced as a direct result of these consultations (ibid., p. 90). More, however, needs to be done in this respect elsewhere. Regular research, not just limited to market surveys, can help to detect the strengths and failures of particular policies, goals and indicators. This would not only give policy makers a basis for future action and innovation, but represents a genuine contribution to grievance handling for the citizen. It is perhaps also important to remember that since public resources are almost always limited, it is important to put them where they will have most impact on customer need and preference.

As we have indicated, a range of devices has been periodically, and spasmodically, applied to assist with grievance redress: so-called 'one-stop' shops, video-monitors in social security offices which run simple programmes about benefit entitlement, customer care managers, the introduction of 'freephone' (usually 0800) facilities, etc. In 1987, we discovered a range of good practices for complaining against local government and most of what we said there is still of value (Lewis *et al.*, 1987). However, since that time, a range of other developments has occurred. The following are selective:

- The chief executive of one Midlands local authority takes direct phone calls from members of the public for one hour every weekday morning.
- A London borough council has a one-stop shop which can deliver at least the first stages of virtually all authority services from one room.

- The National Consumers Council has worked with two, geographically quite separate, local authorities to develop a series of consumer-oriented performance indicators in housing, day-care, library, refuse and street-lighting services.
- In the USA and Canada, voucher systems have been used for such services as day-care and transport for the elderly, thus permitting consumers greater choice of service.
- In Sweden, a procedure known as 'conditional delegation' has been introduced by law in order to increase the influence of consumers in local government decision making. More authority has been delegated to front-line staff, but the right to make a decision concerning certain services is delegated to employees conditionally on their consulting with the consumers affected, before making the decision.
- Another London borough has recently won a consumer award for operating on several fronts: market research, complaints monitoring, staff involvement, consumer consultation groups and corporate information strategy,

but

- The Benefits Agency has discontinued, at least at the time of writing, its consumer-oriented benefit computers (for these and other examples, see Cabinet Office, 1988; Epstein, 1990).

These are all means of either dealing with grievances directly or cooling them out in advance. As such, they are of great importance to citizens. However, if Total Quality Management (TQM) is the current corporate buzzword, then in the public sector what is called for is political TQM. That is to say, traditional politics needs to be reinforced by ancillary, participative mechanisms as well as customer surveys.

CONCLUSION

In this chapter, we have covered a lot of ground. We have tried to show that a range of reinforcing techniques is available and necessary for the disposition of trouble cases – for the handling of grievances real and imagined. Throughout the book, our belief that problems are best handled sensitively within the administration is in evidence. Here we have sought to indicate some new ways of achieving that result. We have also tried to identify some of the criteria for selecting an external mechanism where problems are not resolved within the public agency itself. We now go on to discuss tribunals and public hearings.

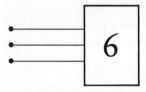

TRIBUNALS AND PUBLIC HEARINGS

The history and use of tribunals has been well documented and much has been said about their contemporary role (Wraith and Hutchesson, 1973). What we provide in this chapter is an analysis of the utility and problems associated with tribunals today. We shall examine other formal opportunities to make complaint or raise objection – the most common form being the public inquiry – to see what scope there is for the extension of such practices into other areas of activity. We shall also address a framework, or variety of frameworks, which will include a tribunal with power to overrule decisions on the merits. Some options will be canvassed. We should note at this early stage, however, that much is happening to the world of tribunals which sometimes makes the tribunal/ombudsman distinction difficult to draw.

A tribunal is an adjudicative technique used to determine a dispute, usually between two parties, after presentation of evidence by the parties and according to a body of rules or principles. In simple terms, they constitute substitute courts, cheaper alternatives to litigation. They can be employed for a variety of tasks, including inquiry and as bodies actively involved in the policy-making process or as recommendatory bodies (Birkinshaw, 1985a, ch. 4).

We should mention at this point that there has been judicial agonizing over the distinction between courts and tribunals: whether a court is a tribunal or a tribunal a court for the purposes of contempt of court (i.e. is it an independent body exercising the judicial power of the state?) or whether a tribunal has power to rule delegated legislation *ultra vires* (*Attorney-General v BBC* [1980] 3 All ER 161; *Pickering v Liverpool Daily Post* [1990] 1 All ER 335; *Chief Adjudication Officer v Foster* [1993] 1 All ER 705; Bradley, 1992, p. 185). The conclusions drawn owe as much to terminology as to immanent quality, especially when one considers that the basic reason for using tribunals is that they are cheaper and quicker than courts even when the same personnel make the decisions (see p. 18). However, the formal trappings of the bodies in question have been responsible for judicial restraint (*Arlidge v Local Government Board* [1915] AC 120 – actually an inquiry case) and judicial activism in the form of controlling tribunals (*Anisminic v FCC* [1969] 2 AC 147). We need only say for present purposes that barring statutory exclusions of judicial review, as in the case of the Interceptions Tribunal and the Security Tribunal, tribunals are subject to very copious powers of judicial review, although most statutory tribunals today are subject to appeal usually, at least, to the High Court on a point of law.

The features of a tribunal, then, are: (1) cheapness when compared with the courts, though much of this relates to the relatively low level of lawyer involvement, and while lawyers are only prohibited from appearing before very few tribunals, e.g. the Service Committees of Family Health Service Authorities (even unpaid), legal aid provisions only apply to a handful of tribunals, making legal representation less than likely unless financed by professional or trade union associations (Genn and Genn, 1989); and (2) informality, i.e. that they should be conducted fairly and not be bound by technical rules of evidence and procedure (see, e.g. *R v IAT ex p Jones* [1988] 2 All ER 65) – although the Council on Tribunals has drafted *Model Rules of Procedure for Tribunals* (1991). In a classical sense, tribunals are adjudicative bodies and sit in public, with powers to go into private session; they do not follow precedent set by previous tribunals though they must act within the law; and they are characterized by a strong lay presence on the adjudicating panel. There has been an increasing tendency to resort to legally qualified chairmen, but lay 'wings' serve to introduce expertise in areas, or to balance what may appear as opposing interests. Having drawn up this list of characteristics, it remains only to say that they can be denied as frequently as they are found and represent only an ideal type.

The Council on Tribunals (see Chapter 4) has jurisdiction over 'scheduled' tribunals, which means it is consulted in the making of rules covering such tribunals and advises on tribunals and their operation. There are thousands of tribunals which are not scheduled, usually of a domestic nature, and over which it has no influence, although it frequently asserts that tribunals should be brought within its jurisdiction, e.g. Housing Benefit Review Boards.

Strong support has been expressed for the virtues of independence of tribunals where they adjudicate between the state and citizens. This relates to a belief in the ideology (i.e. a fundamental idea) of neutrality in the process of adjudication where a citizen's rights or liberties are in question. In some cases, a presidential system has been introduced into tribunal organization with a president at the apex of the tribunal system who is responsible for the operation of the system and making reports. In the past, governments have used the independence of tribunals as a means to facilitate the acceptance of controversial programmes and to transmute clashes in political ideology – fundamental beliefs – into individual disputes about individual entitlement, just as in fact courts are claimed to do. In the past, tribunals were introduced into the administrative process to act as a brake on a minister's discretion and to curb potential arbitrariness (Donoughmore, 1932). Having introduced tribunals to adjudicate on disputes between citizens and the intervening state, they then had to be seen to be operating openly, fairly and impartially (Franks, 1957) which, government claimed, imposed increasing financial, organizational and bureaucratic burdens on the process of administration. Efficient government was being hampered by the time-consuming nature of tribunal decision making. These claims from government were increasingly accompanied by academic work that questioned the use of tribunals in, typically, social security and education administration (see, e.g. Mashaw, 1983; Tweedie, 1986). The basic thrust of this work was that where tribunals were used for large numbers of disputes, they may be good for individual justice but they may have the consequence of promoting individualistic values to get a larger share of what is being provided at public expense. They encourage selfishness. The consequence may be an overall reduction in what is being provided collectively, a diminution in efficiency and no means to ensure that the same problems are not repeated – in the argot, tribunals do not constitute good learning processes for officials. This touches upon points we have already raised in Chapter 3.

The government seems to have been won over by these claims and has increasingly resorted to forms of internal review by officials or adjudication officers (some of whom are under the jurisdiction of the Council on Tribunals) instead of tribunal hearings. Other techniques, as well as cash-limiting benefit payments, include one-man tribunals and the creation of multipurpose investigatory/adjudicatory procedures. All of this has been greeted with consternation by the council, which sees a precious idea being undermined.

In its 1989–90 annual report, for instance, the council noted the trend to 'down-grade and compromise' (Council on Tribunals, 1990, p. 1) appeal procedures for the sake of economizing. In a passage which is notable for its pristine notion of judicial independence and ministerial responsibility – it notes, for instance, the absence of ministerial responsibility for Social Fund

Officials (SFOs) – the council deprecates the government's decision to issue a code of guidance for local authorities on the setting up of 'internal procedures' to deal with complaints from homeless applicants. The council has, along with others, recommended a housing court/tribunal [*sic*] to embrace such matters. Preferring 'independent machinery', it described the proposals as 'highly unsatisfactory' (ibid., para. 1.8). With the pensions ombudsman introduced by the Social Security Act 1990, the council noted that the industry would not meet the cost of a tribunal, but it would finance an ombudsman operating *de facto* as a one-man tribunal investigating disputes over fact and law. Such funding, it felt, undermined independence (ibid., para. 1.12; see also Council on Tribunals, 1991, para. 3.27).

> We believe that where a decision affects a citizen's liberty, livelihood, status . . . particularly where a grievance concerns a decision of a public authority, nothing less is apt for the purpose than a properly equipped independent body able to bring an adjudicative approach to bear on the matter at issue.
>
> (Council on Tribunals, 1990, para. 1.14)

The council seems in fact to be more acerbic in its criticism of government practices. Such criticism covers not only the perceived bypassing of tribunals for other forms of grievance redress, but the failure of government to consult the council on relevant matters or to take any apparent notice of its advice. In the case of Service Committees of Family Health Service Authorities (under the NHS and Community Care Act 1990), the council felt so strongly that it issued a press statement by way of criticism. And despite its criticism, the regulations were not referred to the Standing Committee on Statutory Instruments (Council on Tribunals, 1990, para. 1.21). The Service Committees deal with complaints from patients about doctors, dentists, pharmacists and opticians in the NHS where the latter are alleged to have provided a service falling short of the standards required in their service contracts. Complaints are referred by the general manager of a FHSA to the chair of the appropriate committee. The council praised the fact that, for the first time, complaints could be made orally and the committees were given additional powers of decision as opposed to recommendation. However, its criticism is worth spelling out (the Secretary of State has delegated appellate functions of FHSAs to Regional Health Authorities; Council on Tribunals, 1991, p. 11).

Practitioners can be represented by other practitioners but patients cannot be represented by lawyers, even unpaid, having to make do with assistance from Community Health Councils. The Council on Tribunals also reported that it had observed a member of a FHSA assisting and even representing a doctor before a committee and various other 'undesirable practices' carried out by committees, all of which would have the effect of undermining the apparent impartiality of committees. On its side, the government responded that such practices were isolated or not allowed, assurances which did not assuage the anxiety of the council. More generally, the council has written that an important *informal* task it has undertaken has been to advise departments on the desirability of introducing adjudicative appeal procedures and what form they should take. Early consultation on these non-statutory topics had often prevented problems arising later, the council believed. In 1980, the council published a special report (Council on Tribunals, 1980a) recommending that it possess a general advisory role over the *whole* area of administrative adjudication. The government responded by saying that it would be constitutionally inappropriate to insist by law that ministers consult with the council on legislation they were promoting. However, a code for consultation was agreed between the Lord Chancellor and departments – circulated through ministers' private offices in 1982 and to departments in 1986 (Council of Tribunals, 1987, app. C) – concentrating on the statutory functions and ignoring the informal practices. Civil servants were consequently less aware of the other informal functions, on which the council placed such great store, and which included early advice on legislative proposals. The council has requested that its powers be extended to increase its advisory role in relation to legislation affecting tribunals and inquiries as an exercise in consciousness raising (see Council on Tribunals, 1991, para. 3.51 et seq). On government proposals for replacing the Restrictive Trade Practices Court with a tribunal which would possess, as originally envisaged, adjudicatory, investigatory and prosecuting powers, the council was complimentary on the government's early consultation. This may well have been instrumental in getting the government to remove functions other than the adjudicatory from the tribunal's remit.

There is a tendency, we believe, for the Council on Tribunals to overvalue the virtues of adjudication *vis-à-vis* other forms of grievance redress and to overemphasize the importance of lawyers, the latter of which we deal with below. Many agencies of modern government which carry out adjudicatory tasks, must of necessity perform a variety of roles. These may be advisory, investigatory and regulatory. Examples such as the Office of Fair Trading (to whom the proposed powers on restrictive practices other than the adjudicatory went) and the Civil Aviation Authority stand out. Another is the Commission for Racial Equality, which the courts have had difficulty in accepting because of its mixture, in particular, of investigatory and prosecutorial and adjudicatory powers. What seems to lie at the root of this disquiet is a concern over the dilution of judicial purity; that if people are expected to act as judges, then they should not be expected at the same time to fulfil other, possibly conflicting roles. Stated baldly, the good sense of that sentiment cannot be denied. However, it has to be realized that for tribunals to perform other functions as well as the adjudicative may be not only non-compromising, but may well be beneficial in striking the right balance in the development of policy and its fair application in the process of regulation. Detailed experience of an area of activity gained through one form of administrative oversight may well be of inestimable benefit in adjudicating claims and disputes; providing obvious safeguards against bias or interest and unfairness, are built in where there are disciplinary or criminal or other serious consequences in decision-making.

To repeat, the classical tribunal structure, whereby a body determines a dispute judicially – that is to decide competing claims according to the evidence presented by the application of a body of rules in an independent manner and the tribunal hearing the evidence makes the decision – is a widespread characteristic of contemporary government. It is evident in the work of Social Security Appeal Tribunals, the Immigration Appeal Tribunal, the Income Tax Commissioners, Industrial Tribunals, Rent Assessment Committees and in self-regulatory regimes. Tribunals are frequently utilized in licensing decisions, which may take the form of public inquiries not unlike those operating in smaller land-use inquiries, concerning the decisions of Traffic Commissioners or Licensing Authorities (some of whose hearings do not have rules of procedure). Very often, as in the licensing decisions affecting privatized utilities, 'hearings' take the form of notice and comment procedures, and in the allocation of government-owned franchises, there may well be no public hearings at all. In prison administration, a tribunal system involving lay adjudicators – who also acted as public watchdogs and grievance remedial devices for prisoners – stood at the apex of the disciplinary system adjudicating on the more serious cases involving prisoners which were not adjudicated upon by assistant governors and governors. The prison disciplinary system is currently under review and is examined below. What we can usefully do at this stage is to look at variations in the use of tribunals to assess the problems and strengths of new procedural forms.

The use of tribunals as multipurpose agencies has been well documented in a number of cases and their examination now would take us into the topic of regulation (Birkinshaw, 1985a; Baldwin and McCrudden, 1987). In relation to advisory bodies described as tribunals, the courts have held that they are subject to judicial review and must conduct their proceedings with appropriate standards of fairness. Needless to say, given the importance of the subject matter such bodies (e.g. the Monopolies and Mergers Commission) may deal with, standards of procedural regularity may well become more demanding as a consequence of an increasing number of legal challenges and increasing refinement in the law of judicial review. What we will examine at this juncture is the replacement of tribunals with internal review and we will concentrate on the Social Fund; the use of one-man tribunals which may also perform other tasks, and here we shall look at the reforms in prison administration; ombudsmen operating as tribunals – our example will be the pensions ombudsman (and note our comments in Chapter 6); and we will provide some examples of deficient procedures which are inadequate to do one thing or the other, and here consumer committees with the privatized utilities may offer some useful examples.

THE SOCIAL FUND

One of the more interesting grievance devices – and one which has replaced a tribunal structure – was the review procedure introduced under the Social Fund provisions contained in the Social Security Act 1986. The philosophy behind the Social Fund and its operation have been controversial and certain aspects of the procedure have been successfully judicially reviewed (Social Fund Commissioner, 1990, app. 14A, 14B). The procedure introduced to deal with grievances, however, has novel features in a British context which are instructive for our present inquiry. The relevant provisions, *inter alia*, replace discretionary decisions, which were subject to broad rules and adverse decisions that were appealable to tribunals, by discretionary decisions for payment and loans subject to Secretary of State guidance. These payments are cash-limited, unlike the previous system which was demand-led. A system of internal and higher review by officers in the DSS (Social Fund section) with a further review by a Social Fund Inspector (SFI) has replaced the appeal to an independent tribunal. The SFI's review, as endorsed by the courts, is a two-stage process involving a judicial review-like supervision for errors, and then a check to see that the decision is right in all the circumstances.

The SFI's decisions are monitored by the Social Fund Commissioner, and an annual report is published by the commissioner on SFI reviews. In 1990–91, SFIs received 9775 review applications. In 1989–90, the figure was 7858: 'this is still only 6 pc of the decisions not revised wholly in the applicants' favour by the DSS's reviewing officer at the local office stage'. Fifty-nine per cent of the 1989–90 cases reviewed by SFIs (6238) were sent back for a redetermination (3662) and 10 per cent were substituted (616). In about 35 per cent of the cases sent back for a redetermination, the applicant was made a payment. The Social Fund Commissioner was disappointed that it took longer than she had hoped to clear cases – fifteen days in the case of *crisis* loans, thirty-four days in the case of budget loans and community care grants, including an initial period of two weeks to allow the applicant to see the review papers. Applicants are not normally interviewed by SFIs; only nine were interviewed in 1989–90 at *their* homes. The SFI reviews all the papers and any additional evidence. The commissioner has been critical of SFO procedures, including:

. . . inadequate provision of copy documents provided by DSS. DSS local offices are required to send a copy of the relevant social fund papers with the originals. For much of the year up to 50pc of the cases received by the OSFI required some recopying and a further 10pc of cases had no copies or required substantial recopying. We informed the DSS regularly about these deficiencies . . . rectifying these deficiencies inevitably delayed the clearance of review applications by the office.

The commissioner continues:

The SFI's offer a relatively inexpensive way of providing an independent review of social fund decisions. In my view it is essential to the credibility of the system that applicants receive a considered and reasoned decision within 30 working days of receipt at the OSFI of an application made properly. To meet these objectives the unit must continue to be resourced adequately.

(Social Fund Commissioner, 1990, para. 3.13)

At first blush, the method of monitoring adopted by the commissioner and her four 'team leaders' appears impressive. A legal adviser, whose advice is confidential, has been appointed by the commissioner. In 1989–90, 27.3 per cent of SFI decisions were monitored, and 11.4 per cent of those monitored were not acceptable, although the function of monitoring is to advise and not to direct. The commissioner's management information system is under constant review. Reasons for an SFI review being unacceptable included:

- the monitor was not satisfied that all the circumstances of the case had been considered properly by the SFI (45 per cent from the end of August 1989);
- the monitor was not satisfied that all the essential points were considered by the SFI (34 per cent from 1 August 1989); and
- the monitor was not satisfied that the law and directions had been interpreted correctly by the SFI (21 per cent from 1 August 1989).

The commissioner also encouraged the giving of detailed reasons, in a comprehensive format and in readily explicable language. These recommendations were made after visits by the commissioner to various representative organizations and they further resulted in working sessions with the Plain English Campaign to improve the written style of reasons. Decision letters would contain a brief statement of the result of the review and what will happen next, some general information about the way decisions are made, and a separate document setting out formally, and giving full reasons for, the SFI's decision.

Procedurally, these are encouraging developments. It was also encouraging to see the commissioner recommending that the SFI, who receives a copy of the reasons recorded on the report and decision form by the SFO (and which is more detailed than the microcomputer-produced letter sent to the applicant), should also be sent a copy of the letter as this is the document that the applicant will be addressing his or her comments to. Further, where a case is sent back by an SFI for redetermination, the commissioner believed that the 'applicant's right to know that the SFO has addressed the points raised by the Inspector is fundamental to an open review system'. She recommended that the DSS now consider requiring the Higher Executive Officer (Social Fund) to issue a copy of the decision form SF 614 which records the detailed reasons for the decision to the applicant. Again, encouragingly, she recommended that local rules confining discretion (priority lists) should be properly approved and vetted by managers and checked for defects, and that the DSS give serious thought to the further information on a local officer's budget which should be on the review papers for the sight of an SFI beyond the standard 'insufficient funds'. 'This is likely to be an important point in relation to the legislative changes which you [i.e. the Secretary of State] propose for the control and management of budgets' following a successful judicial review on these points (HMSO, 1991, para. 5.14). Furthermore, in cases of late applications to the SFI or applications for review without accompanying reasons from the applicant, the SFO's papers are not sent to assist the SFI to see whether, for example, the twenty-eight day period in which to make an appeal should be extended. We agree that they should be sent and we heartily concur with the commissioner's criticism of DSS practice. The report was encouraging of good practice and it is not surprising that the work of SFIs has received judicial commendation – even though two of their decisions were successfully reviewed in the courts.

In her 1990–91 report, the Social Fund Commissioner (1991) indicated how training sessions had developed to address weaknesses identified in decision making, e.g. weighing up evidence and assessing the facts. She felt that decision making in about 90 per cent of cases by SFIs was satisfactory. This might appear a little fortuitous given that she was forced, by pressure of work, to appoint as inspectors anyone 'who was suitable'. Given that there are over 125 000 applications for review of social fund decisions to SFOs, and given the mistakes induced by overworked staff and inadequate resources in social security generally, it is obvious that many will feel that with the disappearance of independent appeal to tribunals, a vital safeguard has been removed. However, we are impressed by the efforts of the commissioner to ensure procedural fairness and efficiency in a much discredited scheme.

PRISONER COMPLAINTS AND DISCIPLINE

Another area of highly visible, and too frequently unsatisfactory grievance mechanisms, has been prisons and prisoners. The serious shortcomings were noted by Lord Justice Woolf in his inquiry report into prison disturbances in 1991 (Woolf, 1991). Prisoners had, with varying degrees of success, frequently invoked the courts from the late 1970s as a means of ventilating their grievances. A variety of channels – which included prison staff, governors and Boards of Visitors, the latter bodies also acting as disciplinary adjudicators – had proved less than acceptable from the prisoners' perspective because of a perceived lack of impartiality in their structure. The government did not act upon the Prior Report's (1985) recommendations that an independent tribunal should be established for disciplinary offences. Woolf noted the repetition of inadequate means to obtain redress as a frequently stated reason behind the very serious prison riots of 1990. His solution was the introduction of a contract between prisoner and prison, setting out the prison's expectations of the prisoner and what the prison expected to provide for the prisoner. Contracts would be locally based, not nationally determined. The contract would be discussed with the prisoner and would include those details of the prison regime which are important to the prisoner. It would be reviewed after twelve months. The contract could be maintained, or not unreasonably departed from i.e. 'enforced', by a prisoner obtaining the support of the Board of Visitors or the grievance procedure (*infra*), and ultimately judicial review. Misbehaviour could lead to deprivations of 'expectations' under the contract. The contract would be incorporated into a prisoner's sentence plan. Accredited standards of prior conditions would be set nationally by the Home Secretary. Area managers, by reliance on the contract they have with individual prisons, would ensure that the standards were met. When standards are met, a prison would be granted Accreditation Status by the Home Secretary. Once achieved, they will initially be aspirational, although they may well become enforceable by judicial review.

It is against this background of reform – together with smaller units for prisoners and less crowded confinement – that an independent grievance procedure should be seen. Prisoners would be given reasons when a decision materially and adversely affecting them is being taken. Prison governors would be responsible for discipline and Boards of Visitors would be removed from this function. 'Proper structures are necessary to achieve justice' opined Woolf, who recommended a new grievance procedure. These should be straightforward, expeditious, effective and independent.

Instead of relying upon independent tribunals and outside lay bodies, Woolf recommended greater use of governor grades for grievances, the right to see a 'governing' governor where a deputy governor deals with the grievance and then to proceed to the Area Manager, the right to obtain advice and assistance from the Board of Visitors and, where necessary their investigation, and lastly an independent legally qualified Complaints Adjudicator who would also hear appeals from disciplinary hearings. The fact that it would rarely be used for complaints would not detract from its importance. Woolf believed it would be appropriate to have the same individual carrying out both functions as disciplinary actions and complaints could generate the same sort of response from a prisoner: 'They could also sometimes arise from the same set of circumstances.' The novel dimension of this recommendation, although Boards of Visitors have frequently been criticized for performing both disciplinary grievance remedial work, justifies closer examination.

The Complaints Adjudicator would be appointed by the Home Secretary. For grievances, he or she would recommend, advise and conciliate at the final stage of the procedures. In disciplinary cases, the Complaints Adjudicator would act as a final tribunal of appeal. The adjudicator would not be a prisoners' ombudsman – effective internal procedures rule out such a necessity, Woolf believed. However, the jurisdiction of the Parliamentary Commissioner for Administration (PCA) would not be excluded, although, intriguingly, he observed that because of limitations on the PCA's jurisdiction, the PCA's jurisdiction may not apply to maladministration in the complaints procedure itself (Woolf, 1991, para. 14.353). The Complaints Adjudicator system would comprise a chairman at HQ and three assistant adjudicators operating under him or her. The internal grievance procedure would have to be exhausted. The adjudicator will determine the procedure and may visit prisons. He or she will not have the power to overrule the prison service; the adjudicator's power would be recommendatory and it would be expected that any recommendations would be implemented, even at the Director-General level. If unhappy with the response, he or she would have power to report to the Home Secretary. The adjudicator would not determine matters of policy *vis-à-vis* prisoners generally. He or she would be concerned with individual grievances only and how they are handled by the prison service. Woolf envisaged no special restrictions on the jurisdiction of the Complaints Adjudicator and this would include investigation of the operation of the prison rules and regulations. However, he would not expect the adjudicator to make recommendations which conflicted with the merits of decisions taken by HQ. The role would be a supervisory one in such cases, like the High Court on judicial review 'scrutinising the decision making process'. He or she would establish time limits for responses and acknowledgements and these latter would be accompanied by written reasons for decisions. The adjudicator would also report to the prisoner on the Prison Service's response to any recommendations he or she had put to the Service or to the Home Secretary.

In disciplinary proceedings, the Complaints Adjudicator would have powers of direction which would be binding. Interestingly, the idea of an independent tribunal for disciplinary offences, as suggested in the Prior Report, was not recommended and Boards of Visitors would lose their disciplinary role. However, the duality of responsibility of the adjudicator, such a criticized feature of Boards of Visitors, may cause the adjudicator problems from the perspective of legitimacy in the eyes of prisoners. The recommendation also goes against the frequently articulated argument that the dual responsibilities of Boards of Visitors undermined them. 'The achievement of justice', opined Woolf somewhat hopefully, 'will itself enhance security and control' (Woolf, 1991, para. 14.437).

In its 1991 White paper, the government promised more sentence plans, greater openness and giving of reasons, increased consultation with prisoners on general issues affecting their lives, new prisoner information packs and prisoner 'compacts' introduced on a pilot basis in 'selected prison establishments'. This latter feature followed the Woolf recommendations. The statement, signed by both prisoner and governor, would be factual, not aspirational, and would reflect 'current provision' (p. 78). On the question of complaints and discipline, the government adopted in outline the Woolf proposals – that internal procedures should be topped by a body like the independent Complaints Adjudicator who might also deal with appeals on disciplinary charges. Complaints against staff will be shown to the staff concerned as Woolf proposed. Boards of Visitors will keep their complaints and 'watch-dog role', but their adjudicatory role will go. They will also have a continuing role to play in authorizing removal under rule 43 (p. 94) and the government would consider the appointment of a president for all Boards of Visitors. In 1993, the Home Secretary announced the creation not of an adjudicator, but of a non-statutory prisons ombudsman displaying most of the features discussed. Interestingly he/she will examine *merits* as well as procedures.

CRITICISM BY THE COUNCIL ON TRIBUNALS

The Council on Tribunals has criticized the growing resort to one-man adjudicators in areas as diffuse as student loans under the Education (Student Loans) Act 1990, where an assessor, appointed by the Student Loans Company, will report on disputes between the latter and students. The terms of reference only cover maladministration and breach of obligations under loan contracts; eligibility is a matter for colleges and universities for which no special provision is made. Another example is the Independent Adjudicator appointed under the Local Government and Housing Act 1989, who hears appeals relating to politically restricted posts. Perhaps the greatest concern was expressed over the Pensions Ombudsman (PO) under the Social Security Act 1990.

The Pensions ombudsman is an alternative to the High Court to resolve grievances of pension scheme members. The Council on Tribunals felt that the features of the PO scheme, especially that his determinations were final and binding, that his determinations or directions were enforceable through the County Court and were also appealable on points of law, and that his investigations were to be conducted according to procedural rules, were all characteristics of tribunals. This is true, but it is not true to say that none of these features are to be found in existing statutory ombudsmen; the Northern Ireland Commissioner for Complaints may seek a remedy through the courts or have his/her decisions enforced via the courts. As a one-man tribunal, the PO is under the Council on Tribunals and the rules will possibly provide for oral hearings in public. On these points, the council felt uneasy; it produced a confusion of roles and a down-grading of the quality of appeal procedures (2.51 AR, HC 64 1990–91). The government's arguments in favour of an ombudsman were that the PO concept was 'simple, clear cut and comprehensible to the public' and it was proactive.

Clearly, we are moving towards more and more one-man bands: ombudsmen, adjudicators, assessors or whatever. Where large numbers of complainants are present, this is unavoidable. There is nothing inherently wrong with this providing adequate safeguards exist to protect the full range of interests that may be involved, with greater protection given as the interests become more important. For ombudsmen, we make our recommendations in Chapter 7. In the case of internal review, we applaud the moves towards greater independence and efficiency and fairness in the operation of the Social Fund review officers and their commissioner (though, cf. Council on Tribunals, 1986); our misgivings are directed towards the substance of the scheme itself, criticisms which have been made by others. In social security benefits claims, for instance, increased training and monitoring of adjudication officers of the DSS, who are under a Chief Adjudication Officer (CAO) (Sainsbury, 1989; Wikeley and Young, 1992) and who review decisions of DSS officials concerning relevant benefits, is clearly a beneficial development. Further rights of appeal exist to the local tribunals and Social Security Commissioners. Even so, the CAO has commented that 'adjudication standards remain low on many benefits' (DSS, 1991, para. 1.14).[1]

The problems arise, and here we share the misgivings of the Council on Tribunals, where insufficient consideration appears to have been given to complaints procedures and judgemental decision making. It was interesting to learn, for instance, that the Department of the Environment did not consider that the Director-General of Water Supply would, in the normal course of events, hold oral hearings in discharging his functions including the determination of issues and the resolution of disputes (para. 2.29,

AR HC 114 1989–90). Likewise, consumer committees should be given greater powers than the electricity consumer committees, whose very existence depended upon the discretion of the Director-General and, despite their 'quasi-adjudicative' functions, they were expected to be an integral part of the regulation. Problems arose where an internal appeal procedure was introduced without sufficient safeguards – the fast track procedure under the Asylum Bill (1991–92), for instance. The council was also disturbed by the change of practice introduced by the Employment Act 1989, whereby pre-hearings will take place before an industrial tribunal and for the payment of deposits not exceeding £150 where, *inter alia*, 'no reasonable prospect of success' exists in the appeal. How, the council asked, could this be assessed without reviewing the evidence?

Legal representation

Legal aid to cover the cost of representation only covers three tribunals, with Advice by Way of Representation covering others, including Boards of Visitors. The Legal Aid Act 1988 made no explicit extension of legal aid to tribunals. The Council on Tribunals believes that in appropriate cases legal aid to cover representation should be allowed, although it did not support the Genn proposals for a Government Tribunal Representation Service on the lines of the UK Immigration Advisory Service (Genn and Genn, 1989). Genn and Genn found that *specialist* representation enhanced the chance of success of applicants before tribunals (see Mullen, 1990, p. 230). The position of government is still that every tribunal will be looked at on its individual merits, although there may be opportunities to extend legal aid for representation by way of contract to law centres or by way of franchising beyond the green form scheme.

PUBLIC HEARINGS

The holding of public hearings has been justly acclaimed as Britain's most significant contribution to the jurisprudence of public law. The traditional method is to hold a public inquiry – which often operates as an appeal against, for example, a refusal to allow development – under an inspector (cf. the planning inspectorate are becoming an executive agency), usually appointed by the Secretary of State, to conduct an investigation into the appeal/proposal and to hear objections where proposals have a local, regional or national significance. Under general enabling provisions, inquiries replaced the Private Bill procedure, which proved too cumbersome and prolix. Interestingly, a recent reform involving railways and light rapid transport systems has replaced private Bills with a series of statutory orders to be made after public hearings. The procedures are in a three-tier system covering orders in a hierarchy of increasing environmental significance from local approval, ministerial approval (without reference to Parliament) and those made after the Affirmative Resolution procedure. The minister decides which are to be referred to Parliament. In the case of those subject to local authority approval – the least important in theory – the Council on Tribunals was critical that if the authority acceded to a request to build a relevant rail system there would be no appeal triggering a public inquiry. In the case of the most important schemes subject to specific Parliamentary approval, interested groups will not be allowed to make representations in Parliament.

The basic concept of the inquiry is to allow the appellant/proponent to state their case; the opposing authority, where there is one, to put their case and for appropriate cross-examination, and for the presentation of objectors' cases and their examination at the discretion of the inspector. A report is then made to the Secretary of State who makes the decision either to allow the appeal or to approve the proposal in which his or her department may well have an interest, e.g. the building of a motorway, energy generating plant or nuclear reprocessing plant. This basic model has recently been introduced into the appeal provisions under the Environmental Protection Act 1990 where those wishing to be authorized to carry out prescribed activities or emit prescribed substances, i.e. to pollute, may appeal against a refusal or conditional permit.

The holding of an inquiry is publicized, although many of the consultation provisions relating to planning applications, and which take place before appeals are made if they are made, are discretionary. Regulations for planning inquiries provide details on exchange of case, etc., publicity and the procedure and safeguards for post-inquiry procedure where new evidence is taken by the Secretary of State and so on (Purdue, 1991).

It has to be realized that this basic model of the inquiry has been modified beyond recognition so that there are informal hearings (1175 in 1989–90), a written representation procedure purely decided on paper forms (22 959 in 1989–90, all but 210 decided by inspectors) and, finally, the traditional inquiry as described above, although even here there are special features, as not all of them are decided by the Secretary of State after report (299 were so decided; 2048 were decided by the inspector, making the procedure both here and in the written representation procedure far more like a tribunal). Further, based on a 1988 code, 'shorter inquiries are lumped together in sessional hearings', which has caused concern that parties' and objectors' rights may be curtailed as a matter of practice rather than legal intent. Further economizing measures proposed by the government included the removal of the right to a hearing and the conferral of a discretion on the Secretary of State to decide whether it should be an oral or paper hearing. Proposals were also made to charge appellants for appeals on a graded scale: complexity, written/oral, etc. The Council on Tribunals was furious at the cursory attempts by government at consultation on this matter to remove a right which goes back to 'the 1870s' (actually the eighteenth century), and they could not conceal their delight when the government removed these proposals from the Planning and Compensation Bill.

At the other end of the spectrum there is clearly much scope for reform in the 'Big Inquiries' into major projects proposed by government or government undertakers. The government has merely amended the standard inquiry so that the inspector, usually an eminent lawyer, may be assisted by a panel of experts in sifting through and analysing the evidence. Furthermore, the terms of reference of major inquiries may be extended to allow examination of, for example, economic need, which otherwise would not be examinable. 'Policy' for a proposal or as a reason for refusing to allow a request for development is not considered an appropriate subject for analysis at the inquiry, although questions on the merits of government policy may be answered at planning inquiries if the government representative so wishes. The courts have been generous to government in giving a broad interpretation to policy so that it includes the factual basis behind a proposal and matters which it is simply inappropriate to discuss at inquiries, e.g. the impact on the local economy of raising the toll for a bridge (*Bushell v Secretary of State* [1981] AC 75; *R v Secretary of State etc ex p Gwent County Council* [1988] QB 429). The public can rest assured, courts believe, that these topics will be fully and carefully considered by officials in the government department. It must be appreciated that as the procedure is at the discretion of the inspector, save in so far as rules specify procedure, 'policy' may be raised to prevent presentation of a case, to prevent cross-examination or to exclude material from a report by the inspector to the Secretary of State because it will not assist the minister in his or her task.

We agree with those reports, particularly the Outer Circle Policy Unit (OCPU, 1979), which asked for a novel procedure to deal with major inquiries so that all the implications of complex proposals with national or regional significance can be thoroughly investigated – if necessary in a Project Inquiry and which would be followed by traditional inquiries into site-specific objections. Purists may assert that we are moving from the grievance remedial function into the overtly policy-making process. This it would be alleged would be especially so were we then to explore, as we have done before, suitable participatory mechanisms to assist and flesh out advisory processes in the formulation of policy affecting major constitutional, industrial or economic change and development (Wass, 1984; Harden and Lewis, 1986). This would be with a view to democratizing the policy-making process in a manner that Parliamentary government has not achieved. By feeding the results of such participation into Parliament, we would see the end result strengthening the Parliamentary process, not weakening it. We can only argue the good sense in saying that to allow people to contribute to the shaping of decisions that significantly affect their lives and to allow them to participate in a constructive manner or to raise objections about proposals is far more likely to reduce or remove the cause of later grievance. So much is accepted in British public life, albeit too often half-heartedly and without adequate provision of information to participants or with an assumption, facile or facetious we do not judge, that the necessary skills to contribute effectively are commonplace or easily acquired.

There are numerous opportunities to be consulted and to participate provided by statute and which exist outside the planning and environmental fields or which do not take the form of a public inquiry. In the approval of development plans and structure plans, an Examination in Public has been utilized. This is an open forum with a panel of officials who may answer questions from a selected audience and it takes place after various publicity and consultation exercises. Housing management, for instance, under the Housing Act 1985, offers such opportunities to be consulted, although we have observed how the provisions have been narrowly drawn to exclude vital matters such as rent, how there is no guarantee that officials will take a 'hard look', i.e. give serious consideration to the comments and views of tenants, and how the courts have interpreted over-narrowly the provisions. Subsequent legislation on housing is replete with opportunities to be consulted and to vote on changes of ownership and management and privatization of estates – provisions which, in practice, have been little used and which seem to place indifference in their operation as a precondition for the successful implementation of their programmes.

In many areas of public activity, and without justifiable reason, opportunities to participate are not present. A striking example came with the allocation of television franchises under the Broadcasting Act 1990. No public hearings were held, though no doubt government would point to the previous allocations when, under discretionary provisions to hold hearings, public attendance was minimal. It should be pointed out, however, that only outline documents were provided at the earlier pre-allocation hearings (see *R v ITC ex p TSW Broadcasting Ltd* (1992) *The Times*, 30 March). This compares starkly with the position in the USA and Canada, where pre-contractual public hearings and provision of full information are legal requirements.

In short, we can see much that is of beneficial potential and which goes in some way to fulfilling promises of governing by consent in addition to the ballot box. Why, however, are opportunities to object at a public meeting present in some areas of activity and not others when adequate justification for the distinction is not made? How do we ensure an adequate supply of information to inform participants? How do we best ensure that those making recommendations or decisions take a hard look at the submissions? This means at least explaining why other options were not adopted. What does the way forward require?

THE WAY FORWARD

What we must now discuss is the appropriate mix of bodies to hear appeals from the decisions of administrators, and where appropriate of ministers. We have seen internal avenues for redress within departments and authorities; recently, there has been a tendency to formalize these by the introduction of review procedures. For complaints of maladministration there are ombudsmen. Tribunals cover the range of appeals concerning entitlement, loss or allocation of rights and complaints mechanisms. Tribunals are usually confined by rules or established precepts – they may reverse on the merits but they are rarely given a free hand to review on the merits *tout court*, especially where the authority or official appealed against is high ranking.

It is interesting therefore to remind readers (see Chapter 5) of the Federal Administrative Appeals Tribunal of Australia (AAT), which does possess such a power. The AAT (or GAT) was established by the AAT Act of 1975. The jurisdiction of the AAT is limited to the review of decisions of departments and statutory authorities and ministers listed in Schedule 1 of the AAT Act or by later acts conferring jurisdiction on the AAT. It covers a wide area of activity including customs, insurance, freedom of information, export grants, social security, air navigation, deportation of criminals – though here its powers are advisory not decisional – repatriation and local government matters *inter alia*. The AAT was released from the administrative control of the Attorney-General's Office in 1990 and is now responsible for its own management. It also publishes its own annual report. The growth in its jurisdiction has caused it to resemble the general administrative tribunal recommended by the committees which led to its creation (Kerr and Bland committees).

Readers should also be reminded that the Administrative Review Council's (ARC) Charter includes the role of examining administrative decisions as a class to ascertain whether they should be subject to review on the merits and it is consulted on proposed legislation by the Attorney-General's Department. Guidelines for deciding whether there should be review on the merits were produced by the ARC in its *Eleventh Annual Report* (1986–87) and prima facie review is suitable if the interests of a person will be or are likely to be affected by the exercise of a power; this reflects the standing criteria of the AAT Act. This would cover decisions affecting groups of people, but not where they were of a 'quasi-legislative character', e.g. rules setting standards of care in nursing homes. It will cover review of expert bodies such as the Australian Broadcasting Tribunal and it will cover decisions of ministers. Justification for treating a decision as unreviewable lies in the character of the substance of the decision, not the importance of the person who made it. When the AAT is reviewing the exercise of a discretionary power and there is in existence a government policy to guide the exercise of the power, the AAT will ordinarily apply the policy in reviewing the decision, unless the policy is unlawful or unless its application produces an unjust result in the circumstances of the particular case. Review would not be inappropriate, because in a case such as this, the AAT stands in very much the same position as the primary decision maker (ARC, 1986–87, para. 240). Furthermore, the courts will not interpret the existence of a policy as a justifiable excuse to authorize a bad decision. In other words, where a power is vested in a specific official under statute, a direction from a minister to follow government policy which is deemed unlawful or unfair will not protect the official's decision. Questions of fettering of discretion may also apply on a basis comparable with English law.

The Federal Court in some frequently cited observations, stated that the AAT's job was to determine for itself what is the 'correct or preferable' decision on the material before it (*Drake v Minister for Immigration and Ethnic Affairs* [1979] 24 ALR 577 at 589). The Court continued:

> The question for the determination of the Tribunal is not whether the decision which the decision-maker made was the correct or preferable one on the material before him. The question for the determination of the Tribunal is whether that decision was the correct or preferable one on the material before the Tribunal.

In reviewing the decision, the AAT has all the powers and discretions conferred by statute on the 'primary decision-maker', be that minister, official, board, authority, etc. It is a full power of review, not the more feeble version common in British law. The ARC has indicated the sort of policy issue which is not appropriate for review on the merits:

- management of the economy;
- international relations;
- decisions affecting major developmental projects under the World Heritage Properties Conservation Act, which are likely to have international implications;
- certain decisions affecting mining on aboriginal lands.

The ARC believe that the best way forward is not to exclude subjects as a class, but rather for the minister to issue a certificate stating that review is not appropriate in a particular case – rather like Franks' recommendation for Ministerial Certificates in Official Secrets Act cases – why it was not appropriate in the public interest and the reasons for his or her belief. The certificate would be tabled in Parliament. Precedents exist in Australian law for this practice. The ARC was content to leave to the minister those decisions 'of the highest consequence to government or major political issues' where political processes are available to provide any necessary remedy (ARC, 1986–87, para. 245). Review on the merits will not be appropriate where 'it can be said with some certainty that, because of the nature of the decision making power in question, an exercise of the power will attract Parliamentary scrutiny' (ibid.).

There are decisions which, as opposed to subjects, are not appropriate for review:

- polycentric decisions, i.e. where the polycentric nature of a decision will have immediate consequences for other decision-making processes changing the conditions under which they are made, so that a new basis will have to be found for the other decisions;
- where the reviewing body will have to conduct lengthy inquiries which it is not equipped to conduct, i.e. the nursing home needs of an area;
- where a decision is merely facultative or preliminary or where no appropriate remedy can be given (*quaere* declaration?);
- determination of penal sanctions;
- law enforcement decisions where there are suitable judicial remedies.

This is the familiar problem of defining those decisions which are amenable to review by an independent body that proceeds by an adjudicative process. In the past in the British experience routine decisions were excluded from review because of the mere appellation 'administrative', or because of the supposed benefits of ministerial responsibility and Parliamentary oversight. Too often in the past, and present, this has only served to allow officialdom to abjure responsibility for administrative justice (see Chapter 4).

AAT hearings are usually run on an adversarial basis with the parties defining the issues and the evidence for the Tribunal. However, it may inform itself on any matter and in any way it thinks appropriate. It is primarily concerned with decisions; declaring regulations invalid is considered a judicial function for the courts. The Federal Court has characterized the AAT as an administrative tribunal which does not exercise any part of the judicial power of the Commonwealth, but which is required to act with judicial detachment and fairness. It is linked to the federal judicial system by virtue of a right of appeal to the Federal Court on a point of law 'and by the inclusion of some Federal Court judges as members of the Tribunal' (ARC, 1985, para. 15).

We should observe that despite its wide jurisdiction, there are four specialist Commonwealth review tribunals: the Immigration Review Tribunal, the Social Security Appeals Tribunal, the Student Assistance Review Tribunal and the Veterans' Review Board.

AN AAT FOR THE UK?

Clearly, the AAT possesses a power which is not present in the UK – certainly not in relation to such important decisions and not on a uniform basis. Do we need such a body? If the answer is 'yes', should it operate centrally or regionally?

Arguments in favour would include the fact we do not possess a means to rectify those decisions which offend on their merits but which are technically *intra vires*. Courts are not supposed to review on the merits and ombudsmen are restricted in so far as they are precluded from questioning the merits of decisions taken without maladministration. Judges have indicated that an outright attack on the merits where there is maladministration is not permitted; the decision-making process remains the object of concern, although some ombudsmen have thought differently. Tribunals are subject-specific and their jurisdiction is limited by Parliament or by agreement in the case of domestic bodies although it may include power to review the merits. It would no doubt be argued that review on the merits should not be given to the courts as presently structured without reforming completely the applicable procedure on judicial review to allow for an inquisitorial approach in which the court would be assisted by reporters and fact-finders who would not be hindered by claims of public interest immunity (see Chapter 10). A body representing the public interest rather like the French Commissaire du Gouvernment system would no doubt help where a power to review on the merits was conferred so that all aspects and considerations would be addressed. We have no analogue in our existing practice of administrative justice. We agree with the Council on Tribunals that there should be extension of legal aid to tribunals where the case for such is made out and that this might cover not only private practitioners but also funding for specialist advice centres and law centres. The AAT or its equivalent would clearly be a very strong candidate for legal aid to cover representation before its proceedings where detailed knowledge of legislation is required. This is not to say that all cases would require such representation.

Against the proposal to introduce the right of review equivalent to the AAT would be the fact that the UK has survived without such a system and has a series of considered and well-tested alternatives which are designed to supplement and bolster the political process, not to replace it. The merits of a decision are too close to the sensitive political arena for resolution by an adjudicatory process, and certainly not one that is binding on the executive – the 'Three Wise Men' dealing with cases of deportation on the grounds of national security and diplomatic considerations or for reasons of a political nature is an example of an advisory body operating in a sensitive area. Contentious matters such as these are best dealt with in the political process. Besides, our doctrine of ministerial responsibility is perfectly capable of catering for such matters. A further argument would emphasize that, simply, it is not the British way. The Tribunal would upset that delicate separation of powers which, although not realized in an ideal sense, none the less still separates out the decision-making functions in British public life to a considerable extent. Furthermore, when the crunch comes, the Australian system is not that remarkable; a series of excluded classes of decision were enumerated above, together with inappropriate kinds of decision. Even in the area where the AAT only exercises advisory powers, viz. deportation of criminals, the 1989–89 annual report of the ARC highlights the increasing propensity of the minister to reject the AAT's recommendations and not to provide Parliament with reasons as promised in 1983 in a policy statement to Parliament. The AAT was concerned that a change in policy had taken place without itself being informed (para. 119), (cf. *R v Home Secretary ex p Ruddock* [1987] 2 All 528). In the British system, if matters are that important, they are not up for grabs except through the political process.

These arguments really do not advance the case against to any degree. Drawing the lines on justiciability is never an easy task; that does not mean that the attempt should not be made. The AAT deals with types of cases for which in the UK there is no administrative or judicial remedy. Even in the field of political redress, ministerial responsibility was not designed to cater for grievances and, in any event, it is undergoing profound changes as executive agencies with named civil servants assume more responsibility for the performance of duties and the meeting of objectives. None of the arguments against are that persuasive, especially when one considers that Australia has a governmental system modelled to some extent on the Westminster style of government, that the system of AAT review has not created catastrophe for government and administration and the Tribunal has a prodigious workload. In 1988–89, it finalized 32 915 taxation cases and 3469 non-taxation cases – incidentally, in 116 appeals to the Federal Court of Australia on a point of law, the AAT only lost 10.

We believe that an appeal on the merits is a desirable safeguard. The question is where will it fit in, or what adjustments will have to be made? The first option would be to have the Tribunal sitting at a national level, alongside the review court. The latter would concentrate on legality as at present. The Tribunal's jurisdiction would cover those bodies enumerated in its governing statute as amended from time to time. A difficult question concerns those tribunals currently in existence – would the Tribunal assume their jurisdiction? To make it workable, the answer would have to be 'no'. Tribunals dealing with a high pressure of work are best catered for by their special and specialist tribunals, e.g. immigration, taxation, social security, local taxes, employment would fall under this classification. The Tribunal would deal with areas where there is a tribunal, but with power to review on the merits where such a review is not present below and in those cases where there is no tribunal but where a discretionary decision affects an individual as envisaged by Whyatt (1961). There would be an appeal on a point of law to the Court of Appeal, or possibly the House of Lords, to avoid the

Anisminic problem where an attempt was made to exclude the jurisdiction of the courts. If the ombudsmen are given power to reverse on the merits, there will be those cases which are better suited to a tribunal and which we alluded to in Chapter 5. And, of course, the ombudsmen's jurisdiction will not operate where there is an appeal to a tribunal.

The second option would see a Tribunal operating regionally. It would possess power of review on the merits, as in option one. The virtues are that it would be more accessible and would be easier to fit in with local schemes for representation either from specialists or from law centres or specialist advice centres as described above. The point about tribunals with an onerous workload in option one would be repeated – they would remain as subject-specific tribunals. The point about Ombudsmen would have equal validity and criteria would have to be spelled out pointing a case in one direction rather than another, i.e. private investigatory justice or adjudicative/adversarial justice in public with investigatory powers where necessary. It must be remembered in any case that the introduction of effective internal grievance procedures will reduce the number of cases coming forward for review.

One additional point which we raise at this juncture would be the possibility of regional public law courts to deal with the review of legality and actions involving public bodies. Administrative justice has been London-dominated for centuries. Local public law courts would again make justice more accessible. We would have to give thought to the status of this court, and what would happen to the Crown Office List in London (see Chapter 10).

Further consideration would need to be given to the relationship between the regional Tribunal and the court – clearly the court would not cater for the merits, leaving only the option of the Tribunal. If challenge in the courts is unsuccessful, should there or should there not be a screening process before the Tribunal assumes jurisdiction?

NOTE

1 There are 15 000 adjudication officers working within 485 local offices of the Benefits Agency (an additional 500 are based in the Department of Employment). They deal with Income Support and Contributory Benefits. They decide most claims for benefit. They play a 'complex dual role' as 'independent decision-makers' determining claims and as civil servants 'occupying a particular position in the departmental hierarchy' and subject to Secretary of State control (Wikeley and Young, 1992 p. 240). Their roles, i.e. adjudication (independent) and initial receipt and investigation of claims (as civil servants), are continually mixed up in practice. Of 140 865 appeals against social security decisions disposed of in 1989, 25 per cent were superseded by adjudication officers as a result of internal review.

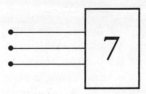

THE OMBUDSMAN

In this chapter, we shall deal primarily with the 'classical' ombudsmen as opposed to the private variety. The classical ombudsman is an independent complaints handler for disputes involving government and the administration of public affairs. They constitute the subjects of interest for the International Ombudsman Institute at Alberta, Canada and the European Ombudsman Institute at Innsbruck.

In some respects, the Police Complaints Authority may properly be seen as an ombudsman system, but its remit is, of course, highly specialized and we have decided to omit it for present purposes. It would require a study of its own to do justice to the issues involved. In like vein, we shall pay only limited attention to the Northern Ireland Commissioner for Complaints, whose main interest for us will relate to the matter of remedies. The Scottish and Welsh Local Ombudsmen are also different from the English in minor respects and we shall concentrate on the English Commission.

BACKGROUND

The ombudsman is Scandinavian in origin and almost 200 years old. From time to time reference will be made to the Nordic ombudsmen systems, whose brief is normally broader than is the case in the UK. It is conventional when speaking of the Scandinavian experience, especially the Swedish, to point out that the ombudsman plays a more significant role in those countries since they do not have a Westminster-style government, and indeed most of the administration is conducted through agencies rather than through government departments. Their system of administrative law is also more highly developed. Correspondingly, interesting though their experience is, any lessons taken from that experience must be chosen with care.

Vastly influential though the Nordic ombudsmen have been, the great surge in what some have termed 'ombudsmania' can perhaps be traced back to the appearance of the first common law ombudsman, the New Zealand Parliamentary Commissioner, in 1962. Britain's interest in the concept is normally associated with the Whyatt Report of 1961. Important though that was, the document was less than bold and is responsible for what many would regard as the present weaknesses of the system. These include the absence of direct access to the ombudsman from the general public (now happily conceded for the Local Government Commissioners, (LO)) and the distinction between 'maladministration' (whatever that is) and the merits of discretionary decisions. This distinction found no place in the Scandinavian systems. Be that as it may, there has been an extraordinary spread of ombudsmen systems across the world, the major exception perhaps being the USA. Not only are ombudsmen here to stay, but their variety helps to place the British systems into perspective. Before discussing the British systems in more detail, however, we need to remind ourselves that ombudsmen are only one way of handling disputes.

As Australia has shown, the ombudsman can operate alongside other methods of dispute resolution and alongside sophisticated methods of public law control. Many people take the view that the British system of public law is inadequate to contain the powers of a very heavily centralized executive. Indeed, the emergence of the Parliamentary Commissioner for Administration (PCA) in 1967 was accompanied by a debate about the need to reform our system of administrative justice more generally. Thus the PCA can be seen as a weak concession to the reformists to avoid a broader re-examination of administrative justice. We should like to take the opportunity of reminding our readers that a weak ombudsman system is more significant in a country like Britain where other safeguards are meagre compared to the record of other advanced democracies.

THE PARLIAMENTARY COMMISSIONER ACT 1967

The Macmillan government had rejected the Whyatt Report, because to adopt its recommendation would 'seriously interfere with the prompt and efficient despatch of public business' (H.C. Deb., Vol. 666, Col. 1124).

The succeeding Labour administration was pledged to introduce the reform but experienced considerable difficulty with officials and indeed with certain ministers. The result is that the Act was very much a compromise. Accordingly, many areas of government were excluded from scrutiny by the PCA as the ombudsman was to be called. Schedules 2 and 3 of the Act list the bodies subject to investigation and those areas which are excluded (see Stacey, 1978).

The government departments and authorities subject to investigation by the PCA have been amended by the Parliamentary and Health Service Commissioners Act 1987. This followed an inquiry into the jurisdiction of the PCA by the Select Committee on the PCA some seven years earlier. In principle, they believed that 'quangos' ought to be included, albeit with some minor reservations. These reservations included advisory bodies, tribunals and certain other limited categories such as professional bodies, charities and the nationalized industries. They believed, however, that other commercial quangos ought to be included. The government largely chose to ignore this latter recommendation, although a number of important bodies have been included since 1987, including the Urban Development Corporations, the Commission for Racial Equality and so on. The Independent Broadcasting Authority (IBA), now the Independent Television Commission (ITC), is not included, nor is the Civil Aviation Authority (CAA). Training and Enterprise Councils (TECs) are not included, since they are bodies operating essentially under contract with the minister, but do not operate as his agent. The 'Next Steps' Executive Agencies will, of course, be subject to the jurisdiction of the PCA.

There are two points worth making here. The first is that it must be unsatisfactory to exclude any public body unless overwhelming reasons can be shown to the contrary. Quite apart from the matter of equity, such a patchwork jurisdiction must lead to confusion in the mind of citizens. Secondly, many erstwhile government functions have been farmed out in recent years to private and to hybrid bodies (see Birkinshaw *et al.*, 1990). The supervisory systems adopted for these bodies must therefore be taken into account and we address the matter elsewhere.

Matters subject to investigation

The 1967 Act says

5. (1) Subject to the provisions of this section, the Commissioner may investigate any action taken by or on behalf of a government department or other authority to which this Act applies, being action taken in the exercise of administrative functions of that department or authority, in any case where –

(a) a written complaint is duly made to a member of the House of Commons by a member of the public who claims to have sustained injustice in consequence of maladministration in connection with the action so taken; and

(b) the complaint is referred to the Commissioner, with the consent of the person who made it, by a member of that House with a request to conduct an investigation thereon.

But excluded are matters where there is a right of appeal to a tribunal or a remedy in a court of law unless the ombudsman decides that it would not be reasonable in the circumstances to pursue that alternative remedy. Schedule 3 lists the matters excluded from investigation, some of which we have already touched upon. In the interests of completeness, it should be added that Section 110 of the Courts and Legal Services Act 1990 provides that administrative functions exercisable by a person appointed by the Lord Chancellor as a member of the administrative staff of any court or tribunal shall, in the normal course of events, be subject to the investigation of the PCA. This ends a long-running dispute over the ability to investigate the actions of court staff.

A word or two of comment may be appropriate here, though we leave a more critical analysis to a later section. First, the 'filter' system has been heavily criticized by some of the ombudsmen themselves, parliamentary select committees and by the Justice Committee. Only the French *médiateur* in the world ombudsman community joins the PCA in resisting direct access from the citizen. Given that our other two formal classical ombudsmen can now be approached direct, it seems even less satisfactory than formerly to retain this particular barrier. Of course, the defence of the position originally was that the role of Parliament *vis-à-vis* the executive was to be strengthened. This, unfortunately, has not occurred. The other explanation for the filter system was that an ombudsman had not, up until that time, been established in any country with a large population. The fear expressed was that the ombudsman would be swamped. Writing in 1978, Stacey was able to say;

> There are strong grounds for saying . . . that the attempt to curtail the volume of complaints to the Parliamentary Commissioner, and to prevent it from becoming a flood, has been much too successful. The actual volume, while being more than a trickle, could not be described as anything more than a small river which the Parliamentary Commissioner and his staff are easily able to handle. (p. 129)

Not a great deal has changed in the years since that was written, save perhaps for the 'Barlow Clowes' affair and its ramifications, to which we shall return later.

Two other matters need to be touched upon here. The first is that, save for the Northern Ireland Commissioner for Complaints, there is no 'sanction' attached to the recommendations of the ombudsman. Solutions need to be negotiated where they are not readily forthcoming. This has not been much of a problem for the PCA, thanks to the existence of the Select Committee but, as we shall see, has caused more problems for the local commissioners where yet another recent attempt has been made to strengthen the legislation to deal with unaccepted recommendations. We shall want to argue that there is no easy solution to this problem.

The second relates to the matter of 'maladministration'. As Birkinshaw (1985a, p. 129) has pointed out, policy was to be the concern of Parliament. The term maladministration was not defined by the Act and is usually accompanied by the celebrated 'Crossman catalogue' of 'bias, neglect, inattention, delay, incompetence, ineptitude, perversity, turpitude, arbitrariness and so on'. Both that and 'injustice' to the individual (another necessary ingredient) were to be worked out in the practical processes of case work. The concern of the PCA was not to be with the technical correctness of the decision, but with the administrative quality of the decision. He rarely comments on the 'bad rule' and is not prepared to condemn a decision purely on the basis that it was 'wrong'. For good or ill, therefore, the brief of the PCA is narrower than it might be. This is especially the case if we recall that the original Whyatt Report had recommended the setting up of a comprehensive system of administrative tribunals, including a tribunal with general jurisdiction. Confining the PCA to maladministration might have been more justifiable in that context. However, that aspect of the Whyatt Report has lain fallow for the best part of thirty years.

The method of working

The investigations undertaken by the PCA are very much of a 'Rolls-Royce' standard. They are high-level reviews with each investigation coming to the attention of the relevant permanent secretary. The investigator is sent to the department concerned to examine the relevant files in person and, where appropriate, to interview the civil servants in question. Most other ombudsman systems employ a less vigorous method of investigation and their staff will only call for files in the more difficult cases and will rarely interview the civil servant concerned. There is both an up and a down side to this arrangement. The up side is obvious but it does tend to delay. We wonder what the state of affairs would look like if the PCA received complaints in the number, say, received by the Commonwealth ombudsman in Australia. Not only the method of proceeding but the organization and staffing of the office indicate the way in which the PCA has been influenced by the office of the Comptroller and Auditor-General. Whether this is entirely appropriate to the office of a citizen's defender is an open question. It may indicate, too, that the role of the PCA is seen, as Stacey suggests, very much as an internal administrative audit. If this is indeed the case, it is unlikely that new standards of administration will be forged by the PCA's office. However, as we have indicated, the *Citizens' Charter* may herald some improvement in this state of affairs.

Section 10 PCA 1967 concerns reports. The PCA sends the report to the sponsoring MP with a copy to the principal officer of the department or authority concerned. Where the PCA finds maladministration which remains unremedied, he may lay before each House of Parliament a special report on the case. He lays before Parliament and publishes an annual report and four quarterly select investigation reports. He has published several detailed investigation reports. All reports are protected by absolute privilege.

The PCA was merely the first of the British ombudsmen and was soon to be followed by the Health Service Commissioner and the Commission for Local Administration. They are all different in their own ways, but the pattern is essentially the same and the influence of the 1967 Act has been crucial. Yet we have already shown that the 1967 Act was a compromise, that it was watered down, that it operated outside a satisfactory context of adequate public law guarantees. The rather muddled British system is not sacrosanct and many people believe it is time to reconsider the whole ombudsman system in the light of our experience and that of other ombudsman systems. We shall return to this issue later. But first, we must briefly describe the other classical ombudsman systems.

THE HEALTH SERVICE COMMISSIONER

When the Parliamentary Commissioner Bill was being debated in Parliament in 1966 and 1967, the most strongly criticized feature was the provision in Schedule 3 which excluded National Health Service hospitals from scrutiny by the Commissioner. In fact, numerous proposals for amending this state of affairs emerged over the years that followed, but it fell to the Heath administration to introduce the necessary reform.

The Health Service Commissioner (HSC), who is in fact the PCA, was created by the National Health Services Reorganisation Act 1973, though see now the National Health Service Act 1977, Part V.

> He reports on complaints made to him from complainants, their relatives or other suitable persons who can make a complaint on behalf of somebody who has died or is unable to act for himself. There *is* direct access to the Commissioner and a health authority can ask the H.S.C.

to investigate a complaint which it has referred to him. The H.S.C. reports to the appropriate Secretary of State rather than to Parliament, though his reports are laid before both Houses. The most important matter excluded from investigation is a complaint which in his opinion concerns 'the exercise of some person's clinical judgment' in the provision of diagnosis, care or treatment. His remit covers 'any failure in the services provided by the various health service authorities listed in the Act, or any other action taken by them or on their behalf'. There must be an allegation of hardship or injustice in consequence of the failure, or in consequence of maladministration connected with the other action.

(Birkinshaw, 1985a, p. 147)

The most striking difference between the HSC and the PCA is that a complainant can go direct to the former without the need for an intermediary. The only limiting provision in this respect is that the complaint must have been made, in the first instance, to the health authority concerned and that the authority is given an adequate opportunity to investigate it before the HSC can investigate. The one exception to this requirement is when a complaint is made by a member of staff or a hospital or health authority, acting on behalf of a patient who is not able to complain himself. This provision was inserted to allow a nurse, for example, to complain directly to the commissioner, on behalf of a mental patient, where complaint to the relevant authority might result in victimization or blocking of the complaint.

The bodies subject to investigation are in effect the health authorities and the former Family Practitioner Committees, now the Family Health Service Authorities (FHSAs). These include the National Health Service Trusts under the 1990 National Health Service and Community Care Act.

It is also perhaps worth adding that the remit of the HSC is, on the surface, wider than that of the PCA in being able to investigate an alleged failure of the service concerned. However, there is little to indicate that the criteria employed by the HSC in accepting jurisdiction are broader than those which he adopts in his capacity as PCA. This may say less about the formula adopted than about the fact that the same person operates the two pieces of legislation and can be expected to provide a degree of consistency. However, there is some evidence that the HSC is more willing to criticize defective procedures than when he operates as the PCA (e.g. *Annual Report 1987–88*, para. 6).

As to matters of clinical judgment, this has been the subject of longstanding controversy and is something to which we shall return later. However, a little needs to be said even at this stage. Some part of this excluded area is now covered by the clinical complaints procedure adopted in 1981. In that year, a procedure called the clinical complaints procedure, or colloquially the 'second opinions procedure', was introduced to deal with such complaints by means of an independent professional review (IPR) of the clinical action which is the subject of the complaint by two independent consultants. The decision whether or not there should be an IPR is a discretionary one, taken by the Regional Medical Officer (RMO). Consequently, the HSC is empowered to investigate complaints that the RMO's decision has been taken with maladministration. He may also entertain complaints about maladministration by the RMO, or the health authority concerned in the procedures leading up to, or following, the decision on an IPR. He can also consider the administrative actions of the independent consultants who conduct the IPR (see Chapter 8).

Each year the HSC has included in his reports cases illustrating problems which have arisen with this procedure. It should perhaps also be said that the 'second opinions procedure' has been quite successful in identifying defects in procedures associated with the cause of complaint. However, it should also be pointed out that the HSC has consistently taken the view that clinical judgment is not the prerogative of doctors and patients. There are occasions when the actions of nurses, midwives and other professionals must be seen as having been taken in the exercise of clinical judgment and therefore as being outside his jurisdiction. In their case, furthermore, there has traditionally been no clinical complaints procedure to fill the gap (*Annual Report 1988–89*, para. 4). However, the Hospital Complaints Procedure Act 1985 came into force in March 1988 [Health Circular 88 (37)]. This seems to be largely left as a back-stop, since in practice internal procedures are used. It is only if the complainant is still dissatisfied after exhausting the informal procedures that the statutory machinery will be brought into play. The Act itself provides no direct enforcement mechanism, so that failure to implement its provisions would presumably be enforceable through an order for judicial review in the High Court only. Whether that provides a reasonable remedy in all the circumstances is something that the HSC would have discretion about if a complaint referred to the absence of an appropriate procedure. Furthermore, although the HSC continues to be excluded from investigating matters relating to clinical judgment, he can presumably hear a complaint that the operation of a procedure adopted under the 1985 Act produced hardship or injustice to a complainant. Furthermore, it should be said that the 1988 circular recommends the designation of a senior officer by each health authority or group of hospitals as the pivotal point of the procedures which should be publicized and monitored. How far the HSC will be able to involve himself in the defects thrown up by the new arrangements it is too early to say. The picture is not, then, one of unrelieved gloom, though it is perhaps over-elaborate and somewhat confused.

The main areas investigated by the HSC over recent years include the care of the mentally handicapped, the registration and supervision of private nursing homes, the operation of the clinical complaints procedure and the behaviour of Family Health Service Authorities. In major respects, the powers of the HSC are similar to those of the PCA. He can require the production of documents by the health authority. He is instructed not to investigate action where the aggrieved person has a right of appeal to an administrative tribunal or a court of law. But in an appropriate case he can waive this requirement. The major matters, then, which are not subject to the jurisdiction of the HSC are:

1 Action taken solely in consequence of the exercise of clinical judgment.
2 Action taken by the FHSAs in respect of medical service committees or the dental or other service committees. These are the administrative tribunals which examine complaints against doctors, dentists, pharmacists and opticians practising in the Health Service.
3 Action taken in relation to appointments or removals, pay, discipline, superannuation or other personnel matters in relation to services under the NHS.
4 Action taken in matters relating to contractual or other commercial transactions.

Perhaps a little more should be said about exclusion. The HSC can investigate other aspects of the work of FHSAs. He can and does, for example, examine complaints about the closure of surgeries, the removal of patients from a doctor's list, etc. Many think it odd that the HSC can look at other aspects of the FHSA system but not the service committees. Even here, however, informal procedures operate, as we shall see in Chapter 8.

THE COMMISSION FOR LOCAL ADMINISTRATION

It was always intended that the kind of powers adopted under the PCA Act would eventually be extended to local government and this eventually occurred under the Local Government Act 1974. The 1974 Act provides that there shall be a body of commissioners known as the Commission for Local Administration (CLA) in England, and a body of two or more commissioners known as the Commission for Local Administration in Wales. A Commissioner for Local Administration in Scotland was established in 1975. The Parliamentary Commissioner is a member of both commissions in order to assist liaison in cases which involve both local government and central departments. The English commissioners are appointed by the Queen on the recommendation of the Secretary of State for the Environment, and the other commissioners on the recommendation of the appropriate secretaries of state.

The jurisdiction of the CLA has changed somewhat since 1974, but it might be useful to begin with the major items which are excluded from its jurisdiction. These are: contractual and commercial matters excluding land acquisition-disposal; personnel matters; internal matters of school management or administration; and where the complainant has an alternative avenue of legal or administrative redress unless in the circumstances it would be unreasonable to insist upon the complainant pursuing such relief. Legal proceedings and criminal matters are outside jurisdiction as are complaints affecting 'all or most of the inhabitants of the Authority's area'. The local ombudsman must also be satisfied that all reasonable efforts have been made to resolve the dispute at the level of the authority before accepting the complaint for investigation.

It should be said that the jurisdiction of the local ombudsman extends not only to local authorities but, since 1988, to the Commission for the New Towns, any development corporation established for the purposes of a new town and, perhaps most importantly, the urban development corporations in relation to their planning functions.

Direct access

Access to the local ombudsman was originally via a local authority member, or directly where a member had failed to submit the complaint to the local ombudsman. This had been the subject of considerable unease and criticism by academics and others and the local ombudsman had himself sought to circumvent the filter requirement by a series of ingenious devices which were, nevertheless, somewhat unsatisfactory. Schedule 3 of the Local Government Act 1988 now allows for direct access. Predictably, direct access has led to a significant increase in the number of complaints (up 44 per cent in 1988–89 and 24 per cent in 1989–90), in their budget and in their staff establishment. Interestingly, in the last year for which we have figures, 83 per cent of complaints from the public went direct to the local ombudsman rather than through a local member. The significance of this figure will not be lost on students of the ombudsman system, especially in Britain.

Sanctions and reporting

None of the UK ombudsman systems provides for a direct enforcement mechanism save for the Northern Ireland Commissioner for Complaints (NICC) Act 1969. This is generally regarded as relating to the sectarian difficulties of administering local services in the province. Be that as it may, the recommendation of the NICC can be enforced through the local county court and from time to time this has occurred. World ombudsman systems inevitably rely upon the legitimacy of their office for the effectiveness of their recommendations and few support involving the courts in these matters. The PCA, after a hesitant beginning, is now satisfied that its recommendations will be complied with, not least because of the practice of reporting an unsatisfactory departmental response to the Select Committee on the PCA, which committee has always proved extremely supportive. The position at local government level has never been entirely satisfactory, the most recent comprehensive study indicating that the number of cases where a critical report has not been accepted in its entirety is almost certainly higher than the official figures (Lewis *et al.*, 1987).

The method adopted for dealing with unaccepted recommendations has been the issuing of reports. In a curious way, too, the whole business has been tied up with the existence of the Representative Body, which consisted of the local authority representative bodies who, until 1989, published the annual reports of the local ombudsman and added their own comments. They also funded the local ombudsman. Since 1989, the local ombudsman has been funded directly out of Revenue Support Grant. The Representative Body had been scathingly criticized in most quarters, most particularly for the fact that it had opposed reforms at every turn, especially in relation to an extension of the local ombudsman's jurisdiction. The 1988 Act and the Local Government and Housing Act 1989 between them have altered the position considerably.

Let us first say a word about the Representative Body. It was abolished by Section 25 of the Local Government and Housing Act 1989. In consequence of its abolition (the position in Scotland is a little different), the local ombudsman will submit his annual reports to the local authority associations. The Commission itself will arrange for the publication of the report. Formerly, the report which the Commission produces every three years on the review of the operation of the Act was to be presented to the Representative Body. Although the legislation is not entirely clear, it appears that the Commission will now present this too to the local authority associations, and, of course, to the secretary of state.

The Representative Body was never particularly supportive of the local ombudsman and so, naturally, did not help a great deal in relation to individual reports which found maladministration and injustice that was not accepted by a local authority. In other words, they did not occupy the role of the select committee in relation to the PCA. There has been considerable constitutional hesitation in bringing aspects of local government directly under the supervision of parliamentary machinery but, for what it is worth, several of the world's national ombudsmen who can examine complaints against local authorities are responsible to their national parliaments. Sweden, Denmark, Norway and France all come to mind. In any event, under the 1989 Act, provision is made for the appointment of 'Advisory Commissioners', whose role is not spelled out in the legislation. At the time of writing, nothing has been done under this provision, but if advisory commissioners were to include representatives of consumer organizations and wider publics, then perhaps the Commission's unaccepted reports could be considered by such commissioners whose independence might carry extra weight. We shall have to wait and see.

A number of changes have been effected in relation to reports in individual cases by the local ombudsman. Originally, the local ombudsman simply issued a second report where he was not satisfied with the local authority response. This provision was frequently criticized and it has now been amended and, many would say, further complicated. The position is now as follows. Local authorities are given three months to notify the local ombudsman of the action they propose to take after the issue of an adverse report with a finding of injustice in consequence of maladministration. The authority is given an additional three months to confirm that action proposed in the initial period has been taken.

The action open to the local ombudsman if he does not receive a response within the time limits, or if he is dissatisfied with the response he receives, is to issue a further report setting out the facts and making a recommendation as to what the authority should do to remedy the injustice caused by its maladministration. The same time limits apply to this further report. Where a local authority decides to take no action, or action which is unsatisfactory, that report must be considered by the whole council, and if the report names or criticizes any member of the authority that member is not permitted to vote on any question in respect of the report. If the local ombudsman is not satisfied with the response to the further report, he may require the authority to publish in a local newspaper a statement in an agreed form detailing the action recommended and, if the authority wishes, a statement of its reasons for non-compliance. In the event of refusal by the authority, the local ombudsman may publish such a notice and recoup the cost from the authority. This procedure is still thought by many to be unsatisfactory and we return to it in due course.

The procedure touches upon the issue of publicity for the local ombudsman's work. We should add, too, that in the normal course of events, the local ombudsman must send a copy of his report to the authority concerned, to the referring councillor (if there is one) and to the person complaining. The authority must make copies of the report available for inspection to the public and must give public notice, by advertisement in newspapers and such other ways as appear to him appropriate that the report will be available for public inspection. The local ombudsman also makes individual copies of reports widely available to the press, scholars and others so that there can be little room to criticize the availability of the reports. The local ombudsman also travels widely in the interest of lecturing and making available information on the nature of the office. In other words, much is done by the local ombudsman to publicize the office. Any failure in terms of public perception must, we believe, be found in the limits of the legislation. Again we shall return to this matter shortly.

As to the procedures for investigation adopted by the local ombudsman, very few criticisms have been voiced. In common with other ombudsman systems in Britain, the procedure is thorough and rarely restricted to an examination of the documents, except in the more straightforward cases. More needs to be said on this matter, since there is thought to be a downside to this thoroughness. In fact, a report on working practices was received from Coopers and Lybrand in 1989. Their report was wide-ranging and dealt with organization, operational procedures, workload, information systems, office location and information technology. The report found that the working practices were sound and that there was no need for any major change in the local ombudsman's approach to handling complaints 'if the present' quality of service was to be maintained' (*Annual Report of the Local Ombudsman, 1989–90*, CLA, 1990, p. 9). The local ombudsman's offices are in London and York, though the decision has recently been taken to relocate one of these to the Midlands.

In the year ended 31 March 1990, the local ombudsman in England and Wales received 8733 complaints. The main subjects of complaints continue to be housing (39 per cent) and planning (29 per cent). Given the historical pattern, there was an encouraging rise in the number of complaints received regarding social services. The time taken to conduct investigations can scarcely be regarded as satisfactory, but given the thoroughness of the investigations and the staff shortage to which the Coopers report bears witness, little blame can be laid at the door of the local ombudsman himself.

Impact upon administration

There has always been a tension in British ombudsman systems between the function of redressing injustice for the individual and improving administration. None of the British ombudsman systems has ever really come clean on the matter, though it is fair to say that the local ombudsman has, in recent years, performed the latter function much more satisfactorily than the PCA. We shall want to argue that one of the primary functions of an ombudsman is to seek out the causes of injustice at the systemic level in the way that a court of law could never do. We shall also argue that much more can be done in this respect than is currently the case. Yet, the chairman of the CLA has gone on record as saying that 'In my view good administration requires that authorities should have effective and clear internal complaints procedures. A failure to have arrangements whereby legitimate complaints may be dealt with speedily and fairly may well in itself amount to maladministration' (*Annual Report, 1988–89,* CLA, 1989, para. 2.15). This is extremely encouraging even if we are doubtful that these admirable sentiments are always evident in the individual reports. However, it has to be said that the courts have done the local ombudsman no service in recent years by taking an extremely unimaginative view of his role and function (e.g. *R v Local Commissioner for Administration ex parte Eastleigh Borough Council* [1988] 3 All ER 151 and *R v Local Commissioner for Administration ex parte Croydon LBC* [1989] 1 All ER 1033); more recently, they have been more charitable to the Building Societies Ombudsman (*Halifax Building Society v Edell* [1992] 3 All ER 389). Of particular interest in this respect is the provision in Section 23 of the 1989 Act relating to advice and guidance by the commissions. This allows them, after consultation with the appropriate bodies, to issue advice and guidance about good administrative practice. Encouragingly, in February 1992, the local ombudsman issued guidance on good practice entitled *Devising a Complaints System* (CLA, 1992; see Chapter 8).

A CRITICAL ANALYSIS

We turn now from the general description of the role of classical ombudsmen in Britain to an analysis of what we perceive to be the weaknesses of the system and to outline alternatives. Again, we shall take each of the ombudsmen in turn but then try to produce something of a synthesis at the end.

The Parliamentary Commissioner for Administration

The first item worthy of comment refers to the number of complaints reaching the PCA. In 1990, 704 complaints were received and of those only 23 per cent were accepted for investigation. For the first time in a number of years, 1990 saw an increase in the number of complaints received, mainly it is thought on account of the publicity received from the 'Barlow Clowes' investigation. In the immediately preceding years, the numbers had actually been falling. Although some of the PCA staff are prepared to defend this record by saying that the rigours of FMI had created more efficiency within government and therefore less reason to complain, most observers regard the position as highly disturbing. Most other ombudsmen receive substantially more complaints than that, institutions as unconnected as those in Austria and Australia affording clear examples. It must be said, however, that the present PCA appears to be seeking a higher profile for his office than some of his predecessors.

To some extent, inadequate publicity may be at fault, though it is by no means the sole explanation for the relatively small number of complaints received. Even so, as long ago as the late 1970s, both Professor Stacey and the Justice Committee were critical about efforts to make the institution better known to the general public.

Let us refer now to the two systems which we have already touched upon: The Commonwealth ombudsman in Australia began life by advertising his existence on milk bottle tops by an arrangement with the milk suppliers. The Austrian ombudsman (the *Volksanwaltschaft*) has a prime-time television slot advertising his wares and explaining cases which he has recently resolved. These examples might seem extreme in a British setting, but they are indicative of different attitudes to the nature of the office. In Britain, the PCA is seen as very much an adjunct to parliamentary sovereignty rather than directly as a citizens' defender. Which brings us naturally back to the question of direct access. It is worth quoting Stacey (1978) at some length:

> The other great weakness of the present Parliamentary Commissioner system is that so few people take their complaints to him. We have seen that he is by far the least used, in terms of population, of any of the Ombudsmen we have surveyed. In part this is due to the inadequate publicity secured for his work. But it is even more clearly due to the fact that he has to be approached through Members of Parliament and cannot take up a complaint direct from a member of the public. We see . . . that in every year since 1972 more people have gone direct to the Commissioner with their complaints, and have had to be rebuffed, than have gone to him through an M.P. But the figure of those who at present approach him direct probably greatly under-estimates the potential volume of complaints.
>
> (p. 170)

It is worth adding that not only has little changed in the meantime but that the Royal Commission on the Constitution, which reported in 1973, had conducted a survey which indicated that an enormous number of unresolved grievances were being nurtured by British citizens. The Justice Committee, reporting in 1977, had also advocated direct access and had cited with approval the practice of the Public Protector in Quebec who would receive complaints by telephone and would hold himself available to see a complainant in person. Since that time, other ombudsmen have assumed the same high visibility and easy accessibility. Once more we shall use the example of the Austrian ombudsman, though it is worth remembering, too, that the Australian Commonwealth ombudsman receives oral complaints and deals with them often in a very informal, though effective fashion.

The striking feature of the Austrian ombudsman is that he is prepared to go out into the country and receive complaints, rather like the old English assize judges (this has also, incidentally, been a practice adopted by the

Irish ombudsman from time to time). He will advertise his intention of sitting in a particular location at a particular time to hear citizen grievances. If they can be dealt with immediately, they will be; if they look like an ombudsman complaint, they will be written down, taken back to Vienna and dealt with administratively. If they are complaints of a different variety, advice will be tendered as to the appropriate course of action. Furthermore, the ombudsman has a direct line to the public which can be used for one schilling whatever the distance and whatever the length of the call. The caller is offered the choice of putting the complaint in writing and submitting it or attending at the next visit in his/her vicinity. It may be worth adding that at the Fourth International (quadrennial) Ombudsman Conference in Canberra in 1988, some discussion centred around the desirability of 'outreach programmes', whereby ombudsmen might be in the business of drumming up business. It may be that ombudsmen outreach is an idea whose time has come. It would scarcely be possible in Britain as long as the MP filter remained. It would almost certainly also require a different culture in the office of the PCA.

MALADMINISTRATION AND IMPROVED ADMINISTRATION

A great deal of discussion has centred around the use of the term 'maladministration' in British legislation and whether it is a constricting concept. The Justice Committee (1977) adopted a robust stance:

> . . . we propose . . . that the Parliamentary Commissioner should no longer be limited to investigating complaints about 'maladministration'. He is more restricted than any other ombudsman in this respect. The New Zealand Ombudsman can investigate any complaints that an action or omission by a government department was 'unreasonable, unjust, oppressive or improperly discriminatory'. The Ombudsmen for the Canadian provinces of Quebec, Ontario, Manitoba, Alberta, Saskatchewan, New Brunswick, Nova Scotia and Newfoundland have similar powers. The Scandinavian Ombudsmen are not limited to maladministration. Neither is the French Médiateur; he is empowered to examine a complaint that a public authority has 'failed in its mission of public service'. This he interprets to mean that the authority, whether a central department, local or other authority, has shown lack of humanity or has acted inequitably.
>
> (para. 19)

We are not convinced that maladministration is co-terminous with defective administration or a failure of administration, quite apart from it being weaker than 'unjust, oppressive or simply wrong'. Indeed, the Commonwealth ombudsman is restricted to defective administration but has interpreted his role much more broadly than has the PCA. The Supreme Court of Canada has also interpreted 'a matter of administration' very broadly as something which:

> . . . encompasses everything done by governmental authorities in the implementation of government policy. I would exclude only the activities of the Legislature and the Courts from the Ombudsman's scrutiny.
> (J. Dickson in *British Columbia Development Corporation v Friedmann*)

Our own discussions with PCA staff indicate that they are not trained to think about the concept of maladministration but, as civil servants, they appear to ask themselves what ought to happen given past practice. The screening officers appear to possess no abstract view about administrative 'justice', but only about traditional administration. It became clear from our discussions, too, that not all departments possess adequate procedures, yet whether that of itself would constitute maladministration is by no means clear. Public pronouncements are one thing; ingrained habit another. Another matter of some concern, given the lack of effective training in the PCA's office, concerns the almost exclusive use of civil servants on secondment. Given that screening of complaints will therefore also be conducted by someone on secondment, there must be some worry that decisions may not be consistent.

The position of the PCA on the 'bad rule' has not been entirely satisfactory either. In a few of the earlier cases some boldness was in evidence, but it cannot be said that the concept of maladministration has been very broadly developed. The select committee itself has not been persuaded to support broadening the jurisdiction of the PCA by adopting, say, the New Zealand formula, though it has urged him to identify any rule which caused injustice or hardship in a particular case, to ask the department concerned to review a defective rule and to enquire what action had been taken to remedy the particular hardship sustained by the complainant. If the rule had not been revised, it would be open to him to find maladministration in an individual case if there had been deficiencies in the departmental review of the rule. There have been numerous occasions when the PCA has asked departments to review their rules, but in our view there has not been a great deal of consistency. We believe that it would be preferable to legislate not only to change the jurisdictional definition of the powers of the PCA, but also to make it clear that he should recommend the reform of rules or policies which were causing hardship.

It must be said in fairness, too, that the decision taken by the PCA in the 'Barlow Clowes' affair has attracted much criticism from government, which believed that he was exceeding his jurisdiction. In agreeing to pay large sums of compensation to investors who suffered losses as a result of the way the investment group was run, the secretary of state made it clear that neither he nor the government accepted the PCA's findings. The PCA took the view that the department had sufficient evidence of the unsatisfactory state of affairs within the firm to withhold their licence. In finding maladministration, he said:

> A regulatory agency . . . ought, to my mind, by definition adopt a rigorous and enquiring approach as regards material coming into its possession concerning an undertaking about which suspicions have been aroused, and also as regards representations made to it on the part of the undertaking in question.
>
> (Parliamentary Commission for Administration, 1989–90;
> see also Gregory and Drewry 1991)

This was indeed a bold strike by Sir Anthony Barrowclough, yet its timing, coming just before his term of office expired, causes doubt that it is the harbinger of a more adventurous policy being adopted. We shall have to wait and see, but our own view is that the office of the PCA needs substantial revision if it is to perform as effectively as other ombudsman systems. Interestingly, at the time of writing, no investigation was under way by the PCA into the Maxwell affair despite several approaches from MPs.

The position in relation to improving administration as such is also somewhat mixed. For instance, the Guidance Note for Non-Departmental Public Bodies, which requests them to liaise with the parent departments in ombudsman cases, seems less directed to contributing directly towards improved performance than to identify cases in which financial recompense may be suggested. The Justice Report came out clearly in favour of the record of overseas ombudsman systems in helping to improve administrative procedures. Since the function of the office is to provide independent assessment and criticism of the operation of the administration the PCA ought clearly to be directed to making a contribution towards improved administration. This is not to say, of course, that the PCA has not produced improvements in administration. He clearly has, as can be seen from reading his reports. However, the circumstances in which this occurs are somewhat unpredictable and unpatterned. It also came as no satisfaction to us to be told by a very senior civil servant just over a year ago that some departments 'don't really have procedures all the time'. In a recent survey of world ombudsman systems, Professor Walter Haller found that 41 out of 43 ombudsmen canvassed claimed to wish to improve administrative practice and the same number also included proposals for improving legislation and administrative rules in the catalogue of their functions (Haller, 1988).

Own initiative investigations

British ombudsmen may only act upon a complaint received. They do not enjoy the power to make investigations of their own initiative where they have reason to believe or suspect that things may not be in good order. The Swedish ombudsman, by contrast, has the specific power to inspect or audit administrative transactions and a number of the more serious cases unearthed have emerged in this way. He therefore acts very much as a permanent commission on administrative procedure and efficiency. The nearest equivalents we have are the National Audit Office for central government, the Audit Commission for local government and the health authorities. Even so, their roles are very different from those of the classic ombudsman. The Austrian ombudsman, is entitled to investigate *suspected* grievances, and the Commonwealth ombudsman also has such powers, though they are very rarely exercised. Professor Haller's survey indicated that the only ombudsmen not to have these powers are the British, the French, the German Federal Petitions Committee (a rather different beast in any event), Liechtenstein and the City of Zurich (Haller, 1988, p. 40). Professor Haller adopts the view that being able to investigate on his own initiative allows an ombudsman to set priorities to his work.

The normal justification for the exercise of such powers is that the weak and the oppressed may be unable to protest in their own interests, especially if they live in a regulated environment – hospitals, prisons, nursing homes and the like. If alerted by press stories, for instance, an ombudsman with his traditional authority would be ideally placed to conduct an enquiry which could alleviate suffering or indeed protect human life. We have no doubt that British ombudsmen should possess such powers.

Organizational and personnel matters

The ombudsman system in Britain requires root and branch examination in our view. We need to begin with the way appointments are made and the general staffing of the ombudsman's office. It is wrong in our view that the appointment of ombudsmen should be in the gift of the government of the day, even if, in recent years, the government has taken soundings from, for example, the Parliamentary Select Committee. If an ombudsman is to be genuinely independent, genuinely a citizen's defender, some other method of appointment ought to be considered. Austria has an interesting system in that it operates a three-person ombudsman board with a Director-General cum chief legal adviser to assist them. They are nominated by the three main political parties. Former politicians are therefore as likely to be nominated as anyone else. They also sit and take decisions as a board.

However the appointment is made, the personality of the ombudsman is extremely important and would become increasingly so were the MP filter to be removed. Australia again provides an example. The first ombudsman, Jack Richardson, a distinguished law professor, built the reputation of the office with remarkable skill and visibility. His successor, the only civil servant so far to hold office there, presided over a falling off of the number of complaints presented and the public's perception of the office. Civil servants ought not to be ineligible but we entertain serious doubts about the desirability of appointing them in general. They enjoy the advantages of insiders but we believe those advantages to be outweighed in the normal case by the Whitehall mentality of protecting each other, the minister and the time-honoured ways. There seems some advantage in appointing *some* civil servants to the establishment, but we would clearly prefer that the body of appointments was made outside the service. We believe that the CLA has shown how extensive the pool of talent is. The mixture of those with local government experience and others from a wide variety of backgrounds seems to us to have been a great success and may account in part for the strides taken by the CLA in recent years. The local ombudsman now looks considerably more effective than the PCA.

The lack of effective training by the PCA has already been remarked upon, but it is exacerbated by the tension between job training and developmental training. Since they are seconded, the staff take the view that they should not be losing out on top management training just because they are having a stint with the PCA. There is, then, little enthusiasm for specific job training *qua* the ombudsman's office.

A final word here may be made about methods of investigating. These comments are, naturally, dependent upon the other reforms already suggested. It is often said that our ombudsman methods of investigation are the best and most thorough in the world. At one level this might be true, but might be borne at too high a cost, not least the delay in the time taken to investigate. The Commonwealth ombudsman in Australia boasts that he adopts whatever procedure is best for the case in hand. If it needs to be formal, then it is made so, but normally this is unnecessary. Telephones and fax machines may be the weapons needed to right some of the simpler wrongs, especially where the citizen is allowed or encouraged to make direct contact with the ombudsman. The Australian ombudsman claims to deal with three times the workload of the CLA with a much smaller population. Even so, he believes his top 100 cases per year compare favourably in terms of rigour with those of the PCA. We have seen too that the Austrian ombudsman works on the basis that requiring written complaints can produce unnecessary legalism while disguising the real issues. We believe that consideration be given to oral complaints being received, which taken in harness with an 'outreach programme' should provide much more widespread justice for citizens.

Exclusions from jurisdiction

Many of the exclusions from jurisdiction are common to the ombudsman systems in Britain and for the sake of convenience most will be dealt with here in terms of the PCA. In the Annual Report for 1990, by far the largest number of rejected complaints, or those which were discontinued after initial acceptance, related to their being not properly referred or not about administrative actions. In reality, this means the MP filter and the limited definition of maladministration. The next category in numerical terms related to bodies outside the PCA's jurisdiction, cases where there was a right of appeal to a tribunal, followed by personnel matters. Surprisingly, perhaps, commercial and contractual matters did not figure prominently.

It may perhaps be added here that the Next Steps agencies should be monitored closely over the next year or so. These agencies are, in one sense, merely the reflections of administrative reordering, but there are several reasons why they ought to be looked at with interest. The first is that the movement is partly driven by the belief that we can separate out policy and administration. That is extremely dubious in reality and divisions of responsibility may occur, while equally complaints may fall between the gaps of the divide. On the other hand, given that the movement is supposed to improve managerial efficiency, it is possible that less maladministration or failed administration will be in evidence. On the other hand, the Social Security Benefits Agency represents the real challenge to the new agencies (and see 27th Report of the Committee of Public Accounts, 1992–3).

Bodies outside jurisdiction
Such nationalized industries as remain are excluded from the PCA's remit. They do, of course, have their own, some would say unsatisfactory, complaints handling systems, but there seems little justification in reality for excluding them any longer. The position with NDPBs is also unsatisfactory. Some were brought within jurisdiction under the 1987 Act on the recommendation of the Select Committee on the PCA. Even so, they recommended the exclusion of professional bodies, advisory bodies, those that could be regarded as tribunals, and charities. The government took a somewhat different view from the committee, most particularly in seeking to exclude bodies which were essentially commercial in character. The result is that the list of bodies subject to jurisdiction in Schedule 2 to the Act is by no means coherent or rational. It is difficult to justify many of these exclusions, but it has to be remembered that commercial and contractual matters have *generally* been excluded from the jurisdiction of the ombudsman. This is almost certainly because of the sensitivity of the Ministry of Defence in 1967, but this is scarcely a reason for extending this exemption to all departments at all levels. Quite frequently it has been

argued that there will, in any event, be a legal remedy available, yet in reality this has not traditionally been the case in Britain. Of particular importance have been tendering procedures adopted by departments. The opportunities for unfairness in such procedures are very marked indeed. Many other ombudsman systems, for example the Australian one, are competent to hear such matters. Incidentally, in his 1988 Annual Report, the PCA took the view that concerning the NDPBs made subject to his jurisdiction in 1987, their functions often include the giving of aid or assistance on terms which may well have a contractual flavour. He regarded that as highly unsatisfactory. It should be pointed out, however, that European Community law now gives some legal redress, though not through the ombudsmen, in relation to procurement practices (see Harden, 1992, ch. 6).

Employment and personnel matters

The Justice Committee was not persuaded of the justification for this exclusion and many others have taken the same view. Service under the Crown has been something of a talisman over the years and it is worth remarking that the European as opposed to the British tradition has been to include personnel matters in the public service as being subject to public rather than private law. The PCA has seen fit to comment on this exclusion on more than one occasion. In 1991 he remarked that he would wait to see with interest whether the new private sector pensions ombudsman would rescue any of the cases which he had to exclude for lack of jurisdiction. Again, we shall have to wait and see. It is doubtful, however, that it could be more than a palliative. It also presents something of an irony given the devolution of many public tasks to the private or hybrid sector in recent years, a matter which we believe in itself requires attention.

Sundry matters relating to the justice system

The Justice Committee had taken the view that the commencement of, or failure to commence, proceedings by the central administration should be subject to the jurisdiction of the PCA. The same comment applied to the conduct of proceedings (e.g. the withdrawal of a prosecution), so long as the jurisdiction of the commissioner stops short of any matter relating to the conduct of proceedings over which the court itself has control. The Scandinavian ombudsmen are fully competent in these matters, as indeed is the Austrian ombudsman.

The other issue which should be raised here concerns prisons. The PCA, to use his own words, is 'in a real sense . . . the Prisons Ombudsman'. However, the trend of complaints from prisoners in recent years has been downwards, a matter which causes the PCA some concern. In remarking that he had done much good work in relation to the cause of prisoners over the years, the Justice Committee nevertheless felt that there were areas of prison life barely touched by the existence of the PCA. This is a complex area, but there is little doubt that having to go through an MP is a strong disincentive for prisoners. Other ombudsmen have had a much greater record of success, with few of them encumbered, of course, by the filter process. Once more, the ability of an ombudsman to investigate of his own initiative may be seen to advantage in such a difficult area of our public administration (see also NACRO, 1989). The Home office has recently amended the rules for handling prisoners' complaints and has deferred a decision on whether to establish a separate prisons ombudsman (see now the discussion on pp. 97–9).

The final exclusion in this section relates to the Training and Enterprise Councils or TECs. These bodies are under contract to the Department of Employment to deliver training services but are not the agents of the department. The PCA is not therefore able to look at the conduct of the TECs directly, but only the parent department if it can be shown that they were guilty of maladministration in their relations with the TEC. This position is plainly silly, especially as the TECs are in every real sense an emanation of the state. Although two-thirds of their directors must be from the private sector, most of the staff are civil servants and they are almost entirely funded out of the public purse and therefore subject to the jurisdiction of the National Audit Office. There is a real danger that we are witnessing a 'contracting state' in more senses than one. The hybrid arrangements for carrying out public purposes should clearly not be outside the jurisdiction of the ombudsmen and we believe that further attention be given to these developments.

In concluding this section, it only remains to be said that the PCA, for all its merits, is not setting the world on fire. It is, by most yardsticks, less effective than the ombudsman systems in operation elsewhere. Almost twenty-five years on, it may be thought that the time is ripe to overhaul the system in favour of something with a little more bite.

The Health Service Commissioner

Many of the criticisms to be made about British ombudsman systems can be made about all of them, so that much of what has already been said represents our thinking about the HSC. However, there are several items that require special consideration.

The first point to make is that the jurisdictional exclusion concerning contractual and commercial matters is particularly unfortunate in the light of the NHS and Community Care Act 1990, which allows health authorities to arrange for the delivery of services through 'NHS Contracts'. The 1990 Act is extremely complex and this is not the place to elaborate on its provisions, but particularly important is the contractual relationship between the health authorities and the new NHS Trusts. At the time of writing, the HSC had made no comment upon these matters but we believe they require further serious consideration.

The issue of maladministration needs to be touched upon again, though in reality the HSC is able to examine a failure of administration. Despite the improvements which he has managed to secure over the years, the feeling nevertheless is that something resembling a 'Code of Good Practice' within the hospital service might have been advantageous.

The matter of publicity is again important here, but it needs to be said that as long as the British ombudsman systems are so littered with exceptions to their jurisdiction, increased publicity is only likely to lead to frustration and disappointment by those who had hoped they had found a champion but had found someone fighting with one hand tied behind their back. The most recent Commissioner, William Reid, has nevertheless pledged himself to do more about publicizing his office. With this aim in mind, he has revised the general leaflet about his office to make it easier to follow and to help people through the procedures involved in making a complaint to him. It should also be said that the twice-yearly volumes of anonymized complaints which he submits to the appropriate ministers, together with their epitomes, are extremely helpful. This is perhaps the nearest he has got to speaking to the issue of good practice. He believes that the reports would prove useful not only as helpful teaching material but also as 'barometers of service quality'.

Clinical judgment

The issue of clinical judgment must detain us for a little while. By far the largest number of complaints rejected by the HSC concern clinical complaints. Perhaps we should add the rejection figure for complaints where there is a legal remedy too, since there is clear overlap in relation to issues of medical negligence.

It is understandable that we should entertain reservations about ombudsmen second-guessing the judgement of professionals. We have also seen that, in recent years, more developed complaints procedures have emerged as a result of official prompting. These procedures include procedures about clinical judgment, a matter which we say more about in Chapter 8.

The HSC has gone on record as saying that the hallmark of a service which cares for its consumers is an open complaints system which provides courteous, critical and thorough investigation of grievances. During the year 1989–90, he investigated 57 complaints about the way grievances were handled and upheld most of them. Even so, such research as presently exists suggests that the record on the ground about the use of complaints or grievance procedures is very mixed. And although authorities are urged to monitor complaints and complaints procedures, it appears not to be done consistently. The officer designated as complaints officer (invariably part-time) rarely appears to examine complaints by looking for trends and systems weaknesses. Nor is this something the HSC can very effectively do without the power to investigate on his own initiative.

As to the 'second opinions procedure', the regional medical officer will first have satisfied himself that the grievance procedure has been properly used. What then appears to happen is that 'minor' clinical complaints will go through the second opinions procedure while the serious ones will be regarded as potential medical negligence suits. On the other hand, some serious ones do appear to go through this procedure, which on the surface appear to be medical negligence cases. Given the pressures put on complainers, according to some sources, it still seems to us highly desirable that the HSC should have the power to examine complaints about clinical treatment without getting into the position of making himself judge on matters which only a professional can make. Research is beginning to emerge in this area which is likely to reinforce this argument.

THE COMMISSION FOR LOCAL ADMINISTRATION

It is probably fair to say that the local ombudsman is our most successful ombudsman on a number of different counts. There are numerous explanations for this, including the fact that recent administrations have demanded more accountability from local than from central government. The local ombudsman has also had a higher general visibility, has been studied and commented upon more frequently and, in consequence, has been statutorily reinforced from time to time as we have seen.

To a considerable extent as well, notes of congratulation need to be sent to the commissioners themselves for their boldness and imagination, especially in recent years, even if we have some doubts about the consistency of decision making. The 1987 Sheffield Report represents not only the most recent detailed work conducted on the local ombudsmen but also the most detailed on ombudsman systems in recent years and much of what we say leans heavily on that.

Despite the new provisions on direct access and despite the attempts of the local ombudsman to publicize his work, there remains a relatively low level of appreciation of his work, a matter not improved by the existence of different sets of ombudsmen with different jurisdictions. We have a few things to say about publicity and reorganization in our concluding remarks to this section, but the lack of visibility remains an important problem.

As to jurisdiction, there are several points to make. First, we take the view, alongside most observers, that the broadest possible jurisdiction should be encouraged save where a clear case for exclusion exists. Secondly, it is worth noting that the local ombudsman performs important and valuable functions in promoting the informal settlement of complaints which are *de jure* outside jurisdiction. So also, we have noted a number of instances where the local ombudsman appears to have bent the rules on jurisdiction in recent years (the commercial and contractual exclusion is one such example). On this, we make two observations. The first is that there is not always consistency. The second is that the local ombudsman should not be put into this position. Both points lead to the same conclusion, viz. that jurisdiction should be extended.

We turn now to the exclusion relating to internal school matters. There is little doubt that this exclusion presents many anomalies. So, for example, it is curious that a child may complain about treatment in a local authority home, whereas a child cannot complain about treatment in a state school. Furthermore, the administration of education departments themselves falls within the ombudsman's remit, whereas administration within the school for which they are responsible may not. Much depends upon the procedures and practices adopted by particular education departments in relation to their schools. If they adopt a high profile over the way schools are run, then the local ombudsman is more likely to have jurisdiction. If they adopt a distanced stance, then the position may be otherwise. In other words, the distinction often seems geographical: if the complaint is about something done or not done in county hall, then the local ombudsman has jurisdiction; if it concerns a school operating under county hall, then it does not. We should also add that the position of grant-maintained schools under the Education Reform Act 1988 is not blindingly clear. For what it is worth, most other complaint-handling officials with jurisdiction over local government have jurisdiction over complaints against school officials, teachers and agencies. We believe this needs to be reassessed in Britain.

As to personnel matters, we have already taken a stand within the framework of ombudsman systems at large. However, it may be worth adding that it does seem odd that delay in paying a housing benefit can be investigated, whereas delay in paying a local authority pension to an ex-employee cannot. Again, the difference between losing an application for a council property and one for a job with the council is not blindingly obvious. Those who work within the local ombudsman's office find this particularly irritating and we sympathize with them in this matter.

Enforcement of remedies

This has been a particular bone of contention for some time with the local ombudsman, and we have already seen that the record is probably worse than the official figures suggest and that further thought needs to be given to the matter. We remain convinced that court enforcement is likely to be counter-productive and that the recent legislative changes are unlikely to remedy the situation to any great extent. At least three possibilities seem to present themselves. The first is for the Select Committee on the PCA to become involved in the matter. The second is for the advisory commissioners under the 1989 Act to become, in effect, a Consumers' Council whose condemnation of a local authority's intransigence might carry some weight. The third is that a sum might be made available to the local ombudsman for *ex gratia* payments to those whose complaints were not adequately responded to. All would require some further thought in terms of detail and repercussions, but it is plainly unacceptable to continue as we are.

Maladministration

We have already said a certain amount about this but a few points remain. The development of the concept has been a very pragmatic affair and not based upon any attempt to draw out principles of good administration. This is not assisted in the local ombudsman's case by the fact that the commissioners do not sit *en bloc* to decide cases, thus risking inconsistency. The local ombudsman's office itself is reluctant to develop precedents, which they believe may be involved in going beyond the pragmatic approach. We doubt that this is well-founded and is probably inconsistent with them drawing up a model complaints procedure in 1978 with the local authority associations. Furthermore, the advice was updated in consultation with the local authority associations in early 1992. There seems little point in us recommending such a procedure if they are to be guided by it or its absence when conducting investigations.

The Sheffield Report has tilled this ground fairly well and we believe that time seems to have borne out the analysis. What is encouraging is the ability now afforded by statute for the local ombudsman to recommend a Code of Good Administrative Practice to local authorities. In our view, it ought to be supplemented by a catalogue of common administrative errors. In either case, the conduct of an authority which infringed the one and/or mimicked the other ought prima facie to be thought to have produced a failure of administration for which they should be called to account.

Injustice

All three classical ombudsman systems in Britain require a finding of injustice before an adverse report can be made. Maladministration without injustice will not require any further action from the authority concerned. Not only does this mean that poor procedures, and indeed maladministration, may be exposed as a result of an investigation without the authority concerned being under any legal obligation to respond, but the meaning given to ombudsman is crucial.

All in all, we have little doubt that the requirement for injustice ought to be removed. This should have the effect, alongside other suggestions which have been made, of directing the local ombudsman (as indeed the other ombudsmen) to adopt a central concern with the adequacy of procedures.

A single ombudsman system

Quite apart from the problems we identify concerning the interface between classical and private ombudsman systems, a case perhaps needs to be examined for a single classical ombudsman system bringing together the three (in effect) which we possess. There is no doubt that confusion is sown in the minds of the public by the separate sets of offices and jurisdictions. Each ombudsman attempts to funnel on the complaints which are inappropriately channelled, but we have no idea how many people get lost in the system. The matter is compounded where none of them appear to have jurisdiction and the culture of the ombudsman office in Britain prevents rigorous attempts to sort out other problems informally.

It is worth adding in this respect that even the PCA has a sizeable number of telephone callers and even personal callers who may not be helped under present arrangements. Other ombudsman systems support integrated offices, oral complaints and the like. We reiterate the advantages which we perceive from a Bench of ombudsmen making consistent decisions, identifying priorities and seeking to improve administration.

There is little current pressure in Britain for the examination of such an idea. Indeed, it seems to us (and we believe to the European Ombudsman's Institute) that there is much to be said for a permanent ombudsman pressure group/commission to press for state-of-the-art ombudsman issues to be taken up within the heart of government. We believe consideration should be given to both these ideas. We do expect that some pressure will be exerted to argue for the entrenchment of the present ombudsman system in any proposed British Constitution emerging from certain quarters. We believe this would be counter-productive without further thought being given to the larger picture.

The ombudsman and law reform

The matter of improving procedures and performance has perhaps been sufficiently ventilated. However, serious attention needs to be focused on the desirability of a statutory power to recommend changes in legislation in order to improve that performance. Let us revert to the Austrian ombudsman who enjoys such a power. Furthermore, he is a member of the Board for Administrative Reforms, which is a high-powered advisory body, not unlike the Australian ARC. His proposals for change are made to the Constitutional Committee of the Austrian Parliament and he informed us that over 100 of the 200 suggestions he had made had been adopted. Section 15 (2) of the [Australian] Ombudsman Act 1976 also empowers the Commonwealth ombudsman to issue a recommendation that a rule of law, provision of an enactment or practice on which a decision, recommendation or omission was based be altered. He may monitor the response of the body concerned, and where necessary exercise his statutory right to report to the prime minister and ultimately to Parliament.

THE OMBUDSMAN: A CHANGING SCENE

The ombudsman is but one form of accountability mechanism available to the citizen and for the administration. We have already suggested that his function *vis-à-vis* other bodies should be more closely examined.

The *Citizens' Charter* is merely the most currently prominent novelty emerging in the search for ways of holding government accountable. The political parties seem to differ primarily over whether a charter should have 'quality auditors' built in or not. What, however, has not been properly addressed is how far there may be overlap between such ideas and the potential of our existing ombudsmen were they to be invested with anything like the powers of their overseas counterpart.[1] Nor at this point does there seem to be much discussion of the impact of American experiments such as the Pennsylvania Public Utility Commission or, for example, the Danish Consumer Ombudsman who has recently examined Danish banking practices. Of course, the Office of Fair Trading may make investigations in some of these areas.

Ombudsman systems worldwide are the jurisprudential discovery of the last thirty years. They are here to stay, but it is doubtful if their full potential is being tapped. This is undoubtedly the case in Britain where we are slow to change and even slower to abandon the conventions on which a number of our institutions are based. As yet our ombudsman systems are seen as ancillary to the primary institutions for seeking justice and do not yet possess the elevated role of a true citizens' defender. Is there any reason, for example, why our ombudsmen should not have special standing to refer suspected illegalities to the courts in the way that we understand the *Volksanwaltschaft* can in Austria? Unthinkable or unthought about (see Widdicombe, 1986)?

What is to be the role of ombudsmen in the new Europe? At least we have a European Ombudsman Institute and the *Kirchhiner Stichting Ombudsman en Democratie* in Holland, which sees the ombudsman system as intimately connected with the commitment to democracy. The Maastricht Treaty embodies the promise to establish an EC ombudsman since, in the words of the British Foreign Secretary, Douglas Hurd, it was 'impossible for national parliaments to watch over the day-to-day activities of the Commission' (*Financial Times*, 12 June 1990). Equally, there is strong movement within the European ombudsman world to establish an ombudsman for human rights. Without prejudice to that idea, what is the mileage for such a development in Britain? Again Austria is very much in the vanguard, for not only does it possess a Human Rights Institute in Salzburg but its own ombudsman is one of the few to have given publicity to the fact that the Council of Europe Human Rights Directorate has asked European ombudsmen for their help in protecting human rights. Perhaps most of the complaints against violation of human rights going to Strasbourg cannot be processed largely for formal or technical reasons. Human rights ombudsmen may be a way around this, but little thought has as yet been given to the matter.

One of the world's leading commentators on ombudsman systems has produced an ideal-typical polarization of the roles which they can occupy in the world community which should give us some food for thought. He describes some who have:

> . . . further narrowed their already restricted jurisdiction and generally taken such a carping officious attitude that they have discouraged people from making complaints. They have made this particular grievance channel yet another official or legal trial for citizens.
>
> (Caiden, 1988, p. 8)

Others have 'aggrandised the Ombudsman office beyond just a citizen's defender or protector into a citizen's advocate, thereby crossing the administrative realm of government into more publicly controversial ground' (ibid., p. 7). He also asked a series of questions about the potential role of ombudsmen: should, for example, they provide special protection for whistle-blowers (Sarah Tisdall, Peter Wright, etc.)? Why have they not done better at exposing official corruption, protecting individuals from inhumane treatment at the hands of the state's agents? And so on. Others have asked whether ombudsmen should be protectors of the environment. Since 1987, the Australian ombudsman has had jurisdiction over telephone intercepts by the security services and others. Our response has been to establish special commissioners and tribunals which are seriously inhibited in these areas. On the more mundane level, he can and does call a complainant in to ensure that the passport he needs for next week and has been unsuccessful in obtaining arrives without further ado.

Given that ombudsmen can range widely, have almost total access to documents, are independent, etc., they perhaps ought to be seen as a real alternative both to the traditional justice system and, even to some extent, to the failed political system. In the days when legal aid is being cut back, the ombudsman's office has an enormous amount to offer. But we have not looked closely enough at the potential of the office. Instead, we have added him to the other conventions of our system and sought to bridle him out of his potential utility.

NOTE

1 On the *Citizens' Charter* and ombudsmen, see Select Committee on the Parliamentary Commissioner for Administration, HC 158 (1991–92).

8

MECHANISMS OPERATING WITHIN GOVERNMENTAL ORGANIZATIONS

Our primary focus so far has been on institutions which operate outside governmental bodies and which are dispensers of justice but which are not courts. Our concern in this chapter is with the internal mechanisms which are used by such bodies to resolve grievances before outside institutions are resorted to. There is in fact a staggering variety of practices from *ad hoc* treatment to semi-formal processes to formal procedures. We do not deal in this chapter with Adjudication Officers (see Chapter 6). What we are concerned with is establishing the more important types of practice rather than an inventory of existing procedures. We shall ask what improvements or changes are required to make institutions more responsive to those with grievances involving their administration. We are addressing very different sorts of institution, with different cultures, sensitivities and political pressure points. It will be difficult, therefore, if not impossible to recommend similar procedures for different tiers of government or different governmental forms. Our plan is to examine government departments, executive agencies, local authorities, health authorities and NHS Trusts. Obviously, we shall have to be alive to the impact of the *Citizens' Charter* in this respect, particularly with regard to the proposed creation of lay adjudicators (see Select Committee on the Parliamentary Commissioner for Administration, 1991–92).

Before we look at government departments, we must spend some time analysing the role of elected representatives. Although they are 'outside' the organization complained against, their intervention often triggers internal devices. In many quarters, it is often assumed that their intervention is invariably of positive effect. Their services are free to the local community and apply to broad sections of the community (Rawlings, 1986b). Whether as a post-bag or referral point for complainants to the appropriate point of contact – and here we should remember that MPs are the first port of call for complaints against scheduled bodies to the PCA and this covers the executive agencies – or whether as the grievance remedial device itself or as an additional prong in a broad-based attack against governmental decisions or policies, the potential importance of MPs is without question. However, there are also examples where too high a profile for complainants, which has been brought about by MP intervention by Questions in the House, Adjournment Debates and the like, can have the effect of freezing up departments and making civil servants cautious and advisers defensive and restrictive with information. However, an MP's letter is an effective method to get into a fast-track lane for access to departmental decision makers, or their analogues in agencies or public authorities. We say this even though there is a vast amount of evidence to suggest that a large proportion of the public is ignorant of the identity of their MP, or, and this was the case in marginals, over 50 per cent of the electorate are unaware of the political party of their MP (*BBC News*, 13 May 1987; 5000 electors were approached).

The point has been made that MPs acquire a great deal of information about departmental performance in the course of their constituency case work. There is a good case to be made for this information feeding into the select committee system; the suggestion has been made that the Select Committee on the PCA should receive this information which could then form the subject of an investigation by the PCA prompted by the select committee on the basis of information it has received from MPs on complaint handling. In open-ended questions addressed to the chairs of select committees in 1990, they were asked whether complaints were made to their committees by complainants. The Transport Committee said that it received complaints from time to time via its chair. These were responses by the public to departmental action following considerable publicity. 'These complaints are about the effect of Department policies on individuals, they are not complaints of maladministration.' The Trade and Industry Committee received complaints from the public, especially when the committee was investigating an issue. But the committee was also asked by members of the public to investigate particular subjects and the volume of this general correspondence has 'certainly increased in the last few years' (25 April 1990). The committee does not have the resources to investigate the individual complaints, but they are considered in the course of the committee's inquiries. Individual complaints covered such subjects as the Post Office. Energy had received complaints relating only to policy matters and they would only refer them to a more appropriate body for investigation or report. The committee had not investigated any individual complaint. The Foreign

Affairs Committee through its chair responded that he very occasionally received letters of complaint against the Foreign Office. 'It has been the Committee's practice not to go into individual cases' (as opposed to policy issues which deal with categories of persons). Complainants are referred to the department or to their own MP. The Environment Committee received complaints but had never sought to resolve such a complaint:

> Indeed it is difficult to see how a departmental Select Committee could carry out such an investigation – not least because committees, like the House itself, do not possess the same powers as the Parliamentary Commissioner to scrutinise internal working documents of Departments.

Without wishing to become involved in the subject of committees' access to departmental papers, it is interesting to note the Foreign Affairs Committee's complaint about a lack of appropriate access to departmental files. The *Belgrano* papers had to be viewed in the Ministry of Defence and had to be recollected from 'corporate memory'. The episode demonstrated the 'unsatisfactory situation which now operates' in relation to the viewing of departmental papers which are not withheld from the committees under the Osmotherly Rules (HC 19, 1989–90, para. 17, Select Committee on Procedure, *The Working of the Select Committee System*).

Education received few complaints and although the Employment Committee received 'perhaps, about one a month', 'the Committee would not usually inquire into the way an individual had been treated; if it became known that the Committee was willing to do this, I am sure that we would receive a large number' (April 1990, letter from the chair). Social Services also receive complaints from members of the public, although like the other committees they would not investigate these but 'such particular instances have been referred to, with the correspondent's permission, in reports of the Committee in order to illustrate general shortcomings or difficulties in policy or practice'.

Many of the committees showed little enthusiasm for departments to establish grievance procedures before ombudsmen or other bodies such as tribunals.

MINISTERIAL CORRESPONDENCE

As part of the doctrine of ministerial responsibility, MPs take seriously their right to take up complaints on behalf of their constituents by writing to ministers directly. Correspondence serves 'both as a means of communicating the Government's policies, and as an aspect of accountability and quality control when queries are raised about poor service or potential maladministration' (Efficiency Unit, 1990, p. 7). Furthermore, each minister has his own private office, and in those that deal with large volumes of correspondence a separate correspondence section exists to deal exclusively with ministerial correspondence. An Efficiency Unit study on the subject which was prompted by MP concern (Efficiency Unit, 1990) found that the volume of correspondence in general to ministers to which they replied personally totalled 250,000 letters per annum. Officials answered well over 600,000 letters addressed to ministers by members of the public. The total annual cost of meeting ministerial replies amounted to about £17.5 million, an average of £70 per letter (ibid., p. 10). The study found that many departments were failing to meet the targets they had set for themselves for prompt response to MPs letters (ibid., p. 4). The recommendations were aimed at making the handling of responses more effective and efficient within a broad framework of best practice which each department can adapt in the light of its own circumstances. These were:

1 Decentralisation of correspondence on operational matters. Does a reply need to come from the ministerial office? Departments should be encouraged to assist MPs to direct their inquiries to the point of government 'which is best able to give them a fast, informed and helpful reply, for example the Chief Executives of executive agencies, or local offices of departments'. MPs are advised on the practices on complaints by the Immigration Department.
2 Better identification of the costs of dealing with correspondence and the points in the system at which delays occur. 'There is a need to eliminate unnecessary multiple handling of incoming letters and draft replies as they are passed along Departmental reporting lines', harnessing the full benefits of computer-tracking systems and word-processing technology.
3 Improved management performance. Targets are generally set on performance for dealing with correspondence but departments regularly fail to meet the targets they set. Too often there is no effective monitoring within departments. Unacceptable delays should be reduced within a more considered framework for setting and achieving targets, improving the management and resources devoted to correspondence, and closer monitoring and publication of performance.

(Efficiency Unit, 1990, p. 5)

In general, departments should do more to keep MPs informed and explain what is happening. Against this recommendation, it should be appreciated that departmental correspondence has increased significantly in recent years, when in many cases the number of officials in a department has decreased. In the DoE, for instance, the study showed that in 1979, the department had 11,300 staff and dealt with 18,500 items of ministerial correspondence. By 1990, there were 6300 staff and 46,000 letters – much of the increase coming in 1989 (poll tax). Furthermore, although MPs usually said they would only write to ministers when 'absolutely necessary', the fact that a ministerial reply seems impressive to the constituent and that a minister has far greater resources for research than an MP were often persuasive factors.

Departments with a below par performance on responses included those with large volumes of correspondence: the DES, Home Office, DoE and the Departments of Health and Social Security. A large number of members of the public were not satisfied with the content of the response received.

From the Efficiency Unit study, two constructive suggestions emerged: the introduction of a booklet on a similar basis to the *List of Ministerial Responsibilities* giving details of all senior officials in departments whom MPs could contact instead of ministers, and also details of executive agency chief executives and officials in local and regional offices. Secondly, a suggestion was made that some form of in-house training should be provided for all new MPs on how to deal with correspondence. New MPs were not used to such volumes of correspondence and had little idea of civil service and government procedures and practices.

MPs are advised to contact executive agency chief executives or local managers for a quicker response than if they wrote to ministers. As Mrs Thatcher stated in June 1990:

> One of the objectives of establishing the Executive Agencies is to respond better to the concerns and demands of Hon and RT Hon Members. Chief Executives and Agency managers will have the immediate detailed knowledge which the Hon Member is seeking as well as the necessary delegated authority to take appropriate action. (p. 17)

It is for the minister to decide whether or not an inquiry should be referred to an agency chief executive. Both the Employment Agency and the Driver and Vehicle Licensing Agency set up early systems to deal directly with MPs' correspondence (see Efficiency Unit, 1990). Where they are exercising powers delegated under a framework document (FD), chief executives should be the point of contact, although some MPs are reluctant to attenuate ministerial acountability (and their constituents are more impressed by a ministerial signature) and others said they had no other option but to write to the minister as they had no available information on points of contact within agencies or departments. The government agreed that such information should be available and ministers should consider asking local offices to write to MPs asking them to contact the office directly with queries/complaints. MPs would not be given any files but they may be sent two letters in the case of DSS matters, one to deal with the complaint and 'open', the other 'confidential', i.e. the complainant is suspected of fraud. The Immigration and Nationality Department proposed that MPs contact the department directly. No reason could be seen why agency chiefs could not deal with policy matters where they had the information, providing the FD did not prohibit disclosure. Where policy was being formulated, a ministerial reply was more appropriate. In general, ministers should:

consider whether there are discrete units within their departments, or external bodies and authorities, which might be further encouraged to develop direct contact with MPs in order to improve the handling of MPs inquiries. Ministers should consider referring to any such units and authorities letters from MPs that could be dealt with at that level in the first instance.

(Efficiency Unit, 1990, p. 22)

Targets should be set, both for official response times and departmental response times, and these should be incorporated within management accounting and information systems. Targets should be 'specific, measurable and achievable' and too frequently the study found they were not (p. 23). The Home Office met its target of response times to MPs in only 25 per cent of cases; the DoE 52 per cent in 1989 rising to 65 per cent for 1990. The Prime Minister's Office asks for a response time of 14 days from departments – in 1990, it was achieved in 20 per cent of cases. In the DSS, targets are set for individual official response times and these are to become mandatory. Targets should be regularly reviewed and published. Performance should be monitored and ministers should be involved in this exercise as well as target setting.

Letters are rarely seen by ministers when they are first received; only those identified as being particularly sensitive or urgent are shown to the minister. The most streamlined procedures for dealing with correspondence were in the Department of Health, DES and DSS. A Correspondence Section decides who should be responsible for replying. This may involve passing letters to the Private Office for decision. Where letters are returned to that office with a drafted reply, it was guessed that 'at least half' of the replies were altered in the Private Office, usually for stylistic reasons. Efficient targeting is a prerequisite for an efficient reminder system and interim replies should be sent to explain the reasons for delay and to indicate, where possible, how long a response may take. Practices differ as one would expect, but in the MoD an interim reply is only sent in response to a personalized letter from an MP, not to a constituent's letter which is only accompanied by an MP's forwarding letter and so on. Further, there is no need to overgrade the reply to a letter concerned with routine correspondence. Standardized campaign letters, which can number anything from 50 to 10,000, will generally receive a standardized reply.

Only two departments, the Department of Employment and the Department of Trade and Industry, undertook central monitoring of 'Treat Officially' correspondence, which is the description of correspondence to ministers from the public. It is treated differently to ministerial correspondence, i.e. that which comes from MPs. It is, for instance, accorded much less priority than the latter. Staff knowledge on 'Treat Officially' correspondence, and whether targets were being met, was sparse and one Grade 5 official stated 'of all the things his branch had to do, correspondence for official reply was one of the least important' (Efficiency Unit, 1990, p. 46). Replies that used standardized paragraphs could be contracted out at a much reduced cost. Importantly, the study believed that 'Treat Officially' correspondence should have the same safeguard of targeting, monitoring and referral to agencies (present practices for which are variable and usually non-existent), local offices, etc., as applies above.

PROCEDURES

Not all correspondence will convey complaints. In the year until August 1990, the DSS received 35,825 letters, of which 18,539 were for ministerial reply and 17,286 were for official reply. However, the department does not count letters of complaint separately (DSS, 20 December 1990, letter), which is surprising. The DSS has units in Central Office dealing with policy complaints regarding, for example, matters raised by the CPAG. Now the Benefits Agency (BA) and Contributions Agency are responsible for administering and delivering DSS programmes formally within the department itself. Letters to the DSS from MPs about the BA are referred to the agency's Parliamentary Business Branch by the DSS. The letter is then sent to a local manager, a section at the Central Office or the Central Services Branch for reply and then signature by the chief executive. It was estimated that about 40 per cent of MPs were writing directly to the chief executive rather than to the minister, a development which has been encouraged, as has sending a letter directly to the local manager, which will 'generally be much quicker' as regards turn-around time. To 31 March 1992, 2592 letters had been sent to the chief executive in the previous twelve months. The BA has developed a number of practices in 'customer care'. It has to be emphasized that the BA's efforts are aimed at producing a quality service to reduce the number of complaints and we need to say a little about this. The BA's Customer Charter spells out the complaints procedure, which we address in a moment.

The Benefits Agency has produced customer care packages and over 200 groups (e.g. CPAG, NACAB and MENCAP) have been contacted to help in their production. The idea is to establish permanent links, not simply isolated contact. Local managers (159 of them) were given discretion to conduct local discussion and consultation on what local 'clients' wanted. These cover such matters as opening hours, situation of offices, means of communication (e.g. numbers of telephones) and so on. The Quality Management Team of the Customer Service Branch has produced *Paving the Way to*

Quality Management (BA, 1992) to explore and identify the benefits and advantages of the implementation of a 'Quality Pays' strategy to deliver a quality service meeting the 'negotiated needs' and 'expectations' of claimants. BA Consultancy Services has produced a report which examines best practices elsewhere and this includes an appraisal of customer perceptions and examination of internal processes checking performance against targets. National customer surveys are conducted (e.g. by N. Russell and S. Whitworth in 1991) and these attempt to establish the overall customer satisfaction rate. Very detailed breakdowns are given but we learn, for instance, that 25 per cent of single parents on Income Support wanted more information. The BA has produced a document about complaining entitled *Have Your Say* (1991), which was not as widely used as the agency had expected.

Complaints of a local nature should be addressed in the first instance to the customer services manager in the local office. A response should be made within seven days. Detailed guidance is given on the level at which a complaint is dealt with and the use of interviews. Cases of mistakes will usually involve adjudication officers (see Chapter 6). Where this fails to assuage the customer, contact can be made with the office manager and then the area manager (of which there are 21). Above the area manager are three territorial directors. In the pre-BA structure, the identity of their analogue – a national director – was not usually released to claimants, but it was not unknown for the most persistent to be seen by the national director.

Opportunity to Improve Service (OTIS) provides an opportunity for customers, by way of questionnaire, to have their say on service. These are fed into relevant operational sections, which analyse them and service delivery points' reaction to their comments. Information from customers and complaints is also fed into the area director's Customer Service Unit. Documents regarding the complaints procedure describe how it is designed to 'achieve better customer service for the general public. It will monitor and analyse complaints and the response to complaints to identify any procedures that need to be improved.'

The Immigration and Nationality Department (IND) split complaints into three categories. Detailed guidance exists for MP representations; these were reformulated in 1988. The first type is a complaint against an adverse decision. In this case, many representations are made directly to the minister. It should be explained that changes in the law make it more difficult for the decision of an immigration officer to be overturned on anything other than a technicality by the Adjudication Officer and the Immigration Appeal Tribunal (see *R v Secretary of State for the Home Department ex p Mundowa* [1992] 3 All ER 606). What this encourages, therefore, is the making of representations to the minister to overrule on the merits. Ministers will be involved where it is a very sensitive case because of its political overtones, or because of media/press coverage. Representations are not rejected out of hand if they are not dispatched from a constituency MP or a relation despite the code of guidance and, naturally, many come from the individuals themselves. Compassionate grounds are the major factor in representations to the minister. The IND were unable to give figures on successful representations.

The second type of complaint concerns those made against an individual, for example, rudeness, racism, theft and the like. Detailed notes are available to officers on the steps to pursue. The third kind of complaint deals with systemic complaints such as delay in the processing of a complaint. This often covers PCA territory. Along with all departments and agencies, special offices exist to deal with PCA investigations (see Chapter 7). These typically set out guidelines which deal with timetabling, intra-departmental liaison, who prepares statements, gathers evidence, consults relevant parties, assembles supporting documentation and submits the file to the Regional Controller or his/her equivalent. Guidance is given on how to prepare a Statement of Events and what the covering minute should contain. That for the Department of Social Security states that the guidance should

> comment on each of the points made in the complaint; identify any errors, omissions or delays for which apologies are due; note any unresolved issues that need to be followed up; consider whether a special payment is appropriate; include any background information that may be helpful for senior officers or the PCA – you may wish to identify extenuating circumstances such as abnormal workload.
> (DSS PCA Guidance Notes, 1989, para. 11)

This minute will not be passed on to the PCA. Extracts from recent draft replies are contained in the DSS guidance, as well as advice on special payments, referral to Ministers and future action.

Complaints raising implications for policy in the Immigration and Nationality Department are sent to other specialist units. In total, 549 letters of complaint were received by the Immigration Service in 1988, as against 475 in 1987. Sixty-two complaints against staff in 1988 were found to be wholly or partially substantiated.

Both the Inland Revenue and HM Customs and Excise (HMCE) adopted a *Taxpayers' Charter* in 1986. HMCE have in 1992 revised their complaints procedure and we examine this below. The Inland Revenue has also instituted changes following the *Citizens' Charter*. These set out to explain, *inter alia*, the part that taxpayers must play in the tax system and their rights to tax allowances and relief. Local offices are grouped into regions. The regional controller monitors the work within his or her region and each local officer in charge of the local office will deal with individual cases, including complaints. Interviews will be given if requested and representation is allowed by properly authorized and qualified representatives. Where the location of a tax office which a taxpayer deals with is inconvenient, an interview at a closer office, or even at the individual's home if disabled, may be arranged. Complaints at regional level are dealt with by a senior officer who calls for the complainant's file. If a complaint is made to head office, it is dealt with by specialists in the area into which it falls. Complaints which come to head office via other sources – MPs, the prime minister, the Queen, etc. – are investigated within the appropriate level of the Inland Revenue and the final report is approved by a senior official. In 1989, 8000 letters were were received by the Revenue's head office. However, not all of these were complaints, 4500 being for ministerial reply. The Revenue has a Correspondence Unit and details are recorded on a computer system. An administrative officer decides which division is responsible for a reply, unless it is really a local matter. Only one division has a correspondence section; letters are directed to and replies cleared by staff at an appropriate level. Targets for reply are set, although they could not be met in some cases, e.g. queries about the budget. In 1990, performance information was not provided for senior officials or ministers (Efficiency Unit, 1990).

Like the IND, there is guidance in the *Inspector's Manual* on complaints to the PCA. Interestingly, it states that the PCA will not accept that a file is missing until an exhaustive search is conducted. Specific examples are provided of how PCA investigations have improved working practices within departments. We deal with this general point in Chapter 7.

There is no doubt that change is afoot, whether prompted by the *Citizens' Charter* or deeper underlying movements. This can be seen in the detailed complaints procedure produced by HMCE. A public notice advises the 'customers' of HMCE on what they can complain about; how they can complain; and how oral complaints and written complaints will be dealt with (a response in either case within 15 days and notification where that is not possible). Where the complainant is dissatisfied with the outcome, he or she may write giving reasons and the 'appeal' will be heard by another senior officer who will be independent in the examination. The complainant will be told within 15 days when he or she will be notified of the outcome and the decision will be a detailed written explanation. Where the complainant is still not satisfied, he or she should write to HQ supplying details of the correspondence.

Internal guidance accompanies the public notice. This is taken to demonstrate 'the Department's commitment to a high level of service to the public, to provide clear guidance to staff on how to handle complaints from the public and to show that all complaints are treated seriously and investigated fairly and impartially'. The procedures should be clear and easy to understand. The purpose of the complaints procedure is three-fold:

. . . to assure Parliament that complaints are being identified and dealt with properly and promptly; investigations are fair to all parties; management is provided with information to help them monitor the quality of service the Department provides to the public.

The guidelines define for their purposes the following items.

Complaint: A written or verbal expression finding fault by, or on behalf of, a member of the public about the handling of their affairs.
Complaint against an officer: Complaints about an identifiable member of Customs and Excise.
Complaint against a system: Complaints against a policy, procedure or system adopted by the Department as a whole or by an office. Complaints against a law or an enactment – whether UK or EC – are excluded.

The guidance advises on how to establish whether a complaint is about an officer or a 'system' or both and how they should be processed. There are also complaints about fairness and accuracy. Complaints are categorized as 'minor' or 'serious'. Minor complaints can usually be dealt with by the officer concerned, or if formal by local managers. All complaints by MPs must be referred to senior management as must all serious complaints, which automatically includes all system complaints. In addition to the Public Notice 1000 'Complaints against Customs and Excise', an outline of the procedure will be published in the *Taxpayers' Charter* (revised in 1991) and the *Travellers' Charter*. Guidance is available in Est. Vol. G2-1A on MP correspondence and on that which is addressed to the chairman or to members of the board. In the latter case, the complaint is dealt with by the Chairman's Private Office (CPO) and a file will be sent to the appropriate collector or head of HQ Division for investigation and preparation of a draft reply. Complaints by MPs and the CPO will be recorded in the collection/division complaints system, like any other complaint. All such complaints are automatically classified 'serious'. Trade associations normally write to the relevant policy division in HQ. They are treated as CPO complaints.

The guidelines may have the effect of adopting local arrangements or creating new procedures, and one should bear in mind possible maladministration if the guideline details are not followed. Officials are advised that it is an important requirement that statistics should be able to be produced, on a six-monthly basis, of all complaints received in a collection/division, whether substantiated or not. A complaints' co-ordinator should be established in each collection/division and senior managers and line managers are instructed on the steps to follow. Appropriate action should be taken within 24 hours of receipt of a complaint which means dealing with complaints at the appropriate level.

Where a complaint is made against a system, which may well have implications for the department, inquiries should establish: what the system is; why the system is in use; how the system works; if there are any known weaknesses or inconsistencies in the system; whether the complainant's circumstances are met by the system, i.e. no system adjustment has to be effected. HQ policy division should immediately be notified if any complaint rectification requires system adjustment with more than local implications.

Interestingly, the guidance spells out the main reasons why people complain:

- they do not understand how the system works;
- the system has discriminated against them;
- the system does not work as intended;
- they were treated rudely;
- they were treated unfairly;
- they are trying to obtain a personal advantage;
- they are trying to distract attention from or mitigate, for example, a revenue offence they have committed;
- they are under stress, whether personally (self-) or departmentally induced;
- they are being malicious.

Copious guidance is provided on recording, logging, investigating and considering criminal or serious disciplinary implications. Time limits are laid down and should be complied with. Officers as well as complainants have a right of appeal (i.e. a right of higher review) against adverse decisions and, in the former case, established disciplinary proceedings may be invoked if formal disciplinary action is taken. Compensation may be awarded for actual loss or inconvenience suffered as a consequence of unreasonable departmental action. The complainant may be asked to quantify this loss. Claims up to £100 may be authorized locally; claims above £100 require PDDS (a special section) approval. It is paid 'without prejudice'. The guidance recommends that complaints files should be kept for three years before destruction. PDDS will ask for statistical returns on all complaints on a six-monthly basis, except for those settled amicably on the spot and which are minor and oral. A particular file may be investigated by PDDS to establish any significant variations in the way complaints are handled across the department and whether the guidelines require amending. It only needs to be said that the department rejected a three-tier division of complaints, viz. minor, serious and very serious, because of difficulties this would pose for classification.

It appears commonplace for departments to have detailed procedures for the handling of grievances, though not so common for these to be gathered together as formal guidelines. Whatever is available is not usually for public consumption. Approaches vary from unit to unit. In one department, the legal adviser voiced surprise at his own ignorance of established practices and, prompted by our enquiry, launched his own investigation. This found that complaints were of two basic kinds: those to ministers and those addressed to the department:

> The most obvious examples falling under the first category are points raised either through PQs or through correspondence sent to ministers by MPs (often, but not always, enclosing letters sent to them by their constituents). In each case, the Minister's office seek advice from officials, usually at Grade 5 (Assistant Secretary) level, who in turn will provide a draft reply. PQs and letters from MPs are of course answered by one or other of the Ministers, as are letters from other important people or major bodies.

Regional or local offices would deal with cases relating to grant or subsidy or where the minister exercises some kind of regulatory function, such as the issue of licences under Regulations. In these cases, complaint recipients are likely to be locally based officials. An established pattern for processing complaints was then followed.

Furthermore, where an entitlement to grant is being withdrawn, by, for example, the Ministry of Agriculture, Fisheries and Food (MAFF), many schemes allow for the right to make representations to a person appointed by the minister. Under the Conservation Grant Regulations 1989, the appointed person is usually chosen from the Regional Panel. No set procedure is laid down; he or she normally receives both written representations and conducts an informal 'hearing'. The report is made to the minister who makes the decision.

LOCAL AUTHORITIES

In a way, we feel back on home base with this topic. It was the difficulty faced by complainants challenging local government decisions which initially prompted us to research the field of grievance redress in the mid-1970s. Much has changed since that time, not least in the position, administration and role of local government. However, local government is still a service provider in a wide range of subject areas and it is still the tier of government with which most people have direct contact.

One of the more important developments in this area, potentially at least, was the Local Government (Access to Information) Act 1985. This statute provided a freedom of information and open government law for local government. It opened up committee and sub-committee meetings to the public, the supply of minutes and agendas likewise, and access to officer reports and background documents – so far as the latter have been relied upon to a considerable extent – which lie behind agenda items. The access provisions are circumscribed by exclusions and exemptions and the evidence shows that the legislation is not widely used or appreciated by the public. The 1980s also witnessed numerous cases in which the common law rights of members of authorities were clarified, generally to the advantage of members on a need to know basis. Certain problematical areas remain with respect to members' rights *vis-à-vis* advisory committees and, for example, when a member may be deemed to have an ulterior motive in seeking access to documents relating to an individual complaint (Birkinshaw, 1981). However, superficially at least, the effect of these developments has been to introduce an element of sunshine into local government administration as a legal requirement which is not present in central government administration.

The Commission for Local Administration (CLA) has produced its own guide on complaints procedures. The exhaustive study of complaints procedures published in 1987 found knowledge of the guide among authorities to be 'patchy' (Lewis *et al.*, 1987). In 1992, the CLA published *Devising a Complaints System*, which emphasizes government thinking on citizens' rights.

This spells out the importance of member and officer commitment to the procedure and those who should be consulted in setting up procedures. It highlights obvious features of a good procedure: easily accessible, conspicuous to users, simple, quick, objective – by independent investigation by individuals from outside the department concerned where necessary – procedures should be confidential and comprehensive, with appropriate modifications for different departments. They should identify what they cover (e.g. not simple requests for information), who can complain, the stages of the procedure, recording of complaints, the form in which they should be made, member involvement, time limits, overall responsibility for co-ordinating complaints systems in an authority and policies on anonymous complaints. It advises on preparatory steps, staff training, publicity, the use of complaints procedures as learning devices for service improvement, good investigative practice and remedial action where a complaint is justified. The commission has frequently expressed the view that not possessing adequate procedures to deal with complaints may, on the facts, amount to maladministration: 'A failure to have one or to rely on one which is incomplete or inadequate may lead to a finding of maladministration' (CLA, 1989, p. 6). In a recent report, the ombudsman wrote 'good administration requires that authorities should have effective and clear internal complaints procedures' (Inv 87/A/453: see also 88/A/0763, where the authority was criticized because there was no evidence to suggest that the complaint had been properly investigated; and also in another case an authority was criticized because it did not adhere to an existing complaints procedure (88/C/1083)). None the less, although the record of many authorities was exemplary in complaint handling, the record of too many others left a great deal to be desired.

There are also numerous examples where detailed provision for complaints is laid down in statute, regulations or guidance. Education has seen the establishment of appeal provisions to deal with appeals against admissions decisions, a process complicated by the virtual abolition of school catchment areas. There are also appeal procedures available under the Education Act 1981 to deal with special educational needs statements and decisions affecting children. The code of practice for these procedures was revised by local authority associations in 1992. These end up with the right of appeal to the secretary of state who may reverse the LEA's decision. It is worthwhile reminding ourselves that 'appeals' or complaints provisions often allow for an appeal from the decision of the local authority to the secretary of state, most obviously under the Education Act 1944 (ss. 68 and 99). Under the Education Reform Act 1988 (s. 23), a complaints procedure is established to deal with complaints concerning the National Curriculum (DES Circular 1/89). This has to be invoked and processed before the secretary of state can be contacted. The object of complaint under section 68 is usually the LEA. Where schools opt out of LEA control, a difficulty has arisen which concerns the emergence of disputes between the Board of Governors and the head-teacher. In the event of a serious breakdown in the relationship, the secretary of state will have to be resorted to.

Complaints procedures have been introduced in provisions under the Children Act 1989, an act which 'fundamentally shifts the onus for review and decision-making from closed, inaccessible case conference planning, review or briefing meetings held by social services departments to a much more open arena' representing a 'most radical shift towards reviewing the exercise of local authority power by the courts' (Robertson, 1989, p. 225). Guidelines have been introduced for social services complaints (see Department of Health, 1990 and see s. 50 NHS and CC Act 1990) and access to social welfare and housing personal records contain provisions whereby an appeal procedure has to be set up for those wishing to challenge an adverse decision. Elsewhere, there are provisions which impose duties to give reasons for decisions which may be expected to generate procedural safeguards in their wake – although in the context of one of these procedures, viz. competitive tendering under the Local Government Act 1988, there would be the obvious need to provide domestic procedures before judicial review was sought; indeed the Act facilitates, even encourages, such challenge through the courts.

We have made the point before that audit provisions provide for full opportunity for objection to be made by local electors and residents and for inspection of the accounts and legal challenge. These provisions have been added to give the auditor a wider range of preventative powers and powers to seek judicial relief. Striking as these features are in the context of consumer voice, they should now be seen alongside the duty of local authorities to appoint 'monitoring officers' to act, basically, as whistle-blowers (Local Government Housing Act 1989, s. 5). The monitoring officer, who has to be provided with such staff, accommodation and other resources as he or she considers sufficient by the authority, is under a duty to prepare a report if it at any time appears to him that any proposal, decision or omission by the authority, etc., has given rise to or is likely to or would give rise to:

> a contravention by the authority, by any committee, sub-committee or officer of the authority or by any such joint committee of any enactment or rule of law or code of practice made or approved by or under any enactment; or

> any such maladministration or injustice as is mentioned in Part III of the LGA 1974 or Scottish equivalent.

The report is made with respect to that proposal, decision or omission. The authority has to consider the report not more than twenty-one days after copies of the report are sent to members of the authority. The authority must also ensure that no steps are taken to give effect to any proposal or decision to which such a report relates until a specified time. The Local Government Act 1992 enacts promises contained in the *Citizens' Charter*, whereby the Audit Commission and the Scottish Accounts Commission will require by direction that local authorities publish information to facilitate performance comparison between authorities in any financial year. The commission may publicize at its discretion information relating to breaches of directions by authorities relating to publicity of its own information.

Informal settlement in the shadow of legislative provisions is then a common feature of local government administration. Interestingly, evidence reveals differences in attitude between departments and citizens and the avenue of complaint. Complainants, for instance, revealed no reluctance to use appeals where the appeal was to the minister or a tribunal, but showed a reluctance to use the courts – not surprisingly, given the potential cost involved. However, the council preferred the courts to other forms of outside appeal in the areas of housing, social services and environmental health. Only education departments voiced a preference for an appeal/complaint to the minister rather than the courts. As Leak (1986, p. 13) rather neatly expressed it, legal remedies were rarely used against the council, but were often sought by the council. In his 1986 report, David Widdicombe QC suggested a role for the CLA in supporting challenges to the courts by individuals whose specified complaints were against an authority. This was not taken up by the government. In those areas where there are active law centres, legal challenge may be more common (e.g. under section 99 of the Public Health Act 1936). Furthermore, a prevailing ethos inimical of individual rights may attempt to discourage legal challenge. This may be described as protecting the 'public interest' by the authority, but it can appear heavy-handed and oppressive, especially in the absence of responsive and effective grievance procedures. In fact, we would argue very strongly that the absence of such procedures has made local authorities easy prey to the consumerist ideology of the government; in the period since the Second World War, too little has been done by authorities to build up local goodwill by involving the public in decisions affecting their future.

THE MEMBER

It has frequently been pointed out that the elected member in local government differs from his counterpart in Westminster in that the former plays an integral role in policy formulation and an essential role in service delivery. Clearly, the reality of local politics today, particularly urban politics, is that business is controlled by an inner caucus of heavyweights as advised by the chief executive and his office. The LGHA 1989 attempted to deal with what the government considered to be abuse of a dominant position by a majority party(ies). MPs have a higher profile than councillors, and many MP's post-bags contain a good amount of correspondence concerning local government, especially where they are 'non-routine cases with no obvious haven' (Rawlings, 1990, p. 40).

Despite widespread delegation of responsibilities to officers since 1972, members are still actively involved in operational decisions, in some cases too much so. The ombudsman has criticized a housing authority where there was too much member involvement in allocational decisions. These sometimes seemed to be based on caprice and whim (Inv 88/A/2329).

Widdicombe (1986, p. 127) did not believe that it was 'practicable or desirable' to leave councillors out of management decisions; it was reasonable that councillors 'should be able to ensure that policies are implemented'. A distinction was drawn between general management policy and day-to-day management intervention. Too much day-to-day intervention could alter the character of councillors making them 'full time administrators rather than people who are representative of the local community which they serve' (ibid.).

Widdicombe found that a councillor spent on average 74 hours each month on council business – 13 hours being spent on constituency business, i.e. electors' problems, surgeries and pressure groups (Widdicombe, 1986, Vol. II, p. 42). Interestingly, Labour and Liberal councillors tended to spend more time on electors' problems than did Conservative ones. Seneviratne (1991, p. 295) found that the role of councillors is sometimes resented by officers:

Although most authorities treat member complaints with particular care, and in some cases have special systems for dealing with such complaints (e.g. members' correspondence to the Chief Executive having special headed paper and arriving via a members' secretariat) giving them special weight, this does not of itself guarantee special treatment. Some officers have complained that member complaints are little more than councillors trying to get around their own policies, and they resent the fact that applicants may receive an earlier response, for example, just because s/he has involved a councillor. Leak (1986) found antagonistic attitudes towards councillor inquiries (p. 260) and in particular there were criticisms of councillors pleading individual cases with officers, when it was as a result of council policy that funds were severely restricted.

In housing and social services, member interference was resented because it ran counter to the professionalism of officers. Widdicombe also noted this resentment among officers of 'more assertive' councillors, particularly between chairs of committees and chief officers (Widdicombe, 1986, Vol. I, p. 67). Widdicombe cited an example of one committee chair reading the chief officer's mail with him. As we have noted before, opposition members may be more likely to take up a complainant's cause to score political points, a feature that will not be lost on the ruling party – only 15 per cent of members are described as independent. A member's common law rights of access to information may be defeated where party political factors are present, forcing the member to invoke his or her less extensive statutory rights. Following Widdicombe, and a White Paper, the government legislated in the LGHA 1989 to remove what it considered to be abuses of dominant political and member power in local government (Birkinshaw, 1990, ch. 3).

As well as evidence of a reduced role for the majority of members in local government, there is evidence of a lack of enthusiasm among the public to resort to members to resolve grievances. Widdicombe found that in his sample only a third complained via a councillor (Widdicombe, 1986, Vol. III, p. 54). In the 1987 Sheffield study, only 27 per cent approached a councillor as opposed to 63 per cent who approached an officer. The study also found that where a department failed to give a satisfactory answer, only 15 per cent mentioned the councillor; 60 per cent mentioned an MP. There is a prevalent feeling that a councillor, especially one belonging to the majority party, is too closely associated with the very policies or administration which are being complained against. Indeed, members may be the very object of complaint, e.g. that they have broken the Code of Conduct for members on how to avoid conflicts of interest. Breaches of the code amount to maladministration. A new code was introduced in 1990. It is to be hoped that the position which Widdicombe found in 1986 is improved, viz. councillors were not as conscious of the code as they should be. Arrangements for induction training were 'patchy'. Unlike MPs, a register of members' interests is available for public inspection as a matter of law (Local Government and Housing Act 1989 s. 19).

The Sheffield study found that it was not the norm to have difficult complaints resolved by committees or sub-committees of members. This was felt to be surprising, as officers' decisions are often of a discretionary nature and ripe for reviewing internally. However, the study found that member involvement was important and useful when they operated as negotiators and conciliators. Some striking examples involved chairs discussing problems with planning officers and applicants, and in housing the chairs discussing such matters with housing letting officers. Seneviratne found that the role of members in dispute resolution can have two distinct aspects:

> Firstly, they can be used as a trigger, to alert the authority to the complaint . . . At the other end of the grievance chain, elected members could be involved in settling resistant disputes which had not been satisfactorily handled at officer level.
>
> (Seneviratne, 1991, p. 87)

However, drawing upon the Sheffield study, she noted that the latter would be a valid role for them:

> . . . as they ultimately have responsibility for the way the authority conducts its affairs, although . . . few authorities have procedures with this level of member involvement.
>
> (ibid.)

SHOULD THERE BE AUTHORITY-WIDE PROCEDURES?

We have long argued that there should be a complaints procedure at the authority level. We would envisage service departments dealing with complaints through officer intervention. We make some suggestions below.

Evidence has shown that it is rare for grievance procedures to exist at the authority level. A grievance at this stage is more likely to contain policy-relevant features for a particular service or for the authority at large. They could provide invaluable information for monitoring of performance and evaluation of service. Local authorities are not self-justifying entities. What was written about Next Steps agencies is equally applicable to local authorities:

> the performance of any operation will be measured not by how much money it spends or how many staff it employs, but how well it delivers the goods and the extent to which it meets the needs of the consumers for whom its services are provided.
>
> (Next Steps Initiative, 1990, ix para. 23)

We should remember that although there is a materialist aspect in insisting that citizens are consumers alone – one we would not go along with – there is a new world in which competition is an essential feature in the provision of service. In some cases, this might mean competition with private providers or indeed privatization. The Audit Commission has expressed this view in the following terms in its support of competition which calls for

'robust monitoring systems' to monitor public satisfaction 'both reactively, by monitoring complaints and proactively, by public opinion surveys' (AC,1989, p. 19).

(Cited in Seneviratne, 1991, p. 152)

The Sheffield study found that local authorities had a long way to go. Even though as long ago as 1978, and repeated in 1992 as we noted above, the CLA had written in its code that arrangements should be made to monitor inquiries and complaints to observe whether they collectively indicate 'trends which require changes of policy, or procedure' and there should be 'simple systems for recording complaints and queries other than those which can be fully and successfully dealt with on the spot'. However, although 59 per cent of housing departments claimed that they recorded complaints, only 14 per cent analysed them; in education, the figures were 39 and 9 per cent, respectively, and in social services 70 and 19 per cent, respectively. It was in social services that officers perceived the utility of formal complaints procedures for managerial efficiency more than in other departments (65 per cent), compared with housing (45 per cent), education (39 per cent) and planning (37 per cent).

Only a minority of authorities in the Sheffield study provided a statistical analysis of complaints, but there was some evidence that senior officers used complaints to review procedures, but only when particular issues came to their notice. In *Performance Review in Local Government: A Handbook for Auditors and Local Authorities* (1986b), the Audit Commission wrote that information for management, including that on complaints, should 'provide benefits which exceed the cost of providing it' (p. 7). It is encouraging to note, therefore, that the CLA has observed an increasing desire among authorities to study complaints to enhance performance, and authorities are increasingly inquiring about good practice (CLA, 1990, p. 30; and 1992).

At the authority-wide level, evidence of statistical analysis of complaints was even thinner. Without doubt, the existence of such a complaints procedure, and regular analysis of the complaints it deals with – which have not been resolved by departmental procedures, whether formally or informally processed – would indicate a corporate commitment to grievance redress and by involving the chief executive's office, somebody who was not involved with the service would assist in resolution.

To repeat some earlier points, an authority-wide procedure would improve effectiveness, viz. the greater realization of policy objectives by the provision of the right services. It would also have a role to play in improving efficiency: provision of a specified volume and quality of service with the lowest level of resources capable of meeting that specification (Institute of Local Government Studies, 1985, p. 59).

As long ago as 1977, we examined the role of executive ombudsmen (i.e. the 'in-house' variety) in US city administration. The Sheffield study conducted a detailed investigation of the complaints procedure operating from the Mayor's Office in Chicago. The study found that the system was difficult to better in terms of publicity. Complainants make their initial approach by telephone – 'one of the best known numbers in the city'. All queries and complaints are logged on to the computer and copies of the entry are printed out and sent to the appropriate department or organization and to the complainant. There is 'a rigorous system of progress chasing' and responses with explanations are usually received within ten working days. In terms of complainant satisfaction, the success rate was almost 100 per cent:

> The unit whose job is to resolve the [complaint] is part of a larger community liaison unit, which has a city wide function of consultation with citizen groups throughout the whole of Chicago . . . seven officers work on complaints, and they function on a territorial basis rather than specialising in particular service areas. They stay with the case until the end, and are, in effect, operating as personal ombudsmen for the complainant.
>
> (Seneviratne, 1991, p. 163)

A statistical analysis is maintained daily, monthly and annually. Each day, the computer is programmed to cross-tabulate automatically in the respective service areas and the electoral districts. By this process, defects in service delivery (e.g. street lighting and sewerage) have been highlighted. Complaints forms are divided into ward areas and have forty-one separate heads of complaint. Analyses are performed to identify trends for quality and systems control. The service, which also deals with complaints about the police, ambulance and fire services, and federal agencies, costs about £1 million a year to operate at 1986 prices.

What makes this practice so interesting is the Heseltine proposals for a mayoral office in English local government to be run by an official. At present, it is a common function of chief executives' offices to launch inquiries into service failure, to send for papers and to interview officers or otherwise to co-ordinate a complaint investigation – very often as a defence mechanism against an ombudsman investigation. In some authorities, the chief executive took the view that it would be wrong for him to interfere with a chief officer's decision. Where the chief executive's department has an officer to investigate complaints, it is not unknown for complainants to view them as their champion, or at least their defender against a bureaucratic department. Sheffield found that 56 per cent of authorities sampled had formal procedures in the chief executive's office to organize CLA responses and most of these used them for purely internal purposes. Only one-fifth made them publicly available. There was a strong feeling that chief executives saw themselves as neutral arbiters and it was not unknown for officers in departments to adopt less defensive postures in investigations where such a complaint existed. In some cases, members were involved, especially the leader of the council and the chair and deputy chair of the committee; in some cases, only the latter and then only to provide information. It was also noted how chaotic the file-keeping was in many authorities when CLA investigations were undertaken.

Only 45 per cent of authorities claimed to possess an authority-wide procedure for complaints; 34 per cent claimed to have a committee or sub-committee as the final link in the grievance chain. The study found these claims to be an over-estimate. And in some cases, not even chief officers realized that a procedure stated to exist existed. Sixty-one per cent of chief executives were in favour of a formal published grievance procedure, but only 3 per cent thought that they should be introduced by legislation. This antipathy to change introduced by statute was also repeated by service departments *vis-à-vis* departmental procedures; in fact, very few departments saw complaints procedures as aids to management efficiency. On the other hand, consumer bodies did view such procedures positively, not least because it would inform them how to complain. Knowledge of the correct procedure would assist them. Publicity for authority procedures that existed was thin: only 18 publicized them (less than one-seventh). Publicity for departmental procedures was as patchy. It is hoped that *Devising a Complaints System* (CLA, 1992) will help to improve matters.

In some authorities, there are executive ombudsmen known as complaints executive officers. The office has jurisdiction over all matters within the competence of the authority. He or she seeks a solution to the individual's problem, which may involve either a fuller explanation or an amended decision. Other examples included pre-printed, pre-paid postcards. It is forwarded on receipt to the appropriate department, and an acknowledgement is sent to the complainant. Complaints against other bodies are sent to those bodies. The Administrative Services Department (ASD) registers all complaints and files them according to wards for ward councillors to inspect. The complaints sub-committee of the ASD monitors complaints and it examines the progress, type and number of complaints in relation to wards. Ward councillors are provided with complaints lists, but there is very little feedback from complainants. It is probably fair to say that the procedure is not well suited to the more serious complaints.

In another authority, a complaints form was used; but there were misgivings about how difficult it was to get into the complaints system – it was only if successfully within the system that the form was presented. It was designed for the more serious complaint. The form is acknowledged within seven days and the complainant is given the name of the officer dealing with the matter. The administration department operates the scheme. Its follow-up provisions required improvement.

In another authority, once a complaint had progressed so far, it was taken up by the head of administration. There was one full-time and one part-time complaints officer. Where not settled by their intervention, it is lodged before the complaint sub-committee. The complainant, the chief officer and the referring councillor if there is one, are invited to attend. The chief legal officer submits a report with the views of the complainant and the chief officer of the department. The committee will either recommend a particular course of action or ask for an in-depth investigation. If the actions of an officer are criticized, the procedure may be suspended to allow disciplinary proceedings to commence. The procedure had met with the support of trade unions.

One serious problem emerging from the Sheffield study merits special attention. This concerns the lack of publicity for good procedures that existed and a reason why in other authorities procedures did not exist. If they were publicized or existed, the authorities claimed they would be swamped. Complaints procedures are useful as a means of obtaining management information. The

> . . . information is needed to see if the system is effective which presupposes a set of goals which are to be fulfilled. Thus, it is not sufficient to equate good administration with cost effectiveness in purely financial terms . . . some consumer input is needed also, to ensure that the goals themselves are adequate. An advantage of complaints procedures is that they give an opportunity to consider the subjective experience of consumers.
>
> (Seneviratne, 1991, p. 200)

Stages in a departmental procedure

The 1992 CLA guidance on complaints procedures split the usual steps of resolution into three parts; interestingly, this follows patterns which we have seen in authorities. The first step would see the service providers deal with complainants and attempt resolution. We have seen a variation on this, where a departmental officer who is independent of the department and answerable to children in care, as it happens, through the members, attempts a resolution. The second stage involves an approach to an identified complaints officer within the department. The outcome is reported to the complainant. In the specific example, it was formally registered with the director who appointed an officer unconnected with the case to investigate. If the complainant remained dissatisfied, the third stage involved outside review possibly by members. The existing procedure had at this stage a hearing before the relevant sub-committee and one independent person who is not an employee of the authority chosen by the chief executive and service chief. A strict time limit is imposed on this final stage.

HEALTH COMPLAINTS (we are indebted to Di Longley for
information on the following)

Under Health Circular 88 (37), formal complaints (i.e. those which are written or made orally as a complaint) which do not raise an issue of clinical judgment are referred to the relevant district health authority (DHA). This circular sets out directions by the secretary of state under Section 1 of the Hospital Complaints Act 1985. No method of enforcement for the Act is contained in the statute; presumably one would have to rely on judicial review. A senior officer will be designated by each DHA for each hospital or group of hospitals to deal with complaints. The processing will be carried out by a member of the unit general manager's staff. There is no uniformity in the occupational status of the officer dealing with complaints in the units or in DHAs. Longley believes that this may have an effect on the way complaints are dealt with, time devoted to, etc., and the use made of grievances for quality control. The guidelines themselves allow for flexibility and there is a wide variation in treatment.

None the less, the guidelines urge authorities to monitor complaints and arrangements for grievance resolution and quarterly summaries of complaints are submitted to the DHA, a committee of the DHA or specified members. Despite Department of Health encouragement, such monitoring that does take place is usually directed to checking the progress of individual complaints rather than system review. Complaints concerning clinical judgment are dealt with by a procedure contained in Health Circular (81)5. The consultant examines the clinical aspects of the complaint and advises the unit manager/DHA of any risk of litigation or non-clinical aspects. Where a complainant is dissatisfied, the matter is referred in writing to the regional medical officer (RMO). The RMO may arrange for a second opinion from an Independent Professional Review comprising two independent consultants. The complainant is informed by the district or unit manager of the outcome. Interestingly, although clinical judgment is not something that can be examined by the National Health Commissioner, the RMO's decision to refer or not is investigable.

Complaints about hospital services fall under three categories: environmental and support services, which includes 'hotel' and other facilities; care, which covers clinical and non-clinical items from medical, paramedical and non-medical staff; and organization, which includes general administration and the handling of complaints. Changes in the NHS have not only unleashed a large degree of grievance, they have also helped to promote up the agenda in DHAs and units the importance of effective mechanisms to redress grievances and to monitor them. However, not all authorities are taking the lead. Most DHAs have produced booklets, leaflets and notices on complaints mechanisms, as indeed they are required to do. However, Longley believes that an anti-complainant culture still persists among many professionals and 'only a small number of authorities provide any special leaflet or training for staff on how to handle complaints or where to refer patients so that matters can be dealt with appropriately' (Longley, 1992).

Most complaints are written but oral complaints are not refused. Complainants are asked to sign a record of the complaint – refusal should not delay investigation. Hospitals and units are encouraging staff to meet with and discuss complaints informally. While this is desirable, care should be taken to ensure that any valuable lessons to be learned from these complaints are not lost. Guidance suggests a resolution time of three weeks, although a significant number fail to meet this target. Patients now have access to health records, a factor which should assist the complainant, although the National Health Commissioner has criticized the poor quality of health records on several occasions.

Some DHAs and Trusts are establishing committees which regularly examine complaints files to identify areas for systematic improvement. Longley recommends the appointment of full-time complaints officers to act as a focal point for resolution and monitoring. It will be interesting to see how complaints relating to preferential treatment for fund holders (i.e. those general practices which budget according to their own fund, which they control) and those from other practices who are refused treatment are dealt with. Certainly the courts have made little contribution where treatment is refused because of inadequate funding.

The health authority will have a chance to deal with a complaint before it is referred to the HSC and complainants may be assisted by Community Health Councils (CHCs), although they cannot make complaints themselves. Complaints against Trusts are subject to the Hospital Complaints Procedure Act; some Trusts have expressed the view that DHAs should have no interest in the handling of such complaints. Longley has pointed out that the deputy HSC has taken the view that monitoring of complaints is a feature of quality assurance and contract negotiation 'and therefore an essential concern for DHAs'. Trusts, like DHAs, are subject to HSC investigation, but contractual matters are excluded. Trusts are, of course, central to NHS reorganization. There are plans for regional health authorities (RHAs) to monitor Trusts as agents of the secretary of state.

Complaints concerning family practitioners are dealt with by the relevant FHSA. The Department of Health issued extensive guidelines in April 1990 following regulation changes in 1990 [NHS (Service Committees and Tribunal) Amendment Regs]. These changes accompanied new service contracts for doctors. They are very detailed and comprehensive, seemingly affording little discretion to complaints officers for their operation. Complaints officers work exclusively on complaints procedures. There are formal and informal procedures, the latter involving a lay conciliator. FHSAs can only formally investigate alleged breaches of terms of service, which may include clinical judgment or other matters. Committees investigate when a formal complaint is made; they can only investigate a breach of contract, not a history of poor practice which falls short of that. Medical Service Committees have three lay and three professional members and a chair. They receive little or no training. An appeal by either party may be made to the secretary of state; responsibility for committees has been delegated to RHAs (see Chapter 6).

Longley speaks of the wide disparity of practice between FHSAs, despite stringent regulations and guidelines. She also believes the absence of a duty to monitor complaints may not endure, as FHSAs are required to oversee GP practices and as audit takes hold, especially under the influence of the *Citizens' Charter*. Furthermore, 'informal' procedures may be developing to deal with non-contractual complaints:

> Complaints Officers may see the resolution of such complaints as part of their job and steadily build up 'unofficial' ways of dealing with certain kinds of complaint with the district's contracted GPs.
>
> (Longley, 1992)

CONCLUSION

In his annual report for 1991, the Director-General of Fair Trading wrote that spending vast sums on advertising and marketing to attract customers was futile if effective complaints procedures were neglected. Many of the consumers of the bodies discussed in this chapter have no choice but to seek the services of those bodies. The comments of the Director-General are no less relevant for those consumers.

Throughout the agencies and bodies we have examined, we have seen a far greater awareness of the importance of complaints and an increased awareness in the importance of learning from complaints to enhance service and delivery of programmes. Writing in 1988, the Cabinet Office noted how

Most central and departmental training is concerned with operational procedures. Much less attention has been paid to training on service to the public. There is no Service-wide policy on training for service to the public, nor does the Civil Service College offer any specialised training.

(para. 3.5)

Performance measures related almost exclusively to departments' administrative programmes and not to standards of service to the public. This point is supported by the London Business School, which in October 1990 reported that executives in 53 companies already or about to be privatized rated customer service and quality as their lowest concern. Today, the target has shifted considerably. All the developments which we have discussed may be part of a successful con-trick on the way to privatization. We suspect that the publicity given to complaints procedures will effect a significant degree of consciousness raising. Our hope is that improved procedures will assist in raising questions about the kind of society we share. Certainly, some of the most searching of questions in the public/private interface concern the activities of the privatized utilities. By privatizing, the government has not unyoked itself from all responsibility for such industries. To this subject we now turn.

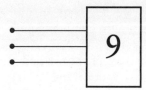

REGULATING UTILITIES AND SELF-REGULATION

The Conservative governments of the 1980s and 1990s viewed privatization as one of their great success stories – although, in this context, 'success' is a highly subjective concept. A large number of state-owned enterprises were sold off along with numerous interests which the government owned in publicly quoted companies. Billions of pounds were raised for the Exchequer, thereby helping to reduce the Public Sector Borrowing Requirement (PSBR) and lending support to the view of the late 1980s that public expenditure was under control. We must pass over the many controversial features of privatization *vis-à-vis* the wisdom of the policy, the pricing of assets and shares in the industries and the relationships between government and the industries after privatization. Our present attention will focus upon the redress of grievances against such industries.

The industries were sold off as monopolies, in some cases without any effective competition. Government desire to make the industries attractive to individual investors led to benign systems of regulation in which, as we shall see, the subject of effective procedures to redress grievances was initially given very little thought. As we write, there are signs that things are changing and government has had to bow to political pressure to take redress and effective standard-setting more seriously. A series of alterations to the operations of the industries by way of licence amendments and codes of practice culminated in changes in the statutory framework in 1992 with the Competition and Service (Utilities) Act (CASU). Furthermore, the point is made with increasing stridency that some of the regulators are adopting an over-confrontational role while not conducting their own duties with an appropriate degree of openness (Veljanovski, 1993).

It has to be said that the industries before they were privatized had an unenviable record from the perspective of consumer redress and government interference. Redress was catered for by a series of consumer consultative committees which operated, though not in every case, locally, regionally and nationally. Details of these bodies can be found elsewhere (Birkinshaw 1985a, ch. 4; Prosser, 1986), although we should note that in the case of rail travel and the Post Office which, though destined for privatization, are still in public ownership, such committees still exist. The procedures for such bodies were cumbersome and convoluted; there was confusion as to their powers, which in any event were very modest, and they were not taken seriously by the industries which had a very bad record in providing information to the committees. Needless to say, such provision was not embraced by legal duties, but by voluntary practices. While some committees made a contribution to grievance redress, their influence on policy was minimal; nor was there any evidence that experience from complaint handling was used systematically by the committees in policy discussions. In the case of existing transport users' committees, the economic case for closing a passenger line is not within the statutory terms of reference of the inquiry into the proposal, though they may be included on a discretionary basis.

As Graham and Prosser (1991, p. 231) have indicated, there was a pronounced feeling that given an effective regime of regulation, the consumer interest would *ipso facto* be satisfactorily provided for. The emphasis was placed upon establishing, in the absence of competition, a suitable pricing formula which would encourage efficiency and, once the licence had been awarded, it would be enforced by the regulator and modified by statutory procedures involving the Monopolies and Mergers Commission and 'notice and comment' opportunities for public contributions. The formulas appear to be relatively straightforward, but they have become extremely complex. The first major utility privatization, that of British Telecommunications (BT), had no separate body to deal with consumer complaints, and we shall examine its regime in a moment. The National Consumer Council (NCC) put up a spirited case for the existence of a special consumer body to help consumers with their complaints and also to press upon the regulator the case for policy changes to benefit consumers, the strength of which would be built upon their experience in complaint handling. Furthermore, without such a body, the regulator would be reliant upon the industry for vital information; a consumer body would at least provide an additional source of information (NCC, 1989, pp. 85–8). They argued additionally that a body representing the consumer interest had to be 'independent of the regulator' (ibid., p. 87). This view was not shared by the government and was not incorporated in the legislation privatizing BT and establishing the Director-General of Telecommunications who heads the Office of Telecommunications (OFTEL). However, although the details differ for gas, electricity and for water regulation, separate consumer bodies were established alongside the regulators. To these we now direct our attention.

TELECOMMUNICATIONS

Under the Telecommunications Act 1984, OFTEL is the grievance remedial body for consumers as well as being the regulator. There are in addition a variety of advisory bodies representing the consumer interest which are established by the Director-General of Telecommunications (DGT). These bodies cover such subject areas as small businesses and the disabled at a national level (i.e. England and Wales); there are also local bodies in various cities. The local bodies deal with complaints – they are in fact the former Post Office Users' National Councils (POUNCs) – although they are not given executive powers. Rather, they are recognized by the secretary of state as representing the consumer interest. They are not empowered to publish their own reports – OFTEL publishes them with its own report – and they have no right of access to information, although the DGT has such power. The Telecommunications Act 1984 in fact repealed s. 9 British Telecommunications Act 1981 under which POUNCs had to be consulted before major changes in supply services were introduced. The other bodies will doubtless operate in an informal capacity in complaint handling when advising the DGT on their respective topics. The DGT will expect BT and the advisory bodies to attempt resolution before he is approached by consumers; they will be effectively screening bodies. An independent arbitration scheme exists with an upper jurisdictional limit and OFTEL and BT review its operation every five years. BT has also promised to have teams of staff in all districts whose sole job will be the investigation of complaints. From 1992, this was a legal requirement.

Following a deterioration in its service in 1987, quality of service became a central issue for OFTEL and it insisted that BT publish more information on its performance. BT publishes six-monthly reports on quality of service and OFTEL publishes an annual report. The two bodies conduct joint surveys on the directory enquiry service and public call-boxes. OFTEL also carries out its own surveys with the help of the local committees: these cover fault repair service and other items (Graham and Prosser, 1991, p. 234).

The two authors are complimentary on the amount of information about BT's quality of service that has been made public as a result of OFTEL's efforts. The most important changes they cite are the changes in BT's contract terms. The DGT had criticized these because they recognized 'few rights for the customer as regards such important items as fault-repair performance; they avoid giving customers a firm date for provision of new service; and they give BT the right to act high-handedly on such matters as changing customers' numbers' (HC 432, 1987–88, para. 1.10). BT agreed, after discussion, to incorporate within its contracts with consumers 'a fixed daily penalty for failure to provide service'. Itemized telephone bills were also introduced. It should be noted that OFTEL has no direct power over the content of the contract; the licence only provides that BT consult with OFTEL on its code of practice for consumer affairs – which is not legally binding – and this has to be consistent with the contract.

The licences issued to telecommunications service providers contain a range of conditions. OFTEL has to ensure these are observed. OFTEL can issue an order where it discovers a breach of condition. These may be provisional or final; the latter require consultation and a period of twenty-eight days in which to object and a further twenty-eight days before confirmation. The DGT can only go to court for breaches of licence conditions where an order has been issued; an aggrieved customer has a right to sue for breaches of an order. Until the order is made, licence holders can breach the conditions with impunity. Under some circumstances, OFTEL can recommend to the secretary of state that BT's licence be revoked; the dramatic consequences following such an act show how hollow the threat is. Enforcement provisions are contained in some licence conditions and may be enforced informally. References can be made to the Monopolies and Mergers Commission (MMC) by the DGT; in fact, a new price formula was achieved by OFTEL without referring the issue to the MMC.

OFTEL possesses the power to modify a licence after it has been issued, but only with the agreement of the licence holder – an obvious incentive to 'deal'. If a modification is required without such consent, a reference must be made to the MMC. The MMC may recommend that the public interest requires a licence modification. The DGT has 'reasonably wide and powerful access to information' in the possession of the operating companies (NCC, 1989, p. 39). The DGT, however, has to know what to ask for. 'In an industry as complex as telecommunications, the problem of knowing what to ask for and/or knowing that certain information exists can itself be a significant barrier to getting information' (ibid.). When it comes to the information that it publishes, it can publish information about the industry except where publication 'would seriously and prejudicially affect the interests of individuals and organisations'. Contrariwise, its *duties* to publish information on the industry to inform the public are very limited (see CASU, *infra*). Notice and comment provisions apply when licences are issued and modified. 'How informed consumers are to be will depend greatly on how the DG interprets his role' (ibid., pp. 40–41). The NCC point out that OFTEL is a very small body compared with the organization it regulates; its budget is about twice the amount of BT's audit costs. 'Although it has tried to develop independent sources, OFTEL has, of necessity, to get most of the information it needs from the industry itself' (ibid., p. 51).

Writing in 1989, the NCC described OFTEL's formal powers as weak. However, it observed that OFTEL had exercised its political powers of regulation with skill in advancing the cause of the consumer. In particular:

> OFTEL has used the threat of future, formal, regulation to gain control (or at least considerable influence) over areas that appear to be outside its formal power. This has made it much more powerful than a purely legalistic interpretation of the act and licence would suggest. Whether this can be sustained over time remains to be seen.
>
> (NCC, 1989, p. 53)

As we shall soon see, increased legal powers followed the *Citizens' Charter* and the 1992 CASU. The decision of the DGT to revoke the code of conduct of the Chatline service of BT and Mercury, thereby forcing their cessation and the decision to investigate BT's *Yellow Pages* service, showed a vigorous approach by the DGT.

GAS

British Gas (BG) was privatized in 1986. It constitutes a monopoly and consumers have no real opportunity to signal their preferences through purchasing choice as they would in a competitive market. The captive nature of domestic gas consumers places them in a very weak position *vis-à-vis* BG. Along with electricity and water, although the position is 'stronger' in gas, and unlike telecommunications, separate bodies were established to deal with consumer grievances. OFGAS is the regulatory authority for BG and the Gas Consumer Council (GCC), whose members are appointed by the secretary of state, is under a duty to investigate complaints concerning gas supply and acts as an adviser to the secretary of state. It has members from each gas region and regional offices in all regions. OFGAS' duty is to ensure that BG complies with its duties under the Gas Act and its Authorization Code. OFGAS is concerned with the supply of gas up to and including the meter. At the point where gas passes to the appliances, any complaints then arising fall within the jurisdiction of the GCC. However, meter tampering and theft are the concern of OFGAS, while cases of disconnection and gas services are the province of the GCC.

> Unfortunately, this division of tasks leaves an unsatisfactory void with relation to standards of service. Theoretically, they fall outside OFGAS' jurisdiction, while the GCC is powerless to force BG to adopt standards of service.
>
> (NCC, 1991a, p. 43)

The GCC's exclusive responsibility is the consumer, but it lacks any power to negotiate with BG. OFGAS, on the contrary, enforces the legislation from two perspectives: the interests of the consumer and the interests of BG. It sees its role as one of 'referee' between the two – a difficult task as the interests of profit maximization by BG and those of lower cost and enhanced service are often not complementary, though as we noted in Chapter 3, there is no reason why efficiency and justice should be incompatible.

The general responsibilities of the Director-General of Gas (DGG) are contained in Section 4 of the Gas Act and include:

- ensuring a gas supply to satisfy all reasonable demands;
- ensuring that suppliers are able to finance their supply operations;
- promote efficiency and economy in the supply of gas through pipes as well as the efficient use of gas supplied;
- protect the public from the dangers of gas transmission;
- facilitation of effective competition in the supply of gas through pipes in excess of 25,000 therms of gas (see CASU, *infra*); this excluded competition in gas supply in the tariff (domestic) market but is subject to change.

Under Section 4(2)(*a*), OFGAS is under a duty to:

> . . . protect the interests of consumers of gas supplied through pipe lines in respect of prices charged and other terms of supply, the continuity of supply and the quality of gas supply services provided.

Other duties of the DGG relate to his collection and publication of information and his interaction with the secretary of state. Under Section 34, the DGG is required to give advice and assistance to the secretary of state or the Director-General of Fair Trading (DGFT) where requested. The DGG arranges to publish information and advice to tariff customers as he considers appropriate. Examples include *OFGAS: Protecting the Rights of the Consumer* and *New Maximum Price for the Resale of Gas*. The DGG can also request information from DG for any investigatory exercise he sees fit to undertake. There has been resistance to such requests although the DGG can seek a court order obliging BG to hand over the information requested (s. 38; and see CASU, *infra*). The DGG is under a duty to produce a variety of annual reports.

The quality of service provided by British Gas has been a cloudy area, although as we shall indicate, CASU will make a significant difference here. No defined standard was set out in the 1986 Act or in the Authorization, although guidelines governing quality and safety are set out in the Act in Sections 16 and 18 (e.g. periodic testing of gas supplied through pipes). Codes of practice cover service to elderly and disabled customers and, since 1989, procedures covering debt disconnection have been incorporated into the Authorization. Both OFGAS and the GCC have attempted to persuade BG to set official standards for all its customers. In OFGAS's 1988 Annual

Report, it asked BG to set standards in three ways: present clear offers of service to the tariff market; set relevant targets relating to the offer: monitor performance against targets. By 1989, the DGG noted that BG had done none of these things.

The Commons Energy Committee in 1985–86 stressed the need for rigorous control of standards of service to prevent the industry evading them to meet efficiency targets or to increase profits. The committee further suggested that because of BG's monopoly, the GCC 'should be given legislative authority in order to safeguard consumer interests on matters such as safety, installation, servicing and repair, appliance quality and performance' (section 5.2 of the Report). This was not accepted by the government and the GCC were given investigatory powers, while OFGAS was given all the legislative power. However, these latter powers did not cover servicing, repair, appliance quality and performance. Pressure from both the GCC and OFGAS caused BG to undertake a nationwide survey of customer complaints; the campaign was known as 'Banishing Gripes', which might say something about BG's perception of the exercise. Two million customers out of seventeen million circulated responded to a questionnaire. In 1990, BG published a booklet entitled *Banishing Gripes*. A customer relations manager (CRM) has been established by BG in each region. The booklet contains a standard of service and there is a compensation scheme for customers disadvantaged through a failure to provide the stated standard of service. OFGAS, the GCC and BG will be monitoring performance against standards.

Although the booklet was produced after consultation, BG's commitment to its customers fell 'far short of expectations' (NCC, 1991a, p. 22). The GCC in particular was disappointed that the document only provided loose guidance rather than 'setting . . . more precise targets that could be monitored, and tell customers exactly what the company will do if things go wrong' (GCC Press Release, 25 April 1990). The NCC felt that many of the commitments were 'vague and non-committal'; for example, if a particular time was asked for 'we will do our best to come at that particular time' (ibid., p. 23). Although CRMs could settle claims up to £5000, there were no published criteria against which a customer was entitled to compensation. 'Appropriate compensation' was left to the discretion of the CRM.

Codes have also been drawn up following consultation with OFGAS and the GCC on *Commitment To Our Older or Disabled Customers* and a variety of information booklets have been produced. In fact, the GCC played a central role in highlighting the purely reactive role adopted by BG in assisting older and disabled customers; when contacted, BG's record was good but too often it did little to inform customers of their special assistance for these groups. Furthermore, the code contained some glaring discrepancies between treatment for the two groups. For instance, in the autumn and winter months, elderly people will not be disconnected; this safeguard does not apply to the disabled. By late 1991, it was still unclear whether the disabled would be given the same protection.

We have already observed the role of the two bodies in grievance redress. The GCC has a duty to investigate matters referred to it, especially in cases where BG is not breaking the law but causing consumers difficulty. These include arrangements for paying off arrears, the amount of deposit demanded or maintenance of gas appliances. A complaint alleging a breach of BG's duty to supply gas, however, is an enforcement matter for OFGAS. OFGAS' enforcement powers only arise when there has been a breach of an obligation set out in the Act or its Authorization. Its powers are not formally operative until a disconnection, although informally it would contact BG before disconnection where notified. OFGAS can make, as in the case of OFTEL, provisional or final orders where it has been notified in writing of a breach of BG's statutory duty to supply. Where there is non-compliance with a confirmed provisional order or a final order, it may be enforced through the courts and damages are payable to a customer on application. BG has resisted orders. In practice, the NCC believe that the legal position concerning a customer's right to damages is unclear where there is an alleged breach of statutory duty (NCC, 1991a, p. 27).

Before looking specifically at the GCC, one glaring example will bring out the weaknesses from a consumer's perspective in having grievance redress split between two bodies. In October 1990, BG changed its gas prices for all commercial and industrial users (i.e. contract customers). The outcome was a sharp rise in the number of complaints from such users to OFGAS (complaints from non-tariff customers do not go to the GCC). Following the DGG's intervention, BG lowered the price of gas for these customers. The contract market accounts for about 19 per cent of the market for BG (1989–90), serving 20,000 customers. The tariff market accounts for about 57 per cent of the market, serving 17 million customers.

> Nevertheless while the price increases in the contract market inspired a flood of complaints to OFGAS and consequently a reaction by the DG which prompted BG to lower their original price increases, the second price increase for domestic customers in September 1990 did not provoke any complaints to OFGAS, because domestic consumers complain through the GCC and the DG's comments were limited to reviewing the price increase in OFGAS' review of the Gas Tariff Formula. The result is that the price increase for domestic customers was implemented without any resistance or serious analysis. Whether it is the case or not, the impression is one of the industry lobby carrying much more weight in the regulator's realm of judgement than the domestic consumer interest.
>
> (NCC, 1991a, pp. 52–3)

The GCC threatened to refer the case to the DGFT, but in the event elected not to. Again, in April 1991, BG altered its price charges in the tariff market with the effect that domestic users faced an increase while business users received a reduction in cost. The GCC issued a press announcement attacking the new prices but felt constrained to do no more, awaiting OFGAS' response to the tariff formula review. This was, in fact, OFGAS' response to the September 1990 price increase. The increases for domestic users have, therefore, 'remained largely unchallenged by both the GCC and OFGAS' (NCC, 1991a, p. 58). The NCC called for 'partisan' representation for the domestic user, otherwise the industry interest will always take precedence. The respective roles of the GCC and OFGAS in this area are unclear. The fault lies with the Gas Act and the government for not delineating the respective roles of the two bodies.

Gas Consumer Council

The GCC was set up in 1986 and replaced the National and Regional Consumer Councils. A council of twenty members is appointed by the secretary of state. Twelve of these are salaried. In October 1991, there were eighty-one staff, sixty-eight of whom were divided among the twelve regional offices. The GCC has the following responsibilities:

- To investigate any matter relating to the supply of gas through pipes and to settle representations made to the GCC by various parties [s. 32(2)(b)].
- To refer all potential enforcement matters to OFGAS or to the DGFT where appropriate (ss. 31 and 32).
- To advise the Director-General of OFGAS on matters referred to the GCC by the DGG or matters on which the GCC considers it should offer advice, or on tariff matters where the DGG's powers may be applicable (s. 40).
- To investigate any matter which relates:
  - to the design, manufacture, importation or supply of gas fittings;
  - to the installation, maintenance or inspection of gas fittings;
  - to the use, or anything connected with the use of gas supplied to customers, or gas fittings [s. 33(2)].
- To send a copy of a report on any of the above, as appropriate, to the DGFT or anyone who will take an interest [s. 33(3)].
- To make an annual report to the secretary of state and to publish this.

Responsibility for gas disconnections (e.g. for non-payment of bills) is not specifically referred to in the Act, but is included within section 32(2). These are monitored carefully by the regional GCCs. A code of practice, a Joint Statement of Intent and Condition 12A of BG's licence provide limited protection for the consumer against disconnections. The GCC uncovered what the NCC (1991a) described as 'sharp practices' in some regions. CASU contains a duty to provide a grievance procedure for disconnections.

The GCC's work comprises two major parts: dealing with consumer complaints that come in through the twelve regional offices and campaigning for improved services on behalf of the consumer. The latter work is conducted through research and policy work in London. In the year ending March 1991, £26,000 was spent on research and policy work (NCC, 1991a, p. 55). This represents 1 per cent of their budget.

The GCC becomes involved in complaint redress when consumers have been unable to obtain satisfactory redress against BG, and BG is expected to possess satisfactory complaints mechanisms now as a matter of law. OFGAS negotiates on their behalf. In 1989, the GCC – through all twelve regions – dealt with 94,000 enquiries and complaints, a 15 per cent decline on 1988. In 1989, the GCC registered 21,178 complaints about BG's services to its customers; this represented a 23 per cent decline on 1988. The main areas of complaint were: accounts, marketing and related complaints, appliances, installation difficulties and fuel debt problems. Billing was the most common complaint with over 6247 complaints. There are variations in the trend of complaints in the regions causing the NCC to suggest that although BG has only one policy on consumer service, that policy seems to be interpreted differently at regional level while also allowing for variations in income and weather. About 16,600 enquiries were made on how to make a complaint itself. The fact that many complaints concerned BG's billing and accounting practices has led the GCC to press BG into a common standard of clarity in its billing procedures throughout the regions. The figures for 1990 show that there were 27,296 complaints (the vast majority against BG) and 75,405 enquiries and 1991 showed a 5.3 per cent increase on these figures. Complaints take the form of category A (those which have initially been taken up with BG) and category B (those which have come directly to the GCC). In the latter case, the complainant is usually advised to approach BG or the company concerned. A

> . . . record of the complaints and enquiries which the GCC receives is fed into a database. The information is reviewed monthly and analysed in detail every four months. This process enables the GCC to keep in touch with the situation of consumers across the country and thus to respond to any significant trends which investigative research uncovers and, where appropriate, to make referrals to OFGAS and/or direct discussions with BG.
>
> (NCC, 1991a, p. 56)

Each regional office has its own computer system and each office can search its database to highlight regional problems, both on cleared and outstanding cases (GCC, 1991, p. 8). The system has been modified and can monitor BG's Standards of Service and the level of service provided by BG staff. This latter records comments received from consumers noting how BG staff dealt with particular cases. The GCC stated that it was very disappointed with BG's Code *Commitment To Our Customers*, observing that it said very little about how BG would deal with customer complaints. In its research, the GCC has highlighted a somewhat bland approach by BG in response to requests, for succinct standards of service and performance targets. Similarly, the GCC asked that the 'mentally confused' as well as the elderly and disabled be entitled to a free gas safety check. BG refused, as their Authorization allowed them to. BG also omitted a GCC recommendation that temporary alternative appliances be supplied where delay was causing hardship, especially to vulnerable groups. This is practised at a *discretionary* level in some regions. In other words, BG his been resistant to transparent standards and enhanced consumer protection.

The seriousness with which the GCC is taken may be gauged from the fact that despite a very comprehensive report on energy efficiency to the Commons Energy Committee, a code of practice on the subject was produced by OFGAS and BG without 'any obvious formal input' from the GCC. Energy efficiency is closely connected with fuel poverty, argue the NCC, and the GCC should have taken a clearer role in the preparation of the code.

The conventional view of regulation is that technical expert analysis provides correct answers. Regulation, however, is a broad-ranging and quasi-political activity and the outcomes of decision-making are a compromise between interested parties whose ability to articulate their views most convincingly will determine the final outcome of decisions. Consumer groups are not sufficiently represented in this scheme if they are not given the resources to fulfil their role adequately.

(NCC, 1991a, p. 60)

Breaches of rules of conduct or operation in the Act are matters for the GCC; alterations to rules causing hardship are for OFGAS. It was deemed inappropriate for both tasks to be within one body; consumer representation must be partisan, whereas regulation must be carried out in the public interest. OFGAS must examine the wider context and act impartially; however, in fulfilling its investigatory and information gathering role to act as consumer watch-dog, the GCC's powers are inadequate, or what amounts to the same thing, it is inadequately resourced. In revising condition 12A of the Authorization – which concerns disconnections – the GCC worked closely with OFGAS and BG to achieve improvement. However, 'Energy efficiency and domestic gas prices are examples of where this has not happened' (NCC, 1991a, p. 61). We shall examine the impact of CASU on targets and compensation shortly. There are, however, problems within BG that legislation cannot attend to; while BG assured the NCC that the contents of the code of practice on the elderly and disabled were well known by their staff, a random check by RADAR revealed that in eight showrooms only one gave accurate information. Furthermore, 'commercial sensitivity' has been used by BG as a reason for suppressing information on consumer affairs (e.g. on testing of meter accuracy and monitoring of disconnection procedures by OFGAS and GCC). The procedures are monitored on a random basis to ensure compliance in each region. Basically, where contact has been made by a consumer with BG, they will not be disconnected forthwith from the gas supply. Disconnections have in fact been a source of judicial reversal for the DGG when on a judicial review he was found to have acted unfairly in not allowing the consumers an adequate opportunity to rebut allegations of meter tampering (*R v DG Gas Supply ex p Smith (1989 1 July) Lexis*). Another judicial review concerned the role of OFGAS and its negotiations with BG and two companies to reduce prices. Other companies who did not benefit objected (OFGAS, 1992).

ELECTRICITY

Both the secretary of state and the Director-General of Electricity (DGE) possess regulatory powers and responsibilities for the industry. The licences were issued by the secretary of state; new licences may be granted by the DGE under a general authority from the former. Their general powers and responsibilities will be dealt with below. The Office of Electricity Regulation (OFFER) has its HQ in Birmingham and its Scottish HQ in Glasgow. It has regional offices. By December 1990, almost 200 staff were in post. Regional offices, with on average nine posts, are responsible for handling consumer complaints, monitoring the policy and performance of local Regional Electricity Companies (RECs) and supporting the work of the regional consumers' committee.

The electricity industry was subject to a massive restructuring operation for privatization, although domestic consumers are still dealing with a local monopoly supplier. Gas may be an alternative for heating requirements, but for many purposes electricity is the only source of energy. The industry was divided up into four main functions: (1) generation, which is performed by three companies, one of which, Nuclear Electric, owns nuclear stations and alone remains in public ownership; (2) transmission (through the national grid); (3) distribution, i.e. transfer of electricity from the national grid and its delivery, via local distribution systems to the consumer; (4) supply, viz. the purchase of electricity from the generators via the 'pool' and its sale to consumers. The National Grid Company is responsible for transmission and is owned through a holding company by the twelve RECs. RECs undertake distribution. In Scotland, the industry is vertically integrated, unlike England, and the two companies have separate licences for these functions.

The RECs took over the role of the former Area Electricity Boards (AEBs). They serve the same areas as the AEBs, but unlike the AEBs they are required to operate their distribution and supply businesses as separate concerns, although supply is dependent upon the distribution system from the grid supply points to consumer delivery points at lower voltage. Distribution accounts for the majority of REC profits; the distribution business levies charges on the supply business and these are reflected in the supply price formula. The vast majority of electricity consumers are connected to the distribution system of a REC and are presented with no choice. Electricity is bought and sold by a REC through its supply business. The 'franchise market' covers all domestic consumers. Most users in the franchise market are supplied on fixed tariffs which are controlled by a set price formula.

From 1 April 1990, competition exists for customers using in excess of the franchise market level of electricity – this level will be reduced to 100 kW from 31 March 1994. Such users can purchase electricity from other RECs or from a generating company. The government hopes that the whole of the supply market will be opened up to competition by March 1998; it remains extremely doubtful that domestic consumers will have a real choice over their supplier.

RECs are governed by the Electricity Act 1989 and by the public electricity supply licences issued to RECs by the secretary of state. A Director-General of Electricity Supply regulates electricity operators according to the Act and licences. The Act provides for the following duties and powers on the suppliers: a general duty to develop and maintain an efficient, co-ordinated and economic system of electricity supply; to provide on request a supply of electricity; a power to recover charges according to a tariff; to request deposits (disputes concerning these are referred to the DGE for determination); to disconnect after giving notice where all due charges have not been made; to supply an appropriate meter. The secretary of state has the power to make regulations for supply and safety.

The bulk of the regulatory system is contained in the licence conditions. These deal with such matters as charge restrictions, tariffs, prohibition of cross-subsidy and discrimination in prices and terms of supply, rights of tariff customers and codes of practice, and elderly and disabled customers. Worthy of special attention are the conditions obliging RECs to achieve overall performance standards as determined by the DGE; requiring RECs to establish procedures for handling complaints after consulting the consumers' committee and which have to be approved by the DGE; and that requiring RECs to provide the DGE with any information he considers necessary for the purpose of performing his duties.

As with other privatized utilities, licence conditions may be modified by agreement between the RECs and OFFER or after a reference to the MMC. The secretary of state has a veto over any modification by agreement. Any part of a licence may be referred to the MMC by the DGE to examine whether it operates against the public interest. Modifications can be made where the MMC believes this to be the case. RECs may also be referred under the Fair Trading Act 1973 on a monopoly or merger and under the Competition Act 1980.

Prices for the domestic supply of electricity are contained in an overall price cap contained in the formula RPI $= X + Y + K$, which is to last until 1 April 1994. In crude terms, RPI constitutes the change in the cost of living between two dates set twelve months apart; X is an efficiency factor initially set at 0, though a figure would be set once there was detailed assessment of the potential scope for efficiency savings; K is a correction factor to miscalculations in RECs' forecasting of demand and costs; Y is a 'cost pass-through factor' comprising electricity purchase costs, fossil fuel levies and distribution charges paid to RECs' own distribution companies. A central component for setting the price of electricity is the 'pool' arrangement controlled by the Pool Executive and the National Grid Company (NGC). Pool prices are set by a computer which matches supply with demand. The DGE has observer status on the Pool Executive Committee and OFFER has encouraged publication of pool prices and has asked the NGC and the Pool Executive to publish as much information as possible as is consistent with commercial confidentiality. This seems particularly tame given the monopoly position of the actors involved. In December 1991, following complaints from industrial customers, the DGE published a highly critical report of the two privatized generating companies who had manipulated the system to fix prices.

In a statement of 18 December 1991, the DGE announced new outline measures to promote greater energy efficiency. The main proposal is for an energy efficiency factor to be built into the industry's price control formula as in the case of gas. It has been suggested in some quarters that performance standards should be set promoting more efficiency.

Performance standards have been introduced by statutory instrument (SI 1991 1344) after prolonged consultation with consumer representative bodies and suppliers. Specific performance standards are effective from 1 July 1991 and these are the same for each company with one or two exceptions. Customers are entitled to compensation where standards are not met. Companies must provide the DGE annually with information on the number of cases in which compensation was paid for each standard as well as the total amount of those payments. Information is also required on the overall performance standards. The DGE publishes information on suppliers' performance standards 'in such form and in such manner as he considers appropriate'. Individual standards, known as guaranteed standards, and sums specified for breach cover, *inter alia*: restoring supplies after faults; notice of interruption to supply; providing a supply and a meter; voltage complaints; meter problems; charges and payment problems; appointments. Disputes on these topics are referred to the DGE by either the company or the customer. It can be determined by the DGE or referred to a relevant consumer committee (*infra*).

Guaranteed standards do not cover the maximum period of interruption to supply, variations in voltage or the frequency of transient variations. In a press release in May 1990, the DGE implied that the standards were unequivocal and comprehensive. However, a supplier can still be exempt from the requirements to meet a particular performance level where it was not reasonably practicable because of a variety of external factors; in other words, the risk is thrown on to the consumer. The DGE did not accept the entreaties of the NCC who wanted strict liability placed on the suppliers. As the NCC said:

> The company is in a much better position than individual customers to evaluate these risks and probabilities, to design the optimum security of supply, and to obtain insurance against these risks if necessary.
>
> (NCC, 1991b, p. 20)

Furthermore, some claims have to be made within one month, not three months as the NCC suggested, leaving them to believe that the industry had prevailed upon the DGE. Again, some payments can only be made after a written claim. It must also be said that the levels of payment are disappointingly low and are unlikely to act as an incentive to the company to achieve the targets set and enhance efficiency.

As well as the guaranteed standards, there are overall standards for eight key indicators. These include items such as: supply reconnection; voltage faults; connections; reconnections after debt payment; meter reading; responses to customers (response should be made to written complaints and enquiries within ten working days). The DGE has written to the chairmen of the RECs stating that their failure to meet these standards may result in him invoking his enforcement powers to ensure their businesses 'are conducted in a manner best calculated to achieve these standards'. Information on the performance of RECs is published each year and is used by the DGE to monitor performance and to make comparisons between RECs to enable consumers to be informed on their REC's efficiency. Standards on appointments will be changed after one year and not three as in the case of other standards. Consumer bodies have asked for specific appointment times to be set.

The DGE is under a duty to investigate complaints. He has encouraged complainants to approach the REC first (and note CASU, *infra*). Where this proves unsuccessful, they may contact OFFER, usually through one of its regional offices, which are listed on the back of electricity bills. In nearly

3000 cases between April and December 1990, the REC was asked by OFFER to respond directly to the complainant keeping OFFER informed. Formal complaints dealt with by OFFER follow a practice whereby OFFER enquires of the consumer and the REC to establish the facts. Its policy is to disclose all information given to it by each party to the other side. As is common elsewhere, a full explanation is all that is required for a friendly settlement. Where a complaint cannot be resolved by either of these means, it is referred to a consumers committee operating locally. The DGE may also have to consider using his enforcement powers.

In the same period as above, OFFER and consumer committees dealt with 10,567 complaints and responded to a further 3397 enquiries about the RECs' services. Nearly half of the complaints concerned disputed accounts or imminent disconnection because of failure to settle a bill. OFFER's recording system is to record a complaint once it has been resolved. Its system is being refined and will be supported by a new computer database, which will help it to identify problem areas and facilitate comparisons in its efficiency studies. Too frequently, OFFER noted in its 1990 report, consumers are not given adequate responses by RECs and OFFER initially rejected codes of practice drafted by the RECs on complaining because of insufficient guidance; they were subsequently approved. As with gas, there are discrepancies between the treatment of the elderly and the disabled, with the disabled being given inadequate protection in the code of guidance.

For customers on income support, Fuel Direct allows the electricity payment to be deducted from a claimant's benefit before payment and sent directly to the supplier by the DSS and is based upon the supplier's estimate of consumption. Companies are required to prepare codes on payment; as of October 1991, only a handful had been prepared. RECs have to offer pre-payment meters to customers who are having difficulties paying their bills so long as safe and practical to do so. The total number of electricity disconnections for non-payment in 1990 was 55,000, down from 100,000 in 1986. There were 21,000 gas disconnections in 1990. The RECs are required to prepare codes of practice on payment of bills. Progress on these codes was dilatory, to say the least, even though Condition 18 of the licence only specifies minimum criteria by way of guidance. For example, Yorkshire's code is user-friendly compared with most of the other draft codes, but even here it stipulates that the elderly will only be disconnected in colder months where they can afford to pay the bills. We are not aware of how this will be ascertained.

Under Condition 19, the RECs are under a duty to establish methods to deal with and ascertain those who 'can't pay' as opposed to those who 'won't pay'. The RECs are not under any obligation to publish the methods they adopt under the condition. Condition 19 is virtually identical to Condition 12A of BG's Authorization and similar criticisms have been made of it (*supra*). It only applies to the 'can't pay' category. The NCC, drawing on Condition H of the Instrument of Appointment of water undertakers, wanted to place the burden of making contact with non-payers on the RECs and to prevent disconnection in 'vulnerable' cases. In the case of water, disconnection cannot be obtained without a court order. The former Electricity Consumer Council found that most customers facing disconnection were in genuine hardship and that any contact between the company and the consumer was 'extremely limited and inadequately recorded' (ECC, 1989).

The DGE has the power to require a licence holder to provide him with information where it appears that a licence condition is being contravened. Compliance with duties in conditions may be enforced by the DGE by provisional and final (or confirmed provisional) orders. Opportunities for representations from the company must be afforded in the case of final and confirmed provisional orders. Provisional orders lapse after three months. Disputes may be resolved by the DGE on a 'determination order'; this order, which is binding on both parties, does not apply to disputes over disconnection of supply or recovery of charges which are enforcement matters and for which provision is now made in CASU (*infra*).

The DGE has to approve various codes of practice which have to be drawn up under the Conditions. Consumers committees must be consulted on the draft codes. The NCC has voiced serious concern about these exercises and the conduct of the regulator. Informally, the NCC and other consumer groups in the Public Utilities Access Forum heard that OFFER was considering draft codes. Only the consumers committees (CC) were statutorily entitled to be consulted, but the Forum was concerned, quite properly, that its members were not being consulted and the newly formed CCs were only being given three months to provide their comments. OFFER acquiesced and allowed a meeting with Forum members who were extremely critical of the drafts. Although eventually the DGE rejected the drafts as inadequate, the NCC was left with an element of disquiet:

. . . it is unfortunate that the process of negotiations between the consumer organisations and OFFER had left the consumer bodies with worries concerning the adequacy and transparency of OFFER's handling of the matter.

(NCC, 1991b, 42)

Guidelines on good practice drawn up by OFFER for the RECs were not placed in the public domain, nor by October 1991 had they been shown to the NCC. Furthermore, OFFER seems to want to place 'minimum information requirements' on the RECs in the monitoring of the codes and a great deal of responsibility will be placed on the CCs. The approach of OFFER to monitoring has been described as 'laid back'; it is placing great reliance upon the CCs. These may well lack adequate resources for these tasks and further reliance upon advice agencies will place a burden upon bodies who invariably are inadequately resourced and networked to obtain reliable and probative information.

The chairs and members of CCs are appointed by the DGE. There are fourteen CCs for England, Wales and Scotland. Each is required to have between ten and twenty members. They are appointed on an individual basis, not as representatives of organizations. They employ no staff and their secretary is a staff member of OFFER in the region, usually the senior complaints handler. There is no national consumer representative body as with the Gas Consumer Council. Under section 53, there is a National Consumers' Consultative Committee. Its role is very limited and it comprises the chairs of the CCs under the DGE and it meets on four occasions each year. It keeps under review issues affecting consumers and facilitates the flow of information between the DGE and the chairs and members of CCs.

The CCs have a variety of general duties, including advising the DGE. The most important role is in complaint handling – a role which they share with OFFER. The CCs investigate 'relevant matters'. These are subjects which are not enforcement issues, i.e. alleged breaches of obligations under the Act and licence conditions. The splitting up of responsibility for complaint handling, although as we discussed earlier it may well be necessary given the regulator's duty to protect the public interest, nevertheless can create considerable confusion in the minds of complainants if the division is not explained in rational and comprehensible terms. It is not sufficient to state, as an OFFER leaflet does, that their regional office will investigate complaints and if they remain unresolved, they may be considered by the CC. Nor is it adequate to declare that OFFER and the CC have wide responsibilities for complaint investigation. This framework is not conducive to a better understanding by consumers of their rights. We have already spoken of the problems facing CCs in their monitoring role over RECs.

The CCs have also expressed concern over price rises announced in April 1991. The CCs have no role in price rises as they are a matter of regulation for the DGE. The NCC highlights a real problem:

> . . . the CCs do not appear to have been successful in their efforts to obtain information from OFFER concerning the validity of the price increases. OFFER was reluctant to share this information on grounds of commercial confidentiality, while the RECs considered that they are only under a duty to supply it to OFFER.
>
> (NCC, 1991b, p. 49)

The committees are under the Public Bodies (Admission to Meetings) Act 1960; this means the public may be excluded where a confidential item is to be taken. The courts have given wide leeway to chairs to exclude the public and, indeed, the NCC has found it extremely difficult to obtain routine papers from CCs, having finally to invoke the assistance of the DGE.

To conclude, the NCC has described the system for consumer representation in the electricity market as 'grossly unsatisfactory' (NCC, 1991b, p. 52). There is no independent national representative body. Regional CCs are appointed by the regulator, serviced by OFFER and have only one salaried member and no proper resources to carry out research. They represent potentially conflicting interests, viz. commercial and domestic users, and advise the DGE on competition policy. Indeed, the regulator has itself faced judicial review when it was criticized by an amalgam of unions and major energy users for not investigating contracts between gas power stations and RECs which were unnecessarily forcing up the price of electricity (*Guardian* 8 August 1992).

WATER

We do not intend to deal with the water industry at such length as gas and electricity. Under the Water Act 1989, thirty-nine companies were 'appointed' to supply the necessary water and sewerage services in England and Wales. These companies are local monopolies. Mergers are investigated by the MMC and this has taken place on several occasions. Section 30 of the Water Act allows the MMC to judge mergers of water enterprises on, *inter alia*, the grounds of whether the merger will adversely affect the Director-General of Water Supply's (DGW) ability to make comparisons on efficiency between water companies. Responsibility for regulating pollution was transferred from the water authorities to the National Rivers Authority (NRA). The Act and licences set out the regulatory scheme and the duties of the companies. Prices are controlled by a formula RPI + K (a factor to represent significant investment programmes) and charges must avoid undue discrimination and preference. The DGW, who heads OFWAT, seeks to act as a surrogate for the market, principally by making comparative studies of performance using the example of the best to encourage the others. A periodic review of K must take place after ten years; it can take place after five years. The reviews involve setting efficiency targets in the light of the results of the most recent comparative studies and reviewing the targets for standards of service.

Customer Service Committees (CSCs) champion the interests of the consumer and a CSC Chairmen's Group meets with the DGW on a regular basis. OFWAT has also commissioned surveys on public opinion to obtain information on what the public wants and expects from the water industry. The CSCs dealt with 4633 complaints in 1990. OFWAT reported that complaints doubled between 1990 and 1991.

Reference was made above to the fact that customers receive protection from disconnection, but in 1990–91 900,000 customers were served with county court summonses for non-payment of bills – this entails an additional £30 payment by the customer. In his 1990 Report, the DGW was critical of companies practices and indicated the wide disparity of treatment of customers: 'The next stage is to identify essential features of good practice in this area and to issue guidelines to companies' (OFWAT, 1991, p. 33). The DGW seems to have learnt from the criticism of OFGAS and OFFER indicating that the guidelines will cover:

- the availability of arrangements for paying bills which recognize the budgetry needs of low income families;
- the provision of clear information and advice to customers about any help the company can give and the consequences of failure by the customer to contact the company or pay the bill;
- the steps companies should take to make contact with customers to avoid disconnection;
- training staff in debt counselling and help from outside agencies.

OFWAT has developed rolling reporting cycles for monitoring and the licences require independent certification. Efficient and effective regulation rests upon reliable information. Under the terms of their licences, companies are required to provide information on a specified series of 'levels of service indicators' of which there are eight: (1) raw water availability; (2) pressure of water mains; (3) interruptions to water supplies; (4) hose-pipe restrictions; (5) flooding incidents from sewers; (6) response to billing enquiries, which identifies the banded response time for meaningful response times to customers' enquiries; (7) response to written complaints, which identifies the banded response time for meaningful response times to customers' written complaints; and (8) response to development control consultations, which identifies the banded response time for responses to development control consultations.

The returns identify details and numbers and the DGW will use them to provide comparative information on companies' performances. The DGW is quick to draw a distinction between levels of service indicators and performance measures: 'Only by considering levels of service improvement over time, and in combination with other financial and physical information, will meaningful comparison between companies be possible.' Reports on levels of service by companies will be compulsory for 1990–91 data. In 1991, reporting requirements also included operating costs, capital efficiency and water quality and leakage. The DGW publishes 'Dear Managing Director' letters, setting out his guidelines to directors on a range of topics. Comparative competition should cover the whole area of customer care, the DGW believes: 'how well for instance, companies explain their services, deal with complaints and develop new ways of meeting customers' wants' (Byatt, 1990, p. 16).

The CSCs have statutory duties and are independent of the companies. There are ten such committees. They deal in policy issues and pursue customer complaints, the more intractable of which are referred to the DGW. The DGW has been sensitive to criticisms that the CSCs are too small and few in number to provide adequate coverage of the companies' activities. His response was not entirely convincing, pointing out that members represent all consumers (domestic and non-domestic) and not any constituency, that they must not own shares in companies and OFWAT provides them with a small secretariat. Their meetings are open to the public.

Their reports to the DGW are published. They have examined company investment programmes and, from complaints of customers, they will be advising companies on customers' priorities. They examined tariff proposals for 1991–92 and considered company codes of practice. The CSCs have discussed a wide range of subjects concerning customers. The DGW chairs regular meetings of the CSC chairs and this helps to 'shape OFWAT policy'. The annual reports of the CSCs show that companies have a long way to go in developing a customer awareness culture.

Most complaints are handled by the CSCs; only a few concerning alleged breaches of statutory duty are dealt with by the DGW. As with gas, the companies are given the opportunity to respond to complaints. Those coming direct to OFWAT are passed on to the company where it is clear there has been no approach to the company and they are expected to reply (and see CASU, *infra*). If the customer is not satisfied with the response, it is referred to a CSC. In the year 1990–91, 4633 complaints were received; 1833 were dealt with by the DGW and the CSCs and 1279 were referred to and resolved by the companies. There is considerable variation in the numbers of complaints coming from the regions. Complaints from customers have helped to identify a number of general issues that require examination and consideration at a national level, such as payment of compensation for service failures and the costs of optional meter installation. A guaranteed standards scheme whereby claims could be made for up to £5 for failures was introduced by statutory instrument in 1989 (SI No. 1159). The amount is paltry for what may be serious interruptions to service and disputes can be referred to the DGW. Altogether, 140,000 leaflets explaining the complaints procedure have been printed and yet in 1990–91 only 880 claims were made and OFWAT stated that only 13 per cent of customers were aware of its existence despite the fact that 90,000 written complaints were made to companies. The low figure for claims may be accounted for by the fact that claims must be in writing. The DGW observed that by May 1992 none of the companies had extended the scheme voluntarily. He therefore issued proposals for new compensation arrangements and a new code of practice and higher standards.

There was evidence that some companies were reluctant to accept without prevarication the decision of the DGW or CSC. To help with the improvement of customer services, codes of practice have been developed under conditions G, H and I of the licences covering customer relations and company obligations, difficulties with payment of bills, and the proper steps to follow to avoid disconnection – although we should note that water disconnections increased by 177 per cent in 1991 to 21,286. A third code covers leakages. 'None of the submitted customer or disconnection codes was sufficiently well written, complete and accurate to meet the basic requirements of conditions G and H.' They were only approved after modifications were provided by OFWAT. The CSCs have suggested additional information that should be contained in bills, etc. OFWAT is conducting a user survey to assess customer priorities and expectations and to use the results in its policy formulation.

Surprisingly, a code of practice on services for the disabled and elderly was not provided for. OFWAT's own survey on the services for these groups found them to be 'disappointing'. Even after prompting by OFWAT, too many companies were complacent, expecting the customer to find out what was provided. The DGW planned to issue his own guidelines after consultations with disability organizations and the companies; the CSCs were not referred to.

COMPETITION AND SERVICE (UTILITIES) ACT 1992 (CASU)

The government explained that the Act would strengthen the various DGs providing them with powers already exercisable by the DGE and additional powers. The DGW and DGT will be given power to set compulsory standards of service to be achieved in individual cases (and in relation to certain customers in the case of gas) and to determine compensation where those standards are not met. However, these empowering provisions may carry important exemptions and in the case of gas suppliers may differentiate in standards. Disputes over individual standards are to be determined by order of the DG or his appointee when referred to the DGs. Regulations for standards will be made after consultation with those affected and 'after arranging for such research as the DG considers appropriate' to discover the views of customers. Both DGs are empowered to set standards of overall performance 'from time to time' – again after similar research and consultation. These are standards which, in the opinion of the DGs, ought to be achieved. The DGG has power to set standards relating to the promotion of the efficient use of gas by consumers and obliges the supplier to inform the customers of those standards and of its level of performance in meeting them. In telecommunications, compliance with standards will be enforced as for a licence condition. In gas, there is a legal duty upon suppliers to conduct business to achieve the standards. Standards may be revised in line with the Electricity Act ss. 39 and 40 (they are prescribed by regulations) for gas and telecommunications. Compensation will be payable for failure to meet individual standards, as is presently the case with water and electricity. The Act requires that customers be informed of the operation of individual standards albeit in somewhat anaemic terms and adds that all private utilities must provide information to customers about overall standards at least once in a twelve-month period. Information shall be collected by the DGs on compensation made by gas, telecommunications and water companies regarding breaches of individual standards and levels of overall service achieved by them in 'relevant services', and companies must provide this information or face prosecution. The DGs are under a duty to publish information collected by them relating to those companies' performance 'at least once a year'. Confidential, especially commercially confidential information is exempted.

All utilities will have to establish customer complaints procedures. There will in effect be a three-tier system: company complaints procedure, consumer committees (the position of BT should be recalled) and DGs. A complaints procedure must be established by the relevant company and has to be approved by the relevant DG. Provision is made for the usual form of consultation in devising such procedures and publicity (i.e. it is limited to consumer committees or is completely discretionary) and the procedure has to be sent to anyone requesting a copy. The procedure, or the manner in which it operates, may be modified by order of the DG, but in this case the consultation provisions do not apply. In the case of both gas and telecommunications, the DG is empowered to determine disputes about terms of supply and, apropos of the latter those concerning charges (including discrimination) for services and deposits. Likewise, all DGs may be given power by regulation to determine disputes over the accuracy of bills. All customers will be protected in their utility supply pending a resolution of their dispute with a company, although there are variations. For instance, water may only be disconnected after a court order is obtained. With electricity and telecommunications, there must be a genuine dispute about charges to prevent disconnection – the direction of the DG is not required except in the case of a new supply in the former, whereas in gas the DG may direct new or continued supply pending resolution of a dispute. Certain enforcement powers of the DGG are enhanced and section 18 provides for preliminary investigations by the GCC into any matter referred to it and which appears to it to be a matter which may be referred to the DGG relating to the determination of disputes, standards of performance in individual cases or regulations made in respect of billing disputes. Where after the preliminary investigation the customer remains dissatisfied, BG will refer the complaint to OFGAS. The DGs are given express powers to demand information in settling disputes (e.g. para. 2, Schedule I CASU). The Act provides for the giving of reasons by the DGs or arbitrators for orders determining disputes and for consultation in the making of regulations on billing disputes or settling criteria for deposits.

Many of the details in the Act have to be filled in by regulations, and as of writing it is not clear whether existing practices in BT or BG on performance standards which have been agreed voluntarily (see above) will be amended significantly.

The point has been made by the *Financial Times* (11 November 1991) that entrusting these powers to the regulators was not a desirable reform, as the handling of disputes – the ombudsman role – did not sit easily with the 'quasi-judicial' duties involved in regulation. The Council on Tribunals has made a similar point which does not appear to have received a satisfactory response (see pp. 100–1 and HC Debs. Vol. 201, col. 1174; see also Justice Committee, 1976). In the latter task, the regulator determines the industries' pricing formula in the light of information on its rate of profit return and the need to promote greater efficiency and competition. Into these judgments, he can build quality criteria and specify non-financial targets such as energy saving. But to confuse the roles of ombudsman and regulator 'could reinvent the sorts of conflicts which bedevilled ministers responsible for nationalised industries; the goal of better services was all too frequently obscured by the desire to minimise politically contentious price rises'. Indeed, the correspondent suggested that in regulatory hearings where complaint redress was not at issue, formal representation and examination of interested parties – consumers, both individual and corporate – could take place in public. The Act does raise questions about the decision-making processes of regulators and their transparency and their own accountability. We agree that increasing the transparency of regulation should be placed high on the political agenda. Information which the regulator uses and the criteria he adopts should be publicly available, especially so when the subject of regulation is powerful state-created monopolies. Also worthy of consideration would be: annual reports and examination of the reports of DGs by parliamentary select committees; fixed-term and non-renewable appointments for DGs; and decennial, or quinquennial, fundamental scrutiny of each industry by the MMC.

Part Two of the Act deals with competition in the water, sewerage and gas industries. Regarding gas, the secretary of state may reduce or remove the threshold of 25,000 terms per annum in the Gas Act up to which suppliers have a statutory monopoly of supply and above which a supplier may offer gas on contract rather than tariff terms. In other words, it increases the possibility of competition in the commercial and even domestic market. This threshold featured in the OFT investigation into British Gas when contract customers complained about the price of gas.

SELF-REGULATION AND CODES OF PRACTICE

The Office of Fair Trading (OFT) has played a pivotal role in regulating the marketplace both with a view to maintaining competition and protecting the position of the consumer. In the area of utilities, the DGFT may exercise powers concurrently, or in consultation, with the other regulatory agencies; on certain matters, only the OFT has competence (e.g. BG's contract market). The major responsibilities of the DGFT under competition law involve detection of the existence and operation of monopolies, reporting to the secretary of state on proposed mergers, policing the market for anti-competitive practices and for restrictive practices, and advising the secretary of state on competition policy. He stands between companies and self-regulatory bodies such as the City Panel on Takeovers operating its own code on the one hand, and the Monopolies and Mergers Commission (MMC), the Restrictive Practices Court (RPC), the Secretary of State and DG IV of the European Commission, which polices European markets, on the other. Much of the OFT's work is taken up by negotiating agreements or undertakings with commercial bodies whereby formal references, or recommendations for references, to the MMC or RPC, or consequential ministerial orders may be avoided. In relation to mergers, this process has been facilitated by legal changes effective from 1990. The Financial Services Act 1986 (FSA) places a variety of advisory duties upon the DGFT and under the Broadcasting Act 1990 he examines the networking arrangements made by Channel Three licensees and their implications for competition. The licensees may *appeal* to the MMC. The DGFT also has to ensure a sufficient percentage of independent production of programmes for BBC television. A great deal of the information which the DGFT relies upon comes from individual complaints, which is also largely true for the DTI's Companies Investigations Branch which investigates allegations of fraud, breaches of company law and other criminal corporate offences (Guardian, 21 December 1988).

The OFT's main responsibilities under consumer affairs include:

1 *Regulatory*: credit licensing and taking warning or enforcement action against businesses that cause difficulties for consumers including under the Control of Misleading Advertisement Regulations.
2 *Consumer policy*: proposing changes and amendments to the law where consumer interests are being harmed.
3 *Information*: giving consumers information and advice they need. The DGFT's efforts are concentrated on those situations where consumers are least able to look after themselves, e.g. by targeting on those most in need through careful marketing and research.

The DGFT has encouraged trade associations under Section 124 (3) of the Fair Trading Act 1973 (FTA) to prepare codes of practice for their members which provide guidance in safeguarding and promoting the interests of consumers in the UK. The codes are voluntary and do not set legal standards. They cannot be enforced against non-members and are difficult to enforce against members. By 1991, twenty-nine codes had been produced, twenty-five with arbitration schemes. The codes have sought, *inter alia*, to make a certain level of transparency mandatory where information is obscure because it is incomplete or because the consumer is swamped by it. However, one of the most significant developments in this area was effected not by codes but by regulations under the Consumer Credit Act 1989. Where a code is agreed by a trade association, the DGFT may, paradoxically, have to seek the permission of the secretary of state not to take it to court under the Restrictive Trade Practices Act – no such permission has ever been refused. A detailed code of advertising practice exists which is enforced by the Advertising Standards Authority – a self-regulatory body – and it is the DGFT's duty to support and reinforce such a code under the regulations. A code of practice exists for misleading price indications which the OFT has a role in monitoring.

A great deal of the information, and many of the complaints which lead to action being taken by the DGFT, come in via Trading Standards and Consumer Protection Departments of local authorities (their relationship is well networked), Environmental Health Departments, CAB and other advisory bodies. In his 1990 annual report, the DGFT noted that 700,000 individual complaints were recorded in the report (OFT, 1991a, p. 14). The successful operation of Part III FTA, under which the DGFT can ask traders who have persistently disregarded obligations under criminal or civil law in a manner which is detrimental to consumers to give assurances about future good conduct, has largely depended upon such information. Court orders may be sought by the DGFT where assurances are not forthcoming or are broken. The DGFT has recommended that the available power should be augmented to cover misleading, deceptive or unconscionable practices with a power to issue cautions and take action in the civil courts.

The DGFT has been active in promoting the benefits of Alternative Dispute Resolution which we looked at in Chapter 2. The emphasis upon codes, effective and fair self-regulation and effective redress of grievance should not blind us to the fact that the OFT's role in consumer protection is really a strategic one and the:

> Office is neither a price commission, nor some sort of super consumer advice centre able to sort out individual problems. Our efforts therefore are largely concerned with *preventing* problems and *improving* the trading environment.
>
> (OFT, 1991a, p. 18)

As we have shown elsewhere (Birkinshaw *et al.*, 1990), self-regulation can take a variety of forms. It can mean at one extreme self-government; it may take the form of self-regulation without any statutory constraint; or it may mean self-regulation under a statutory umbrella. In this last form, the regulation is usually carried out by a domestic body approved by government but whose rule books or codes of practice are supervised by government within the context of a loose, discretionary, statutory framework. These may be supported by 'Statements of Principle' as under the amended FSA [s. 47A(3)]. It can be seen that the DGFT has a crucial role in self-regulatory schemes; under the FSA as we saw, the DGFT advises on the implications for competition of the rule books of bodies seeking recognition as self-regulatory organizations, investment exchanges and clearing houses. The DGFT advises similarly on rule variations and the operation of the rules by these bodies which regulate their particular markets. The regulators are market professionals. Likewise, under the Courts and Legal Services Act 1990, the DGFT advises on the rules concerning rights of audience and the conduct of litigation drafted by the professional bodies regulating solicitors and barristers, viz. the Law Society and the General Council of the Bar. In both these cases, independent ombudsmen to deal with consumer or client complaints had to be introduced as part of the package of reform.

Self-regulatory schemes were not adopted for the privatized utilities. They are regulated by regulatory agencies, although as that name might suggest, this does not involve detailed regulation through statutory provisions controlling the rate of return of the utilities as in the USA. In the UK, as we saw above, the government opted for a 'light-touch' form of regulation which sought to shape and influence standards of service, practices and efficiency through a pricing formula, which was subject to variation, and through the development and approval of codes of practice by the industries. As we saw, legislation was required to give more satisfactory protection to consumers.

Codes of practice

'Soft Law' or 'Reflexive Law' theory has been in the ascendant since the mid-1970s in providing explanations for the role of law in the contemporary state. As state institutions are no longer able to implement policy programmes themselves, the state promotes instead what is known as regulated autonomy. Groups at an intermediate level between the individual and the state are responsible for regulating their own affairs, the state's role being to oversee the design and functioning of their self-regulatory systems and relationships between themselves. Or, as in the case of SROs under the Financial Services Act, a statutory duty may exist to provide adequate arrangements and resources for the effective monitoring and enforcement of compliance with their rules concerning investment business. The basic theme of reflexive law is that public accountability of such systems can be sufficiently ensured by 'external' organization and monitoring of the 'internal' procedures by which groups carry out delegated public policy functions. As we have pointed out, the concerns of the existing literature seem to neglect the constitutional dimension.

We would not wish, on the other hand, to be thought to be adopting a position which suggested that regulated autonomy and negotiated regulation are antinomian *per se*. Much of the legitimacy of the outcome depends upon the level of transparency and openness adopted in the decision-making process and the degree of public access to that process in terms of participation opportunities, information provision and investigation.

Codes of practice are a substitute for legislation or statutory regulations and arguments supporting codes state that legislation frequently only sets minimum standards and cannot supply the detailed content of general policies in specialized areas. Legislation which requires constant updating will clog up the legislature or impose rationality overload on government. Legislation is costly to enforce, especially where it seeks to regulate vastly differing industrial and organizational practices. Legislation may not draw sufficiently on those who have expertise in a particular area and so on. Advocates for self-regulation press the case that codes have none of these disadvantages. Furthermore, bodies such as the National Consumer Council have claimed that self-regulatory arrangements have enhanced standards and have given consumers protection beyond the law itself. They refer to the Advertising Standards Authority and the Code of Advertising Practice. The OFT encourages trade associations to include conciliation and arbitration provisions (NCC, 1986, p. 1). Non-OFT codes contain arbitration schemes, e.g. those of professional groups, some nationalized and privatized industries and the National Housebuilding Council. Other advantages of OFT codes have included prohibition of contractual limitation or exclusion clauses. Ombudsmen within self-regulatory bodies, such as insurance and banking, have also been praised by the NCC, although in the latter case there was a stinging report from the DGFT in 1991 on anti-competitive practices towards small businesses by banks.

The NCC was clear, at least in those areas where protection of the consumer was paramount, that the starting point for determining the nature of the institutional arrangements for self-regulation must be the policy objectives in intervening in the marketplace. What is being sought will determine the detailed arrangements. The need and rationale for intervention in the market should be clearly thought out and the rules which are going to be imposed must first be identified as objectives. 'There may be bargaining and negotiation about the balance between regulation and self regulation, but that should follow after the optimum objectives have been set down' (NCC, 1986, pp. 15–16). The NCC said that the scheme should be based on clear statements of principle and standards, preferably a code. Further desiderata for the accountability of self-regulatory bodies included:

- The scheme should command public confidence and ideally be linked to a form of public approval procedure; this might involve in some cases oversight by a regulatory agency.
- There should be strong external involvement in the design and operation of the scheme.
- So far as is practicable, the operation and control of the scheme should be separate from the managers of the industries.
- Consumers and outsiders should be fully represented on the governing bodies of self-regulatory schemes.
- There should be clear, accessible and well-publicized complaints procedures where breach of the code is alleged.
- There should be adequate sanctions for non-compliance.
- The scheme should be updated and modified in the light of changed circumstances and expectations.
- There should be a high degree of publicity for its operations, preferably an annual report (NCC, 1986). This happens with both banking and insurance ombudsmen schemes.

Codes often worked best where they were given legislative support, even if the mandatory requirements remained vague and general. However, the strong 'ideal world' feel to the NCC framework can be gauged from the fact that the document itself identifies five categories of codes on a 'mode of adoption' spectrum. These cover a wide range: from those where there has been no consultation with outside bodies in their production; those codes where there has been such discussion and possibly outside participation in the operation of the scheme; those drawn up under the FTA 1973 and approved by the DGFT; those given statutory status outside the FTA (e.g. various professional codes and those under the Insurance Brokers Act 1977). An interesting variation here would include the provisions covering arbitration of disputes between BT and customers which do not involve complicated points of law. The provisions are derived from a requirement in BT's licence awarded under statute. The last group comprises those codes which flesh out broad statutory duties and are drawn up by either a government department or a non-departmental body. Examples here include those drawn up by the Health and Safety Executive under the Health and Safety at Work Act 1974.

However, the NCC found that arbitration schemes in codes, for instance, are rarely used either because there was little publicity about them or there was a lack of sufficient confidence in them by consumers (NCC, 1991c, p. 4). Some codes are well-publicized, e.g. that of ABTA. Further, the voluntary nature of OFT-approved codes means that they cannot be enforced against the recalcitrant. In a case involving the Consumer Credit Trade Association arbitration scheme, when a consumer tried to invoke it, the member firm in question refused to comply leading to its expulsion. Then, of course, the problem is augmented as the unscrupulous are less likely to subscribe to the values inherent in a code. The NCC also found that many consumers found conciliation a 'waste of time' (ibid., p. 26). The OFT has also supported 'documents only' hearings for arbitration, although most claimants would have preferred a personal element, i.e. oral presentation (OFT, 1991c, p. 54). In other cases, criticism was made of the rules under which schemes operate; with BT the scheme is mainly concerned with applying BT's standard contract, but the scheme cannot be used to challenge the terms of that contract, even though OFTEL considered some of the terms unreasonable (NCC, 1991c, p. 56). The NCC also proposed that the informal discussions between arbitrators on the operation of the schemes should be put on a formal basis and that there should be annual reports on the work of arbitration under codes as in the case of the banking, insurance and building societies ombudsmen. The OFT should also take a far more active role in monitoring how codes' redress procedures are operating. In reviewing codes, it should evaluate 'how far the redress procedure provides accessible, quick, cheap and fair solutions to consumers' problems' (ibid., p. 62). It is deflating to report, however, that the NCC noted so many qualifications about the operation of arbitration schemes in codes, that it recommended that all schemes advise consumers of their rights to go to court as well as arbitration (cf. Consumer Arbitration Agreements Act 1988). This view was endorsed by the OFT (1991b, p. 9) despite the manifest failure of the courts in the field of consumer protection. Having said that, it is interesting to read the details of the EC draft Directive on Unfair Contract Terms which appears to allow class actions to be brought by representative bodies in courts to test the validity of contract terms.

The OFT agreed that more publicity should be provided about the operation of arbitration schemes and an annual report, preferably by the Chartered Institute of Arbitrators, should be produced. There should be greater publicity for schemes and trade associations should consider joint action, especially where associations are small and operate in related areas (e.g. they should set up common facilities for dealing with consumers to advise them of conciliation and arbitration facilities and to operate common redress schemes which would both lower overheads and enable greater publicity to be given to the schemes). Serious thought should be given to the conciliation process being conducted by persons who were independent of the industries/trades concerned. It further recommended that there may be scope for a manual setting out of the details of the various redress schemes, possibly looseleaf or computerized. It had started to prepare more detailed advice for consumer advisers and it wanted to see further research on good practice on conciliation and arbitration. The OFT was considering the possibility of enabling 'suitable consumer organisations in the UK' to undertake legal action on behalf of consumers and, finally, it canvassed the possibility of the creation of a forum on consumer redress as an opinion former and consciousness raiser. This is all very agreeable but perhaps a little too anodyne.

CONCLUSION

In this chapter, we have addressed some of the difficulties posed for the citizen/consumer in the public/private divide. Privatization has not of itself fostered a climate of efficiency and competition, enhanced performance and service delivery. These will have to be achieved via increasingly appropriate regulation through 'independent' agencies, although ministers still retain powers of direction [e.g. Telecommunications Act 1984 s. 47(3); Gas Act 1986 s. 39(2); Electricity Act 1989 s. 96; Water Act 1989 s. 170] and intervention (Water Act 1989 ss. 131–3). The increased scope and extended nature of regulatory activities makes it vital that a body such as the Administrative Review Council (see Chapter 5) has the bodies discussed in this chapter and their activities within its remit so that justice systems operate effectively in the extended state. The regulators themselves require supervision, guidance and, if need be, control.

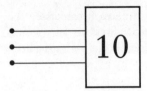

THE COURTS

Before we conclude, a few words must be devoted to the place of courts in our programme of reform. We do not personally belong to the school of thought which places courts at centre stage on all occasions for all purposes. In line with our approach throughout this book, our present task is to ask what is the optimum place for the courts when citizens complain. We are not primarily concerned with the existing technical weaknesses or problems affecting judicial review and, although we have a little to say about procedure, we only touch upon the procedural and substantive points which are either being investigated by the Law Commission or which are subject to widespread comment (Woolf, 1992, p. 221, Law Commission, 1993). Nor do we take on board the role of a constitutional court charged with the duties of interpreting a written constitution, although it will be pertinent to point out the pressures, usually from but not restricted to Europe, which make the continuation of our process of government under an unwritten constitution unlikely in the long term. What we offer in this brief chapter, and in too compressed a form, is a critique of the role of the courts in the structure of grievance redress; we offer some suggestions for fundamental change in procedure and organization, not simply incremental alterations to existing procedures.

However, a few salient features need to be mentioned. First, there is the widespread perception of the coming of age of public law in judicial as well as academic circles. Judicial review, that is the process by which judges keep powers exercised on behalf of the public within their allotted legal bounds, has expanded not only in quantity (in 1981 applications for leave for judicial review numbered 533; for the years 1989 and 1990, the number of applications was 1530 and 2129, respectively; it should be noted that 905 and 902 were allowed) but also qualitatively. What the latter refers to is the growing sophistication and subtlety of judicial review following the reform of Order 53 in 1977 and the elevation of those reforms to statute in 1981 (Section 31 Supreme Court Act 1981). Despite those reforms, we are still dogged by serious problems *vis-à-vis* judicial review – some practical, some intellectual. The intellectual problems concern the conflict over the public/private distinction – by this we refer to the debates over what are matters of public law and what are matters of private law. Latterly, the judges have opted for an expanded concept of the state, and thereby the 'public' for judicial review purposes while simultaneously limiting the breadth of the scope of the public law procedure by insisting that 'private' law items be brought under private law process even though the object of attack is a public body or a surrogate for the state. The fact that liability – that is, compensation for wrong – and, as a consequence of decisions of the House of Lords, judicial review are under different jurisdictions is messy and is not a happy or elegant compromise. It owes more to nineteenth-century ideology than to functional efficiency for today's state apparatus or convenience for the citizen. Nor is the provision allowing transfer from public law process to action as if begun by writ, nor indeed the informal and apparently unauthorized reversal of this procedure 'where a case has merit' (Woolf, 1990, p. 27), adequate to overcome these impediments to a fully developed system of public law.

The theoretical impoverishment in our approach to public liability is coming home with a vengeance. It is manifest in the absence of 'law' relating to the contracts of public bodies (Harden, 1992). There have been very significant developments in public procurement law under EC directives, but these address the pre-contractual position, not the question of performance. Liability under tort is governed by common law principles as is the whole question of restitution. The position of public bodies being sued by individuals, citizens or otherwise, is characterized by obfuscation and deviously complicated law; it is the result of fictionalizing a public actor as a possessor of public powers while acting as a private individual. Other systems are not without their difficulties, but at least they have addressed many of the central problems and have decided, as in the case of the French, to place the risk of public activity on the shoulders of the state or, in the case of the Americans, to provide what is still a wide 'sovereign immunity' from tortious liability for the actions of federal government (though not for contractual liability).

These are important issues, but they run parallel to our present preoccupation which is really concerned with the procedural framework within which our administrative justice operates. What we would personally endorse would be a procedure accommodating both review and liability in one application. The existing power to couple a request for damages to a review application is not adequate and rarely successful. Subject to what we say below, applications which concern review will not be accompanied by detailed pleadings, that is written specifications and details of the allegations or case; we make proposals which, if implemented, would have an important bearing on fact finding and which would assist litigants. Where a question of liability arises, or forms the central feature of the gravamen, then it would be pleaded in detail as appropriate. We would add that serious consideration must be given to new bases of liability being established which would place the risk of activities conducted by the state or those who operate on behalf of the state, and which have been conducted ostensibly negligently, on the shoulders of those best able to support that risk, i.e. usually the state or its surrogates. Size, resources and individual circumstances would be crucial, so that in the case of a commercial organization for instance, it may be more appropriate for ordinary principles of negligence to obtain. A Lonrho is not the same as a widow! As we shall see in a moment, it may well be that EC law will force our governors to re-chart our law of public liability (*Francovich v Italian Republic*, Case C690, 19 November 1991). Against this backcloth, what do courts do better than anyone else?

Most obviously, they provide considered analysis of legislation and prerogative powers and other legal instruments. Many bodies dispense justice and correct maladministration or redress grievances. Higher courts are better than these bodies at determining the law and setting the broad matrix within which administrative justice operates and in which rights provide security. While on the one hand the rulings of the courts must be principled and authoritative, they must also be flexible in interpretation to provide guidance in what will be a potentially infinite variety of circumstances. So much is obvious, and yet achieving the balance remains particularly challenging in public law litigation, a factor which accounts for the widespread attraction of the subject of judicial review for academics and senior judges.

By their training and practice, judges in the higher courts are expected to be adept at settling the more intricate or arcane points of law. It may well be that the law they produce is not ideally suited to the requirements of administrators or citizens: a reluctance to intervene on behalf of citizens may encourage arbitrary and ill-considered action by governors. Conversely, over-frequent intervention can, as we saw in Chapter 3, induce inefficiency. It must be said that the basic test applied by courts in English law to review the exercise of a discretionary power – the *Wednesbury* test – is seriously deficient in providing guidance to administrators on how they should exercise their powers within the law or in acting as a barometer anticipating judicial decision and reaction in a multiplicity of subject areas. The bluntness of the test, viz. a body must not act so unreasonably that no reasonable person could come to that decision and that considerations must be relevant and relevant considerations must be considered, makes it a crude instrument for the task of honing administrative justice and too frequently acts as a convenient shroud for judicial prejudice. A test which would have provided more subtle instruments for review of discretion rather than a 'pick 'n' mix' basis was rejected comprehensively by the Law Lords in the *Brind* decision ([1991] 1 All ER 720) in so far as it was argued that proportionality existed in its own right as a separate ground of review. The court ruled that the doctrine of 'proportionality', which is commonplace in legal systems in Europe as well as that of the EC, has no place as a discrete entity in British law but is part of the *Wednesbury* test. The doctrine allows a far more probing examination of the circumstances and background behind a decision to ensure that powers are exercised for a proper purpose and not in an exaggerated or heavy-handed manner and certainly offers a more probing examination than *Wednesbury* would usually provide (cf. Craig, 1989, p. 291 *et seq.*). The case for it will no doubt emerge in future litigation. For the time being, *Wednesbury* prevails in English law. Hence the importance of getting it right before the courts are invoked in order to minimize disruptive litigation. Widespread resort to the courts is more likely to occur where there are inadequate opportunities to ventilate complaints or redress grievances and/or where there is serious service or performance deficiency.

A crucial factor in judicial review is whether the basis of judicial decision making is as well informed as it ought to be. Does the existing procedure for judicial review in particular provide sufficient information for judges to make their decisions and to provide best guidance on the expectations of the law and for them best to fulfil their role as overall quality control mechanisms? One of the major reasons why there is widespread scepticism over the integrity of judicial review relates not to the fact that judges are biased for or against government or tiers of government. It relates rather to the feeling that review is largely programmed to avoid examination and investigation of all relevant facts in the exposition of the law. The large numbers of applications coming before the courts, a fact bemoaned by judges as much as anyone else – except the public law bar – seems to indicate not so much faith in the courts as a failure to provide adequate opportunities for explanation and redress within authorities and their surrogates themselves before outside agencies are resorted to. It is not reducible to such nostrums as 'More courts and judicial review good' or, conversely, 'less judicial interference better'. Our concern has been to secure that institutions do their best job in relation to complaints and grievance redress and that they do the job for which they are best suited.

To repeat, making decisions on the law and in making those decisions laying down guidance on the necessary content of justice, fairness and legality seem the appropriate tasks of courts. In making such decisions, where the factual background behind a case is relevant – as it inevitably will be – procedures and opportunities should be available to examine relevant documentation. We take comfort from the fact that some of the most helpful contributions in this area have come from the extra-judicial writings of a senior judge (Woolf, 1990, 1992). Furthermore, although the doctrine of 'ripeness' (i.e. courts will not interfere until the matter has exhausted domestic channels) is not as emphatically present in England as in the USA for instance, judicial reluctance to interfere where there are suitable alternative remedies is a well-established reason for not allowing judicial review in deference to domestic or other remedies. In other words, even at this early stage in this chapter, we should emphasize that by allowing greater access to facts and evidence, this will not mean courts being swamped if appropriate grievance institutions are in operation and whose existence we have supported throughout this book.

A further advantage of courts over other bodies concerns the enforcement powers, especially the interlocutory enforcement powers, of courts. The remedies available under judicial review, and remedies available under private law against central government, suffer from well-known defects *vis-à-vis* such enforcement. Chief among these is the fact that public law and equitable remedies are discretionary; that there is no such animal as an interim declaration; that injunctions will not issue against the Crown unless the latter is in breach, or allegedly in breach, of EC law; and that while the forms of relief that were developed by the courts to keep public power within its lawful domain (i.e. certiorari, mandamus and prohibition) possess certain qualities akin to powers of enforcement, the orders suffer or are qualified by their complexity, their discretionary nature and the fact that until December 1991, ministers of the Crown were not susceptible to the contempt jurisdiction of the courts. In a welcome judgment, the Court of Appeal ruled that ministers could be held to be in contempt where they failed to carry out a court order (*M v Home Office* [1991] 4 All ER 97). Other welcome developments have seen the emergence of a legal doctrine which makes public officials abide by their representations and promises where parties have acted on the basis of those promises. The doctrine, known as 'legitimate expectation', has been invoked to enable parties to be consulted in a widening range of circumstances where decisions affecting them are going to be made and even to prevent policies being altered unfairly – though clearly the courts will exercise reserve in this latter area. Furthermore, the courts have shown a greater alertness to the desirability of governors and officials giving reasoned decisions for decisions although the trend reveals some inconsistency.

SPECIFIC ITEMS IN AN OVERALL PERSPECTIVE

First, how will courts fit into an enlarged system of grievance redress as we have described it in the preceding pages? For instance, the greater accessibility afforded to the ombudsmen by our proposals will make them, or at least will have the effect of making them, more easily contactable and more widely used by the public. Figures on direct access to local ombudsmen show distinctly the considerable increase in the numbers complaining to those ombudsmen since the 1988 Local Government Act came into effect. But these ombudsmen will only operate as an external grievance body after internal procedures have been used, many examples of which we have examined. Furthermore, a body operating along the lines of the AAT to hear appeals on the merits will doubtless be an attractive alternative to the courts and the comparative rigidity of judicial review. An example of the latter was revealed in the litigation involving the Hull University lecturer, Edgar Page, and his dispute with the university over the tenured nature of his employment. In that case, the House of Lords, reversing both the Divisional Court and the Court of Appeal, refused to accept jurisdiction over the Visitor where he acted under an error of law. Judicial review is always hemmed in by technicalities, whether the reviewing court is in an expansive mood or a restrictive one. Certainly the Page decision is against the grain of decisions since the 1960s in which the courts' jurisdiction over inferior tribunals and administrative and judicial bodies has been expanded. Much of the case turns on its specific facts and the somewhat rarefied relationship between a Visitor and a university. However, it reveals how equally rarefied legal reasoning over jurisdiction can deprive a citizen of a judicial ruling on a point of law and construction, let alone a decision on the merits which is what the AAT provides (see Chapter 5). By allowing challenges to take place on the merits, the AAT proposal will at least open up an avenue of challenge that does not exist at present, however innovative a court may be inclined to be. Recommendations for more specialized tribunals in areas such as homeless cases would considerably ease the pressure that operates on the supervisory jurisdiction of the High Court at the moment.

Finally, the basic thrust of much of our analysis has been in the direction of effective, efficient and responsive complaints and grievance procedures operating within departments, agencies and authorities. We have argued since 1976 that the proper forum for most grievances is an internal one which is able to operate fairly and quickly. We welcome the fact that the *Citizens' Charter* has adopted this theme. What we expect from this is a variety of results

1 Complainants will be expected to have ventilated their grievance through the appropriate channels before approaching the courts. This is expected currently, but there would, from a complainant's perspective, be a more satisfactory mix of procedure.
2 The role of the courts would be clarified. At present, they alternate between 'hands off' and 'hands on' approaches in their task of review. With

an AAT individuals will be less inclined to attempt to use the courts to exercise a merits review, a task which courts might, or might not, be willing to perform via the back door at present.

3 Courts will be concentrating on the task for which they are best equipped. That is not as a body to deal with all and sundry grievances and alleged abuses of power – a role envisaged long ago by Chief Justice Coke (*Bagg's Case* 11 Co. Rep. at 93a) – but as bodies laying down and interpreting the broad parameters within which political power operates.

As a corollary of what we have said there will be a consequential reduction in court work. We find this a desirable prospect, but opposing views may well be advanced. For instance, advocates for more judicial involvement might argue that there will be an increase in second-class justice through non-judicial fora. There is no reason why this should automatically follow, especially given our recommendations to ensure the responsiveness and accessibility of the procedures. Nor indeed is there any reason to suppose that simply because an issue is before a court, the best answer as a matter of justice will necessarily be achieved. Yet a further argument against the decrease in judicial decision making involves the fact that the public will potentially be deprived of a good number of judicial decisions on important subjects; in other words, the jurisprudence of public law will be diminished. The vast majority of cases are settled long before they arrive at court in any event and the argument seems to suggest that simply because a case is before the court it deserves to be there. Many would accept that judicial review as presently devised is not an appropriate remedy for many of the cases coming before the courts on Order 53 applications. Rather, it would be seen that because of the paucity of procedures elsewhere in the various entities under challenge, judicial review is the only feasible remedy, or it may provide a useful staying device (e.g. to prevent someone's removal from the jurisdiction). Most judicial review applications, although naturally enough of personal importance to the applicants, are routine cases in terms of legal significance. They could and should in a large number of instances be satisfactorily resolved before judicial intervention. The application for leave to apply can doubtless act as a screening process in some cases and may help to weed out those cases that should be so settled but which at present simply fall by the wayside in the absence of appropriate domestic procedures. It is probably true to say that what the complainant invariably needs is good advice and a good domestic remedy, not a court.

Thirdly, and to lead on from the second point, the optimal position of the courts is as quality control checker and the ultimate provider of justice. Here one would have to qualify that by saying 'Justice according to law' whereas other bodies may simply dispense justice.

The fourth point relates to the quality of justice and specifically the fact-finding process that leads up to the decision on the law. As we have said at various stages throughout this work, fact-finding if one of the weakest features of our judicial review procedure. The position was improved with the Order 53 reforms whereby discovery, interrogatories and cross-examination were allowed. However, they have rarely been utilized by the courts because judicial review is meant to be a speedy process, a review on the papers and affidavits; it is not a trial of fact in the commonly understood sense of that term. One would have to delve into legal annals to see why this was so, but a convenient hypothesis might be that if the courts excavated into the factual basis of governmental decisions too deeply, they might interfere with Parliament's role as the grand inquisitor of the nation, let alone interfering with processes of inquiry over which a minister usually has some degree of control whether by setting the terms of reference or by acting as the executive power after recommendations are received from the inquiry. Whatever the cause, judicial review is concerned with correcting errors of law which are generally perceived in a narrow technical sense, although the doctrines of procedural fairness and legitimate expectation have added breadth to the judicial armoury. Without a fact-finding heritage behind it, it has been too easy in the past to allow the administrative process to close in on itself and to present itself as the 'inscrutable face of the Sphynx' when faced by judicial challenge. Devices such as the recording of as little evidence as possible on the record of proceedings and the more drastic curtailing of judicial review by a variety of parliamentary devices helped that process, as did the general protection of secrecy in our 'public' life (Birkinshaw, 1988, 1991).

Procedure for judicial review as it currently operates has its detractors (Justice-All Souls 1988) and its supporters (Woolf, 1990). Woolf in fact has suggested that the existing *modus operandi* largely works satisfactorily; so that, to give two examples, affidavit evidence is often copious and frank avoiding the necessity thereby of discovery and cross-examination and departments invariably abide by a *status quo* until final court order. So much depends upon trust and integrity, qualities which might all too easily be compromised in the absence of adequate safeguards. The fact remains that a citizen is at an enormous disadvantage when taking on the state, especially in its ever developing and protean form. The disadvantage is reinforced by the absence of a Freedom of Information Act affecting central government, an absence which the present Major government seems adamant to maintain. The supervisory/adversarial nature of judicial review and its limitations as a reliable fact-finding process is illustrated clearly when compared with the French system of judicial review as performed in the *tribunaux administratifs* and especially the *Conseil d'Etat*.

The procedure has recently been described in detail by an English commentator (Bell, 1991) and the salient features include the following. First, it is very cheap to invoke. Secondly, a good deal of the responsibility for evidence gathering and fact-finding falls on the staff of the courts, the *rapporteurs* who are not hindered, indeed would be non-plussed, by claims of public interest immunity to the extent that an English litigant would be. Public interest immunity allows information to be withheld from a litigant by virtue of a minister's certificate. The certificate may be overruled by a judge, but there is a reluctance to do so. Nor are they confronted by the same barriers that would stand in opposition to a litigant in the UK who was tackling bureaucracy: the onus of proof is on the applicant in England as it usually is in France, but in England and, notwithstanding Woolf's assurances, there are no external pressures upon departments to assist a litigant, as numerous episodes exemplify. The court/tribunaux in France may order an expert's report. A file or *dossier* is built up for each case. Furthermore, the *public law* nature of the proceedings in France is emphasized by the fact that, unlike English proceedings, where the contest is seen as one between citizen and state institution, a third party representing the public interest takes part in the proceedings. The party, known as the *Commissaire du Gouvernement*, helps to put the litigation into a wider context. As the designation 'public' indicates, the litigation is perceived to involve interests beyond those of the two protagonists. The commissaire's duty is, *inter alia*, to 'relate the case to the broader body of case law of the Conseil and to develop principles' (Bell, 1991, p. 221). They are also expected to make case law on a particular area, and if need be cases may be grouped together on similar themes before the same hearings. The commissaire is expected to take a role which is uninfluenced by government; he or she is not their representative, unlike our own Attorney-General, but seeks instead to operate as a representative of the public interest.

The French procedure, with its mixture of adversarial, inquisitorial and investigative techniques, offers an interesting comparison with judicial review procedure in England. This is not to suggest that judicial review cannot get beneath the surface when that is required. The history of judicial review in England displays the English judiciary in their most independent and tenacious spirit; it has also revealed them on occasion to be more executive minded than the executive. There is a problem, however, about method and system in fact-finding which we must address.

The fifth point concerns assistance to litigants through the offices of an official. Here Woolf has made a valuable contribution in his recommendations for the establishment of a Director of Civil Proceedings (DCP) to assist litigants against public bodies; and we would spell out that this includes those of central and local government as well as their agencies and surrogates and public/private hybrids. It is in fact of such importance that we think it better to flag the suggestion up at this stage and to return to it in greater detail in our concluding chapter where we suggest various reforms. Suffice to say at this stage, the DCP would be outside party politics and would hold office independently and irrespective of the government of the day.

The sixth item we wish to raise, and here we address a matter which has been widely alluded to by others, concerns access to the courts, as indeed do the following two points. The specific issue concerns the test for *locus standi* for public law applications. The test of interest is laid down in section 31(3) of the Supreme Court Act 1981 and stipulates basically that the applicant has a sufficient interest in the matter to which the application relates. After fairly liberal interpretations of this formula by the Court of Appeal and House of Lords (*National Federation etc v IRC* [1982] AC 617), Schiemann J gave a judgment on *locus standi* which we regard as unhelpful to those with a genuine grievance. The case concerned the remnants of the Rose Theatre in which some of Shakespeare's plays were first performed. The remnants were uncovered during redevelopment. The applicants before the court were a preservation group seeking to challenge the decision of the secretary of state not to schedule the remnants under a relevant statute to give them protected status against developers. The judge held that the applicants did not have standing, largely because a statutory commission was the only body named in the statute which the secretary of state had to consult and their interest as a representative group was not sufficient. It is an unsatisfactory decision (Cane, 1990, p. 307; Schiemann, 1990, p. 342).

It is of course pertinent to point out that if the recommendations for the DCP come to fruition, he or she would have a significant role to play in cases where there is or might be a problem over standing. Even with the existence of the DCP, we would hope for a return to the more open spirit of standing which was present in the *National Federation* case. This would certainly be in line with developments elsewhere, notably in private law. For instance, under the proposed Council Directive of the EC on Unfair Terms in Contracts, member states must ensure that in the interests of consumers, competitors and the public generally, adequate and effective means exist for the control of unfair terms in consumer contracts. Such 'means' include provisions of law whereby persons or organizations, where under national law they have a legitimate interest in protecting consumers, may take action before the courts or before an administrative authority to determine whether the terms are inconsistent with the provisions of this directive (cf. *R v Secretary of State for Employment ex p EOC* [1993] 1 All ER 1022).

In Chapter 6, the reader will recall our views on the establishment of regionally based courts to deal with public law matters. We are of the view, as we expressed in that chapter, and this is our seventh point, that our present system is too centripetally based as far as judicial review is concerned. We recommend, albeit with mixed enthusiasm, that regional courts for public law disputes should be established. We would argue for special courts which exercised both review and compensatory powers; and as we suggested at the beginning of this chapter, we believe that the rules on state liability require redrafting. Nevertheless, it makes perfectly good sense for such matters to be dealt with by the same court, especially as many private actions now involve matters of public law, whether it be *vires* such as misfeasance of public office, discretion as in breach of statutory power or, and increasingly, EC law as in breaches of EC provisions (*Francovitch* (1991), *Marleasing* (1990)) or discrimination or competition provisions of EC law. Such a measure would save on expense and make the courts, where required, more accessible. It would not be necessary to have a High Court judge sitting in each case – a jurisdictional division could be drawn between serious and less serious cases. Judges would be appointed for their proven expertise in judicial review and litigation involving public authorities. Woolf has suggested that a method of expediting proceedings on review is to have paper hearings only as on application for leave. A request could be made for an oral hearing or for an appeal with the requirement for leave. We would feel much happier with this state of affairs if the fact-finding processes of the *Conseil d'Etat*, or ones which were equally effective – which we touched upon above – were in existence.

The eighth point relates to advice and cost (and see Chapter 11). We have adverted at various places to the growing demands of the Treasury for cost-cutting and greater efficiency in the provision of legal services. The profession has felt, and to some extent has fought off, the demands for greater competition from the government in the provision of legal services. The profession will remain bifurcated for the foreseeable future. A statutory ombudsman for the professions has been established under the Courts and Legal Services Act. Attempts have been made to make courts more consumer-friendly and judges have been requested to keep time charts to record the amount of time spent in court – a request made by the former Lord Chief Justice. Legal aid has come under enormous pressure; estimates from a variety of sources suggest that as many as 15 million people have fallen out of the eligibility range for legal aid since 1979. With the legal aid bill for the state approaching £1 billion, efforts taken to reduce legal aid payments have resulted in increasing numbers of solicitors refusing to carry out legal aid work, especially in the criminal law field. There are also well-documented case histories of criminal legal aid work being carried out by inexperienced clerks as opposed to qualified solicitors with a consequential deterioration in the quality of service (McConville, in press).

It has been pointed out on many occasions that the criteria adopted by the Legal Aid Board to determine the award of legal aid are inherently individualistic, a factor which in itself renders it more difficult to obtain legal aid for many public law areas. Indeed, contrary to Woolf's assurance, it has been decided that where leave for judicial review has been obtained, it does not automatically follow that legal aid will be granted (*R v Legal Aid Board ex p Hughes* [1992] *The Independent*, 27 August). Granting of leave did not automatically satisfy the relevant test: 'is there a real chance of success for the application such that a solicitor would advise a client to proceed if the client were paying for the litigation out of his own pocket?'. Not only does the material benefit to the applicant have to be considered but also the *ultimate* benefit of the application to the public. If others are interested in the application (i.e. a representative application), then there is the possibility that the Legal Aid Board may seek contributions from those others.

Legal aid is not the only area to have suffered as a consequence of the Treasury bludgeon. Law centres suffered a spate of closures in the 1990s. Providing advice and assistance to those who were either unlikely to use solicitors, or who lived in areas where solicitors were unlikely to have practices or whose problems were not catered for by traditional practice, law centres were frequently disliked by both central and local government (see *New Law Journal*, 1992, p. 1165). If support were present:

> . . . then the workers who staff them would not be paid less than their clients. There would not be a steady stream of closures, and those law centres which manage not to close would be open for more than a few hours a week.
>
> (Editorial, *New Law Journal*, 15 March 1991)

Other developments include cutting the number of advice agencies and giving a contract to the local CAB allowing it to allocate sub-contracts between various advisory bodies with the consequential loss of funding for assistance with litigation or representation; advisory centres would be precisely that, they would be confined to general advisory work. A recommendation came from the Legal Aid Board in 1990 that centres should be funded to 50 per cent from central government funding. The Lord Chancellor's Department has not acted upon this. Plans by the government to take legal aid away from private practitioners and devolve funds and responsibilities on to specialist agencies such as UKIAS have placed a worthwhile organization under a blaze of adverse publicity which ended with the collapse of the proposals and the near collapse of the service.

It is over 21 years since the first law centre was established. That was a period when 'access to justice' was a far more prominent theme than it is today in terms of commitment to opening up access by extending novel forms of legal service rather than simply by way of rhetorical contributions. If the Rule of Law is not simply to add to that rhetoric, then it must mean equal access to justice and advice. Work has shown how the legal profession does not serve whole segments of the community and how the quality and nature of its service decline as the lawyer descends to clients in the lower socio-economic groups (Campbell and Wilson, 1972; McConville, in press). We do not expect to see change in the foreseeable future, but if justice itself becomes just another market commodity, then the state will have turned its back on one of its most fundamental duties: the duty to provide justice to its citizens. Justice is worthy of investment. To repeat a point we have made before, our commitment to justice would mean grievance procedures throughout institutions serving the public, and justice would not be located simply in the courts. However, citizens need advice and centres or places where worthwhile advice may be given. A sense of community does not exist in many of our urban landscapes; a sense of alienation will not be overcome by simply providing procedures if people remain largely unaware of how they can be utilized or lack the skills or resources to use them meaningfully.

Our final point concerns the codification of our administrative procedure. The Americans, after all, have had an Administrative Procedure Act since 1946. As stated, this is a more comprehensive task than simply codifying judicial review, a task which the Australians have undertaken but which Woolf did not think appropriate for this country. Basically, Woolf believed, the codification would deprive judicial review of its current flexibility and might encourage an ossified system. That depends upon how the legislation is drafted. Certainly, the UK has participated in the setting of Minimum Standards of Good Administrative Practice through the Council of Europe. Recommendation No. R (80) 2 from the Committee of Ministers concerned the 'Exercise of Discretionary Powers by Administrative Authorities'. These were summarized by Justice-All Souls (1988) in the following manner: power should be exercised for its proper purpose; objectivity and impartiality should prevail in the exercise of discretionary power; equality before the law; proportionality; action should be taken within a reasonable time; guidelines should be applied consistently; guidelines should be published; departures from guidelines should be justified by reasoned decision; there should be ultimate independent control over discretionary decision making; a failure to act should operate against an authority in the absence of good reasons; there should be an unimpeded supply of information to the independent controlling authority.

What we have in mind is a code of good administrative practice embracing these safeguards which would be placed in legislation. This would set out the general duty to act fairly, the duty to provide grievance and complaints procedures, the duty to avoid bias and self-interest in establishing such bodies and a general duty to provide reasons for decisions. The Competition and Service (Utilities) Act addresses some of these points, e.g. complaints procedures. Tribunals and inquiries are of course covered by their own statute. That Act of 1971 (now 1992) deals with the easy parts of administrative justice, not the submerged part of the iceberg. The legislation would give broad guidance on the issues we have identified and would draw upon the experience of the ombudsmen and the Council on Tribunals. Furthermore, it would establish the UK ARC (see Chapter 4) and AAT (see Chapter 5). The proposals we made for a regionally based system of public law would require legislation.

On balance, we would prefer legislation which left the scope of review on its existing basis, but which would include as a ground of review 'proportionality', which was rejected by the Law Lords as a discrete head of review under English law in 1991, as noted above. Under the Council of Europe resolution, proportionality requires public bodies to 'maintain a balance between any adverse effects which a decision may have on the rights, liberties or interests of persons and the purpose which it pursues' to ensure that action does not interfere with rights and interests more than is strictly necessary. It would also provide rights to reasoned decisions.

The legislation would set out a public law of public liability to cover not only negligence and contractual liability, but such subjects as compensation for *ultra vires* action which has caused damage. It is appropriate for such legislation to provide for the award of an injunction against the Crown. On both of these subjects, decisions of the EC Court have made striking developments. In *Francovich* [(1991) *The Times*, 20 November] it was established that where a member state of the EC fails to implement legal obligations contained in a directive, the state will be liable for damage suffered by individuals for non-implementation even though not directly effective. *Factortame* establishes the primacy of EC law so that where the performance of legal duties under EC law was prevented by an Act of Parliament, the Act must be disapplied, by injunction from domestic courts if need be. The legislation would establish a satisfactory basis of restitution after *ultra vires* payments and contracts (*Hazell v Hammersmith LBC* [1991] 1 All ER 545; *Woolwich BS v IRC* [1992] 3 All ER 737).

This list is a tall order, but it is no more than citizens deserve and they all deal with problems which judicially made domestic law has left in an unsatisfactory condition.

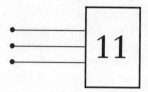

11

CONCLUSIONS

Most of our argument has already been made, but we need both to provide some kind of overview and to add a few remarks by way of supplement. We have so far said little about resources. In a recent study, it has been said that while the means of state administration have grown larger, becoming more bureaucratized, specialized and technical, the means of representation have lagged behind. Consequently, 'many citizens, and especially the disadvantaged have found it increasingly difficult to participate in the proliferation of state policies and functions' (Stephens, 1990). It may be thought, then, that despite increasing the institutional opportunities for redress, little real citizen advantage would accrue without paying attention to resource issues, especially in relation to the representation of citizens before the new bodies advocated. There is some merit in this argument and it cannot be pretended that justice comes cheaply. We do not expect it in relation to the funding of the police or, perhaps to a lesser extent, in terms of our criminal justice system. Even so, some of the suggestions we have made ought to mitigate the worst features of a state/citizen imbalance. We will not list them again here but invite the reader to think through the impact of these suggestions as we rehearse individual items.

The first thing to say is that the time is not propitious for an increase in the legal aid budget. Not only is the present administration seeking to reduce public spending but the Lord Chancellor, Lord Mackay, has sought savings in the legal aid budget and is continuing to do so at the time of writing. It has to be said that in the last ten or so years the proportion of the population qualifying for legal aid has dropped from around 80 per cent to somewhat less than 50 per cent. Most of the others are in a legal poverty-trap: too 'rich' to qualify for legal aid, but too poor to pay for legal assistance out of their own pockets. We are moving towards 'safety net' legal aid. The *Magna Carta* proclaimed that 'to no one will we refuse or delay right or justice'. It cannot in all seriousness be said that we are currently anything like honouring that pledge, and in order to satisfy it a great deal of rethinking of our justice system needs to be done. We doubt that subsidizing lawyers in general on a case by case basis represents the most valuable use of resources, yet the few law centres we possess appear to be in constant fear of extinction. On the other hand, some of the Lord Chancellor's suggestions for cheaper and simpler alternatives to litigation might alleviate some of the problems and would chime well with much of what we have had to say (see, e.g. McKay, 1991).

Where there is no real alternative to the courts – where important points of law or principle are at stake – we have already spoken of the idea for a 'Citizen's Defender' or Public Interest Advocate, perhaps attached to the Ministry of Justice, who could take over a case from a complainant and prosecute it at public expense (see Woolf, 1990, ch. 4). Such a figure, who would have wide access to documentation, could relieve the citizen of the burden and expense of litigation while at the same time vindicating important points of law and constitutional principle. This might need such a figure to liaise with the ombudsman, operating, of course, under the extended jurisdiction which we suggested in Chapter 7. Various forms of lay advocacy need to be considered and extended, since if we are not seeing the court system as the *usual* method of citizen redress, then we ought to get used to the idea that legal skills may be employed by people outside the traditional legal profession. These and other matters aimed at making justice against the state for the citizen more accessible might well be considered as a matter of some priority for the Standing Administrative Conference which we recommended in Chapter 4. It might be useful, for example, to remind ourselves of the recent work of the Australian ARC in its *Multicultural Australia Project*. There are also experiments elsewhere to which such a study could turn. Much, for instance, has been written about public interest law in the USA (e.g. Handler *et al.*, 1978), while across Europe the most enriching experiments are occurring in relation to working for the consumer/citizen in the public services (see, e.g. Epstein, 1990). Whether in Spain, Sweden, France or indeed in Britain itself, renewed emphasis on the rights and expectations of the citizen can be seen – in the form of advocacy, citizen representation on management boards and so on (ibid.).

Be this as it may, a systemic approach is what is needed. As has recently been said, consumerism cannot be a bolt-on extra to be attached when everything else goes on as before (Pollit, 1988). The Local Government Training Board (LGTB) has pointed out that no single method will do, that a comprehensive multi-faceted strategy for change is needed (LGTB, 1988). The OECD, too, runs an on-going programme examining the relations between public administration and its citizens. There is therefore a great deal of advice available. The reforms which we have advocated earlier would facilitate the systems-flexible approach which such commentators call for.

Leaving aside for a moment the central role which we envisage for an enlarged ombudsman system, it is worth laying stress on some other proposals for the cooling out of disputes within the administration without the necessity of calling in third parties. First, we reiterate our belief in the necessity for legislated complaints procedures for all public bodies, including central government departments. Complaints procedures are springing up on the statute book with remarkable frequency these days. For example, we only have to look at the Competition and Service (Utilities) Act 1992. Procedures for dealing with complaints are required for telecommunications, gas supply, electricity supply, water supply and sewerage services. The provisions also require both consultation and publicity. From April 1992, health authorities and NHS hospitals will have to publish details regularly of both the number of complaints received and how long it has taken to deal with them. We are bound to welcome such developments even though the precise shape of the arrangements is unclear at the time of writing. Allied to information with respect to levels of performance expected and in fact achieved, there ought to be a greater emphasis than in the past on customer needs and satisfaction. The local ombudsman, too, is joining the debate by calling occasionally for legislative changes to protect complainants and, for example, to extend appeals committees within the field of education (see, e.g. CLA, 1991, pp. 5–7).

Staying with local government, customer care and quality assurance are high on the list of priorities for many local authorities these days. The Association of County Councils has recently published a guide on customer service, the Association of District Councils has issued a customer care guide especially for councillors and the Association of Metropolitan Authorities has produced an introductory guide to quality assurance for local authorities. The CLA, in its 1990–91 Report, expressed the view that the attention which local authorities are paying to customer care and quality assurance is being reflected in the number of complaints to them which are being settled locally. Now some of this change is being driven by central government, some elsewhere and some represents a genuine conversion. In any event, the ability of the citizen to complain is gaining greater visibility than ever before. However, it still seems to us a shame that a *general* statutory requirement for all bodies in the public domain has not been required.

There has for some years been, as we have seen, a renewed interest in improved managerial performance in the public services through Rayner, FMI, Next Steps and the like. Others can argue whether the main thrust is inputs, outputs or outcomes; is it, i.e. the objective, the progressive reduction of public expenditure, value-for-money or a debate over the services which are preferred? Certainly, the last-mentioned is underdeveloped and we have noted an increased reliance by government on sounding out customers through market research surveys. Whatever views are taken about present trends, such developments *can be consumer-oriented*; if they were, then the formal justice system might have much less to do. What we do know is that, however much improvements are being sought, there is much more work to be done. The Ministerial Correspondence Efficiency Scrutiny, to which we have already referred, has recently spoken of unacceptable delays, inadequate or non-existent monitoring and the like. This requires constant vigilance, but the larger point we would make is that public lawyers need to be aware of advanced management techniques for protecting the interests of citizens, in addition to the formal and informal justice mechanisms. That said, we have drawn attention to the down-side of exploring customer preferences through market research techniques and believe strongly that such 'information' needs to be supplemented through genuine consultation devices where customer views are adequately and systematically represented.

Although we have paid considerable attention to third-party agencies in helping to resolve resistant complaints and grievances, we have some optimism that a new administrative culture can be created whereby complaints can be seen to be taken seriously by government itself. In this respect, we should not overlook the requirement to state reasons for decisions, supported by the facts which have influenced the decision maker. Overseas experience has suggested that although such a requirement is likely to lead to an increase in the equivalent of judicial review applications in the short term, these gradually diminish as the administration adapts to its new responsibilities. The requirement has been found to stimulate the decision maker to consider action more carefully to avoid errors and to ensure that the decision rests on a rational foundation. In Australia, we have seen that the improvement in decision-making standards has been attested to by senior administrators. Remember also, that if such a duty was backed up by an appeal to accessible tribunals at the local or regional level, the administration might be less careless than otherwise would be the case. This may well represent the undoing of the so-far-untried *Citizens' Charter* in Britain, where the chartermark and a system of monitoring is expected to secure compliance. We retain reservations on this matter. In particular, the Charter development has not been accompanied by a root and branch review of justice against the state. There is so far no real attempt to ask what a just system would look like and then try to produce reinforcing and interlocking arrangements to try and produce it.

To buttress our belief that most complaints can and should be attended to satisfactorily internally, we strongly recommend that serious consideration be given to the idea of a consumer advocate within the larger departments and organizations along the lines of the US Postal Service. Complaints officers in some areas, especially local government, are currently the nearest we get, but a great deal more could be done.

THE LONG-STOP

Whatever reforms are adopted by or forced upon state organs there will remain dissatisfaction, justified or not, which requires access to third-party intervention: a long-stop. Too often this is the courts, which are expensive and inaccessible to most people. Even so, the present overcrowding and delay in the Divisional Court is hardly acceptable (see, e.g. Woolf, 1992, pp. 221 *et seq.*). We shall have more to say about the ombudsman in a moment, but let us dwell briefly on the courts/tribunal end of things.

We believe in general that an appeal on the merits should lie from most discretionary decisions. Exceptions would be for Parliament, assisted by the SAC to determine. We also believe that some version of an AAT is desirable for this task, without prejudice to high-volume jurisdictions such as social security being treated differently. In a country as densely populated as Britain, we also believe the tribunal should be regionalized to give easy access to complainants. It is our belief that this would take the strain off the divisional and higher courts. Even so, the divisional court would need to be the first level of constitutional quality control and should also be there to resolve problems of law of particular importance (see Chapter 10). It will be recalled that we envisage some use of a Citizen's Defender or Public Interest Advocate. There is no clear agreement between the two authors on whether the divisional court ought also to be regionalized as part of the process of reform. Although we are agreed that accessible justice is a primary consideration, we should not want to overburden the system with a plethora of institutions; a position which some readers might think we are already guilty of. Even so, with an entrenched Ministry of Justice and SAC, we should be in a better position than presently to address such needs over the mid- and longer terms.

We should perhaps also reiterate our point that for all the developments in public law jurisprudence over the last two decades, we entertain considerable unease about the executive deference shown by the courts, most particularly in the field of ministers and central government departments. The so-called *Wednesbury* standard of supervision is, in our view, far too lax for a modern democracy, allowing ministers and others to take decisions without clear explanations and without disclosing the factual basis of their decisions (see Chapter 10). We believe that this imbalance ought to be addressed by Parliament or its agents since the die has been cast too far back for the courts to adopt new conventions towards the behaviour of 'responsible' ministers. It would be more difficult for the government of the day to reject recommendations along these lines given the other institutional changes which we advocate.

REGULATION AND THE PUBLIC UTILITIES

The regulation of the public utilities is relatively new and is a changing scene. Even as we write, the full effect of the 1992 Act cannot be clearly envisaged (see Chapter 11). However, a number of key problems have been identified which need constant supervision. The first is that the machinery for registering complaints and grievance is convoluted, heterogeneous and confusing. At the very least, some semblance of order needs to be introduced to leave the general public less bewildered. A broad Regulatory Act might be considered which sought to adopt common standards across the utilities for both the redress of grievances and for consultation over the larger issues. Although this has not been at the centre of our concerns during this work, the way in which the regulatory framework operates is less than open. It appears that a great deal of bargaining occurs between the regulator and the regulated, which never comes into public view. The nearest we come to understanding the tensions and the disagreements is through a close reading of the *Financial Times*. Valuable service though that is, it does not represent open government. Adding to these rather shadowy dynamics are the equally shaded discussions which go on between the regulators and the relevant minister. We are a long way from 'Government in the Sunshine' as practised by the Americans (see Birkinshaw *et al.*, 1990, pp. 267–8).

A more fundamental point concerning grievance handling by the utilities is the dual role of the regulator; that is to say he is frequently both regulator and individual grievance-handler. Now even though grievance-handling may be one useful form of performance monitoring, it may be considered that the person who has bargained prices, objectives and standards may not be sufficiently disinterested to hold the ring as between the utility and its customers. These are not easy matters to resolve, especially from the outside. In any event, a number of commentators believe that a more limited role for the regulator would enable him to do a difficult job more effectively, leaving the last-resort grievance-handler a utilities ombudsman, who could be appealed to when internal mechanisms were exhausted.

THE OMBUDSMAN

At this point we must return to the ombudsman, whom we do see as being a central figure in our scheme of things. At present, we have not even begun to think about the potential of our ombudsman system. We repeat that short of a few jurisdictional changes, there is little wrong with the local ombudsman. It is the PCA which causes us most concern. Even given the limited brief which is implicit in the nature of the office, he would be a much more effective Citizen's Defender if the public could always approach him direct, if he had regional offices and if he could take oral complaints and advertise. Without such developments, he will remain marginal to our constitutional arrangements.

However, ombudsmen are capable of doing much more than this. They are a genuine alternative to the courts in a whole range of circumstances, which we have spoken to at length in Chapters 5 and 7. There should be fewer restraints on complainants to use the courts in preference to the ombudsman. We should think seriously about an ombudsman for human rights. We should encourage, perhaps statutorily, the developing practice of meetings between the ombudsman, the NAO, Audit Commission and others. Their respective experience of administrative performance and value for money on the one side and grievance redress on the other might be pooled to suggest improvements in public service delivery. The pooling of justice and efficiency.

In conclusion, we would support an expanded role for ombudsmen as recommended in the Multicultural Australia Project so that the ombudsman could act as a central reference point for complaints, could adopt a leading role in the dissemination of information about forms of redress and so on. As a leading figure attached to the new SAC, he could assist with a constant reassessment of both his own role and other parts of the justice system.

SUMMARY

Any concluding remarks in a work which seeks to cover as much ground as we have are bound to sound somewhat limp. Let us therefore restrict ourselves to just a few points, all somewhat by way of reprise. First, to offer citizens effective ways to complain against the state, to provide a system of justice, we must range much more widely than the traditional court and tribunal system, for all their intrinsic value. This is fortunately beginning to be recognized, but it is occurring in the absence of effective machinery which can examine the problems in the round and which have enough human and other resources to make an effective contribution. Systems of justice must not be reactive but must be mutually reinforcing responses to a clear concept of justice for each citizen. Secondly, we need to take advantage of the relatively recent drive to improve management in the public service and to honour canons of customer care by feeding in from the other end innovative, clear and accessible ideas for delivering, on systems which combine fairness with efficiency. Finally, we need to repeat our concerns about the 'contracting state' and the privatization of our public affairs. How can private deliverers of public services be held accountable for fairness and quality through the use of standards, criteria, tendering processes, contract terms, monitoring, complaint opportunities and enforcement remedies? This is a nettle which will have to be grasped at some time in the near future. After all, the state is not being rolled back as any casual reader of the statute book will perceive. It is merely being reformed. We shall need to reform our system of justice alongside it if our citizens are to be entitled to complain effectively.

CODA

We append a kind of dream flow-chart to summarize the main strands of our reform agenda. These ideas are not concrete, not immutable but are intended to identify the nature of the problem as we perceive it. An anatomy of justice against the state could resemble the following (see over).

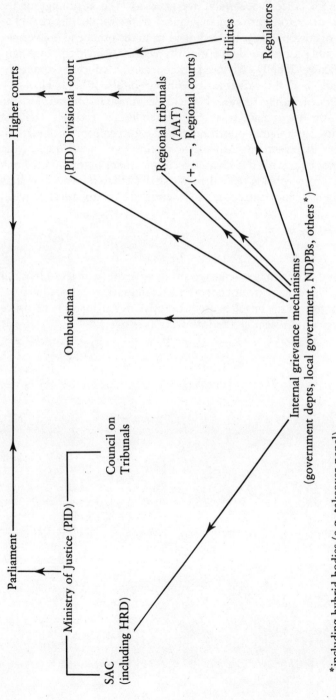

*including hybrid bodies (e.g. takeover panel)

Key:
SAC = Standing advisory committee
HRD = Human Rights Division
NDPBs = Non-departmental Public Bodies

AAT = Administrative Appeal Tribunal
PID = Public Interest Defender

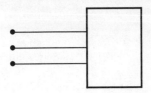

REFERENCES

Administrative Conference of the United States (1985) Quote from *The Federalist*, No. 51. In *Federal Administrative Procedure Sourcebook*. Washington, DC: ACUS.

Administrative Conference of the United States (1991) *A Guide to Federal Agency Rulemaking*, 2nd edn. Washington, DC: Office of the Chairman, ACUS.

Administrative Review Council of the Commonwealth of Australia (1985) *The Relationship Between the Ombudsman and the Administrative Appeals Tribunal*, Report No. 22, Canberra: ARC.

Administrative Review Council of the Commonwealth of Australia (1987) *Eleventh Annual Report, 1986–87*. Canberra: ARC.

Administrative Review Council of the Commonwealth of Australia (1991a) *Report to the Attorney-General. Review of the Administrative Decisions (Judicial Review) Act: Statement of Reasons for Decisions*, Report No. 33. Canberra: ARC.

Administrative Review Council of the Commonwealth of Australia (1991b) *Fifteenth Annual Report, 1990–91*. Canberra: ARC.

Administrative Review Council of the Commonwealth of Australia (1992) *Administrative Review*, No. 32. Canberra: ARC.

Audit Commission (1986) *Making a Reality of Community Care*. London: Audit Commission.

Audit Commission (1986a) *Managing the Crisis in Council Housing*. London: Audit Commission.

Audit Commission (1986b) *Performance Review in Local Government: A Handbook for Auditors and Local Authorities*. London: Audit Commission.

Audit Commission (1989a) *Managing Services Effectively – Performance Review*. London: Audit Commission.

Audit Commission (1989b) *Housing the Homeless*. London: Audit Commission.

Audit Commission (1989c) *Preparing for Compulsory Competition*. London: Audit Commission.

Audit Commission (1990a) *Footing the Bill*. London: Audit Commission.

Audit Commission (1990b) *Calling All Forces*. London: Audit Commission.

Audit Commission (1990c) *Urban Regeneration and Economic Development*. London: Audit Commission.

Audit Commission (1991a) *Healthy Housing: The Role of Environmental Health Services*. London: Audit Commission.

Audit Commission (1991b) *How Effective is the Audit Commission?* London: Audit Commission.

Audit Commission (1992) *The Citizens' Charter Performance Indicators*. London: Audit Commission.

Baldwin, R. and McCrudden, C. (1987) *Regulation and Public Law*. London: Weidenfeld and Nicolson.

Barron, A. and Scott, C. (1992) 'The Citizens' Charter Programme', 55 Mod, LR 526.

Bell, J. (1991) 'Reflections on the Procedure of the Conseil d'Etat', in G. Hand and J. McBride (eds) *Droit Sans Frontieres*. Birmingham: Holdsworth Club.

Birkinshaw, P. (1981) 'Freedom of Information, the Elected Member and Local Government', *Public Law*, p. 545.

Birkinshaw, P. (1985a) *Grievances, Remedies and the State*. London: Sweet and Maxwell.

Birkinshaw, P. (1985b) 'Departments of State, Citizens and the Internal Resolution of Grievances', *Civil Justice Quarterly*, 4, 15.

Birkinshaw, P. (1988) *Freedom of Information: The Law, the Practice and the Ideal*. London: Weidenfeld and Nicolson.

Birkinshaw, P. (1990) *Government and Information: The Law Relating to Access, Disclosure and Regulation*. London: Butterworths.

Birkinshaw, P. (1991) *Reforming the Secret State*. Milton Keynes: Open University Press.

Birkinshaw, P., Harden, I. and Lewis, N. (1990) *Government by Moonlight: The Hybrid Parts of the State*. London: Unwin Hyman.

Bradley, A.W. (1985) *Constitutional and Administrative Law*, 10th edn. London: Longman.

Bradley, A.W. (1992) 'Administrative Justice and Judicial Review', *Public Law*, p. 185.

Byatt, I. (1990) *The Regulation of the Water Industry*. Edinburgh: David Hume Institute.

Cabinet Office (1988) *Service to the Public*. London: HMSO.

Cabinet Office (1991) *Citizens' Charter*, Cm 1599. London: HMSO.

Caiden, G. (1988) 'The Challenge of Change', in *Proceedings of the Fourth International Ombudsman Conference*, Canberra.

Campbell, C. and Wilson, R.J. (1972) *Public Attitudes to the Legal Profession in Scotland*. Edinburgh: Law Society of Scotland.

Canadian Law Commission (1987) *Towards a Modern Federal Administrative Law*, Administrative Law Series. Ottawa: Canadian Law Reform Commission.

Cane, P. (1990) 'Statutes, Standing and Representation', *Public Law*, p. 307.
Commission for Local Administration (1978) *Complaints Procedures*. London: Commission for Local Administration.
Commission for Local Administration (1988) *Annual Report 1987–88*. London: Commission for Local Administration.
Commission for Local Administration (1989) *Annual Report 1988–89*. London: Commission for Local Administration.
Commission for Local Administration (1990) *Annual Report 1989–90*. London: Commission for Local Administration.
Commission for Local Administration (1991) *Annual Report 1990–91*. London: Commission for Local Administration.
Commission for Local Administration (1992) *Devising a Complaints System*. London: Commission for Local Administration.
Common, R., Flynn, N. and Mellon, E. (1992) *Managing Public Services: Competition and Decentralization*. Oxford: Butterworth Heinemann.
Commonwealth of Australia Ombudsman (1982) *Fifth Annual Report, 1981–82*. Canberra: ARC.
Council on Tribunals (1980a) *Special Report*, Cmnd 7805. London: HMSO.
Council on Tribunals (1980b) *The Functions of the Council on Tribunals*, Cmnd 7809, Session 1979–80. London: HMSO.
Council on Tribunals (1986) Cmnd 9922. London: HMSO.
Council on Tribunals (1987) *Annual Report, 1986–87*. London: HMSO.
Council on Tribunals (1990) *Annual Report, 1989–90*. London: HMSO.
Council on Tribunals (1991a) *Annual Report, 1990–91*. London: HMSO.
Council on Tribunals (1991b) *Model Rules of Procedure for Tribunals*, Cm 1431. London: HMSO.
Craig, P. (1989) *Administrative Law*, 2nd edn. London: Sweet and Maxwell.
Davies, A. and Willman, J. (1991) *What Next? Agencies, Departments and the Civil Service*. London: Institute for Public Policy Research.
Department of Health (1990) *Representations*. Consultation Paper No. 17. London: HMSO.
Department of Social Security (1991) *Annual Report of the Chief Adjudication Officer 1989/90*. London: HMSO.
Dewar, D. (1991) 'Customer Care as an Aspect of VFM', *Ripa/Mori Seminar*, 6 November.
Donoughmore, Earl of (1932) *Report of the Committee on Ministers' Powers*, Cmd 4060. London: HMSO.
Electricity Consumer Council (1989) *Annual Report 1990*. London: ECC.
Efficiency Unit (1988) *Improving Management in Government: The Next Steps*. London: HMSO.
Efficiency Unit (1990) *Scrutiny of Ministerial Correspondence*. Cabinet Office. London: HMSO.
Epstein, J. (1990) *Public Services: Working for the Consumer*. European Foundation for the Improvement of Living and Working Conditions. London: RICA.
Franks, Sir Oliver (1957) *Report of the Committee on Administrative Tribunals and Enquiries*, Cmnd 218. London: HMSO.
Gas Consumer Council (1991) *Annual Report, 1990*. London: GCC.

Genn, H. and Genn, Y. (1989) *The Effectiveness of Representation at Tribunals*. London: Lord Chancellor's Department.

Goldsmith, A. (ed.) (1991) *Complaints Against the Police: The Trend to External Review*. Oxford: Clarendon Press.

Graham, C. (1991) *The Non-Classical Ombudsman*. Sheffield: Centre for Socio-Legal Studies, University of Sheffield.

Graham, C. and Prosser, A. (1991) *Privatising Public Enterprises*. Oxford: Clarendon Press.

Gregory, R. and Drewry, G. (1991) 'Barlow Clowes and the Ombudsman', *Public Law*, pp. 192 and 408.

Haldane, Viscount (1918) *Report of the Committee on the Machinery of Government*, Cd 9230. London: HMSO.

Haller, W. (1988) 'The Place of Ombudsmen in the World Community', in *Proceedings of the Fourth International Ombudsman Conference*, Canberra.

Handler, J.F., Hollingsworth, E.J. and Erlanger, H.J. (1978) *Lawyers and the Pursuit of Legal Rights*. New York: Academic Press.

Harden, I. (1992) *The Contracting State*. Buckingham: Open University Press.

Harden, I. and Lewis, N. (1982) 'Law and the Local State', *Urban Law and Policy*, 5, p. 65.

Harden, I. and Lewis, N. (1986) *The Noble Lie: The British Constitution and the Rule of Law*. London: Hutchinson.

Hay, D. *et al.* (eds) (1975) *Albion's Fatal Tree*. London: Peregrine.

Her Majesty's Treasury (1991) *Competing for Quality: Buying Better Public Services*, Cm 1730. London: HMSO.

Hill, M., Walker, J. and Cracknell, S. (1992) *Citizens' Grievances about Local Authority Services*. London ESRC.

Home Office (1991) *Custody, Care and Justice*, Cm 1647. London: HMSO.

Institute of Local Government Studies (1985) *Good Management in Local Government*. Birmingham: ILG.

Institute for Public Policy Research (1991) *The Constitution of the United Kingdom*. London: IPPR.

Justice Committee (1976) *The Citizen and the Public Agencies*. London: Justice.

Justice Committee (1977) *Our Fettered Ombudsman*. London: Justice.

Justice-All Souls (1988) *Administrative Justice: Some Necessary Reforms*. Oxford: Oxford University Press.

Law Commission (1993) *Administrative Law: Judicial Review and Statutory Appeals*. London: HMSO.

Leak, A. (1986) 'Appeals and Accountability', PhD thesis, University of Sheffield.

Lewis, N. (1989a) 'Regulating Non-governmental Bodies: Privatization, Accountability and the Public–Private Divide', in J. Jowell and D. Oliver (eds) *The Changing Constitution*, 2nd edn. Oxford: Clarendon Press.

Lewis, N. (1989b) 'The Case for a Standing Administrative Conference', *Political Quarterly*, 60, p. 421.

Lewis, N. (1992) *Inner City Regeneration: The Demise of Regional and Local Government*. Buckingham: Open University Press.

Lewis, N., Seneveritane, M. and Cracknell, S. (1987) *Complaints Procedures in Local Government*. Sheffield: University of Sheffield.

Llewellyn, K. (1940) 'The Normative, the Legal and the Law Jobs: The Problem of Juristic Method', *Yale Law Journal* 49, p. 1355.

Local Government Training Board (1988) *Learning from the Public*. London: LGTB.

London Business School (1990) *Privatisation: The Implications for Cultural Change*. London: London Business School.

Longley, D. (1992) *Public Law and Health Service Accountability*. Buckingham: Open University Press.

MacKay, Lord (1991) *Access to Justice – The Price*, 20th Upjohn Lecture. Association of Law Teachers.

Mackie, K. (ed.) (1991) *A Handbook of Dispute Resolution: ADR in Action*. London: Routledge/Sweet and Maxwell.

Mashaw, J. (1983) *Bureaucratic Justice*. New Haven, Conn.: Yale University Press.

Mullen, T. (1990) 'Representation at Tribunals', 53 Mod, LR 230.

Multi-cultural Australia Project (1992) Administrative Review Council 16th Annual Report 1991–92, para. 87, embracing the ARC's report no. 34 entitled 'Access to Administrative Review by Members of Australia's Ethnic Communities', September.

National Association for the Care and Rehabilitation of Offenders (1989) *The Ombudsman and Prisoners' Complaints*. London: NACRO.

National Consumer Council (1986) *Self-regulation*. London: NCC.

National Consumer Council (1989) *In the Absence of Competition*. London: NCC.

National Consumer Council (1991a) *The Gas Industry*. London: NCC.

National Consumer Council (1991b) *The Electricity Industry*. London: NCC.

National Consumer Council (1991c) *Out of Order*. London: NCC.

National Consumer Council (1991d) *The Citizens' Charter*. London: NCC.

Next Steps Initiative (1990) *Treasury and Civil Service Committee, Eighth Report, 1989–90*. London: HMSO.

Office of Fair Trading (1990) *Annual Report, 1989–90*. London: HMSO.

Office of Fair Trading (1991a) *Annual Report, 1990*. London: HMSO.

Office of Fair Trading (1991b) *Consumer Redress Mechanisms*. London: OFT.

Office of Gas Supply (1989) *Anual Report, 1989*. London: HMSO.

Office of Gas Supply (1992) *Annual Report, 1991*. London: HMSO.

Office of Water Supply (1991) *1990 Report of the Director-General of Water Supply*. London: HMSO.

Osborne, D. and Gaebler, T. (1992) *Reinventing Government*. Addison-Wesley.

Outer Circle Policy Unit (1979) *The Big Public Inquiry*. Justice/OCPU.

Parliamentary Commissioner for Administration (1989–90) *The Barlow Clowes Affair*, HC 76. London, HMSO.

Peters, T. and Waterman, R. (1982) *In Search of Excellence: Lessons from America's Best Run Companies*. New York: Harper and Row.

Pirie, M. (1991) *The Citizens' Charter*. London: Adam Smith Institute.

Pollit, C. (1988) 'Consumerism and Beyond', *Public Administration*, 66(2), p. 217.

Prior, P. (1985) *Report on the Prison Disciplinary System*, Cmnd 9641. London: HMSO.

Prosser, A. (1986) *Nationalized Industries and Public Control*. Oxford: Blackwell.

Purdue, M. (1991) *Planning Appeals: A Critique*. Milton Keynes: Open University Press.

Rawlings, R. (1986a) *The Complaints Industry: A Review of Sociolegal Research on Aspects of Administrative Justice*. London: ESRC.

Rawlings, R. (1986b) 'Parliamentary Redress of Grievance', in C. Harlow (ed.) *Public Law and Politics*. London: Sweet and Maxwell.

Rawlings, R. (1990) 'The MPs Complaints Service', 53 Mod, LR 22 & 149.

Robertson, I. (1989) 'The Children Bill: Children, Parents and the Local Authority', *Family Law*, p. 225.

Sainsbury, R. (1989) 'The Social Security Chief Adjudication Officer: The First Four Years', *Public Law*, p. 323.

Scarman, Lord (1974) *English Law: The New Dimension*. London: Stevens.

Schiemann, K. (1990) 'Locus Standi', *Public Law*, p. 342.

Select Committee on the Parliamentary Commissioner for Administration (1991–92) *The Implications of the Citizens' Charter for the Work of the Parliamentary Commissioner*, HC 158. London: HMSO.

Seneviratne, M. (1991) 'Complaints Procedures in Local Government', PhD thesis, University of Sheffield.

Social Fund Commissioner (1990) *Annual Report, 1989–90*. London: HMSO.

Social Fund Commissioner (1991) *Annual Report, 1990–91*. London: HMSO.

Stacey, F. (1978) *Ombudsmen Compared*. Oxford: Oxford University Press.

Stephens, M. (1990) *Community Law Centres: A Critical Appraisal*. Aldershot: Avery.

Street, H. (1975) *Justice in the Welfare State*. London: Stevens.

Sunstein, C. (1990) *After the Rights Revolution*. Cambridge, Mass.: Harvard University Press.

Thompson, E.P. (1975) *Whigs and Hunters*. London: Peregrine.

Thynne, I. and Goldring, J. (1987) *Accountability and Control: Government Officials and the Exercise of Power*. Sydney, Australia: Law Book Co.

Tweedie, J. (1986) 'Rights in Social Programmes: The Case of Parental Choice of School', *Public Law*, p. 407.

Veljanovski, C. (1993) *The Future of Industry Regulation in the UK*. London: Lexecon Ltd.

Waldegrave, W. (1992) *The Citizens' Charter, First Report: 1992*, Cm 2101. London: HMSO.

Wass, Sir Douglas (1984) *Government and the Governed*. London: RKP.

Whyatt, Sir John (1961) *The Citizen and the Administration: The Redress of Grievances*. London: Stevens.

Widdicombe, D. (1986) *The Conduct of Local Authority Business*, Cmnd 9797. London: HMSO.

Wikeley, N. and Young, R. (1992) 'The Administration of Benefits in Britain: Adjudication Officers and the Influence of Social Security Appeal Tribunals', *Public Law*, p. 238–62.

Woolf, Sir Harry (1990) *Protection of the Public: A New Challenge*. London: Stevens.

Woolf, Sir Harry (1991) *Prison Disturbances*, Cm 1456. London: HMSO.

Woolf, Sir Harry (1992) 'Judicial Review: A Possible Programme for Reform', *Public Law*, pp. 221–37.

Wraith, R. and Hutchesson, P. (1973) *Administrative Tribunals*. London: George Allen and Unwin.

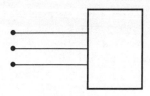

INDEX

NO SUCH THING AS SOCIETY?
INDIVIDUALISM AND COMMUNITY

John Kingdom

Margaret Thatcher's imperious declaration 'There is no such thing as society' captured the essence of a political vision and opened an era that was to bear her name and bequeath to the 1990s a legacy which cannot be ignored. This book argues that there *is* such a thing as society and that the creation of political structures which enshrine communal values is vital. In developing this argument, the author examines the intellectual and moral underpinnings of the Thatcherite doctrine which seemingly found in modern British political culture a deep vein of individualist sympathy.

The book is deliberately polemic and intended to engage, challenge and promote thought and debate. Its theme is of central relevance throughout the social sciences and its lively and accessible style makes it a stimulating read for anyone concerned with politics and society in the 1990s.

Contents
The masturbatory society – The roots of individualism – Towards the communal state: creating social democracy – The sins of the fathers: did social democracy fail? – The Thatcher assault – The myth of the market – The false logic of collective action – Reasserting the communal ethic – Restoring the communal state – References – Index.

144p   0 335 09726 X (Paperback)   0 335 09727 8 (Hardback)